2

D0290383

WITHDRAWN

I.C.C. LIBRARY

DEMCO

China

China

The Pessoptimist Nation

WILLIAM A. CALLAHAN

I.C.C. LIBRARY

OXFORD
UNIVERSITY PRESS

DS
779
.29
.C35
2010

OXFORD

UNIVERSITY PRESS

Great Clarendon Street, Oxford OX2 6DP

Oxford University Press is a department of the University of Oxford.
It furthers the University's objective of excellence in research, scholarship,
and education by publishing worldwide in

Oxford New York

Auckland Cape Town Dar es Salaam Hong Kong Karachi
Kuala Lumpur Madrid Melbourne Mexico City Nairobi
New Delhi Shanghai Taipei Toronto

With offices in

Argentina Austria Brazil Chile Czech Republic France Greece
Guatemala Hungary Italy Japan Poland Portugal Singapore
South Korea Switzerland Thailand Turkey Ukraine Vietnam

Oxford is a registered trade mark of Oxford University Press
in the UK and in certain other countries

Published in the United States
by Oxford University Press Inc., New York

© William A. Callahan 2010

The moral rights of the author have been asserted
Database right Oxford University Press (maker)

First published 2010

All rights reserved. No part of this publication may be reproduced,
stored in a retrieval system, or transmitted, in any form or by any means,
without the prior permission in writing of Oxford University Press,
or as expressly permitted by law, or under terms agreed with the appropriate
reprographics rights organization. Enquiries concerning reproduction
outside the scope of the above should be sent to the Rights Department,
Oxford University Press, at the address above

You must not circulate this book in any other binding or cover
and you must impose the same condition on any acquirer

British Library Cataloguing in Publication Data

Data available

Library of Congress Cataloging in Publication Data

Library of Congress Control Number: 2009934135

Typeset by SPI Publisher Services, Pondicherry, India
Printed in Great Britain
on acid-free paper by
CPI Antony Rowe, Chippenham, Wiltshire

ISBN 978-0-19-954995-5

1 3 5 7 9 10 8 6 4 2

The past is never dead, it's not even past.

William Faulkner

To my parents, who love a good story

Contents

Preface   ix
Acknowledgments   xi
List of Figures   xiii

1. Introduction: Soft Power, Pessoptimism, and the
Rise of China   1

2. When Is China? (1): Patriotic Education and the
Century of National Humiliation   31

3. When Is China? (2): Producing and Consuming
National Humiliation Days   61

4. Where Is China?: The Cartography of National
Humiliation   91

5. Who Is China? (1): Foreign Brothers and
Domestic Strangers   127

6. Who Is China? (2): Trauma, Community,
and Gender in Sino-Japanese Relations   161

7. Conclusion: How to Be Chinese in the
Twenty-First Century   191

Notes   219
Character List   259
Index   261

Preface

While I was reading an article in 1998 about the South China Sea disputes between China, Vietnam, and the Philippines, I came upon an unlikely reference. In an otherwise hard-nosed analysis of the issue, a prominent Chinese strategist cited a book called *The Atlas of Shame*. This odd juxtaposition of security studies, geography, and emotion piqued my interest, so I asked a friend in Beijing to track down this curious book. Once I got a copy of *Maps of the Century of National Humiliation in Modern China* (the actual title), I was fascinated by how it combined politics, history, and identity in the very deliberate celebration of national *insecurity*.

Like most people who study Chinese politics, I had encountered the phrase "national humiliation" [*guochi*] before – but I didn't take it very seriously. Once I started looking for national humiliation discourse, however, I found that it is actually quite common. Although it doesn't receive much attention in Western analysis, it turns out that there are textbooks, novels, museums, songs, films, and parks devoted to commemorating national humiliation in China.

This is a great topic for a book, I decided, because it allows me to eavesdrop on conversations in China that discuss the country's past, present, and future.

It is actually a controversial topic. On the one hand, many colleagues in the West dismiss it as a distraction; they insist that China's emotional outbursts about the Century of National Humiliation are largely a thing of the past, especially with the success of Beijing's more rational and pragmatic foreign policy. On the other hand, many colleagues in China complain that a critical analysis of national humiliation discourse is disrespectful because it denies the crimes of imperialist powers while presenting a negative view of the People's Republic of China (PRC) as a vengeful country.

Luckily for me, China's foreign ministry keeps highlighting the importance of emotions in foreign affairs: It regularly chastises foreign critics for "hurting the feelings of the Chinese people," and cites cleansing national humiliation as a major policy objective. In a reversal of the grassroots feminist slogan – the personal is political – the Chinese state seems to take international politics *very* personally. Its public statements amount to more than simply words; I write this preface just after Beijing cancelled the 2008 EU–China summit, which was supposed to address the global economic crisis, because French President Nicolas Sarkozy "hurt the feelings of the Chinese people" by planning to meet the Dalai Lama.

Chinese foreign policy thus entails much more than the pursuit of wealth and power; we also need to recognize how the more symbolic issues of Beijing's search for respect and status drive the PRC's foreign policy.

When Prime Minister Wen Jiabao visited the United States in December 2003, he noted that there was a serious knowledge gap between the two countries: "If I can speak very honestly and in a straightforward manner, I would say the understanding of China by some Americans is not as good as the Chinese people's understanding of the United States." This statement, which has been repeated many times by Chinese scholars and officials, assumes that as the world gets to know "the real China" it will criticize the PRC less.

But I think that the opposite is more likely to be the case. While few bother to comment on the domestic politics or foreign policy of small countries, great powers attract lots of attention, simply because they are consequential. Many of China's new leaders expect that the world will be nicer and more respectful to them as the PRC becomes more powerful. But the opposite is likely to ensue: as China becomes more important, it will become the focus of more commentary, including more provocative criticism. In a way, Chinese leaders and opinion-makers should be happy that people around the world are taking the time to write serious criticisms of the PRC; this activity actually confirms China's new stature on the world stage.

Australian Prime Minister Kevin Rudd, who is also a China studies expert, addressed China's new relationship with the world in his speech at Peking University in April 2008. Using a classical Chinese reference, he explained that a "true friend" [*zhengyou*] is a critical friend: "A strong relationship, and a true friendship are built on the ability to engage in a direct, frank and ongoing dialogue about our fundamental interests and future vision."

Perhaps Irish playwright Oscar Wilde put it best when he observed that "There is only one thing in the world worse than being talked about, and that is not being talked about."

William A. Callahan

Acknowledgments

Over the past decade, many people have read this manuscript in various forms. For their critical comments – most of which I have followed – and generous support, many thanks to Mark Aspinwall, Elena Barabantseva, Patrick Bell, Sumalee Bumroongsook, David Campbell, Chaiwat Satha-Anand, Gordon C. K. Cheung, Kelvin Chi-kin Cheung, Rey Chow, Paul A. Cohen, Arif Dirlik, Cynthia Enloe, Mary Erbaugh, Edward Friedman, Bryna Goodman, Robert Hathaway, Yinan He, Kevin Hewison, Shiping Hua, Christopher R. Hughes, Jia Qingguo, Alastair Iain Johnston, David Kerr, Robert J. Kibbee, Richard Curt Kraus, Kirk W. Larsen, Liao Shaolian, Liu Hong, Duncan McCargo, Manjari Chatterjee Miller, Rana Mitter, Daniel Bertrand Monk, Michael J. Shapiro, Shi Yinhong, Chih-yu Shih, Elizabeth Sinn, Richard J. Smith, Somchai Phatharathananund, Song Xinning, Julia Stapleton, Suwanna Satha-Anand, Marie Thorsten, Thongchai Winichakul, R. B. J. Walker, Wang Gungwu, and Stephen E. Welch.

For taking the time to read the whole manuscript again, I would especially like to thank Richard Curt Kraus and Yinan He. Michael J. Shapiro also offered moral support and helpful advice at critical moments of this project.

Many thanks to the librarians in China, Taiwan, Hong Kong, the United States, and Britain who cheerfully located obscure materials for me – especially the early-twentieth-century Chinese maps. Thanks also to Richard Baum for running the China Politics e-mail list, which is always a lively source of information and opinion.

I would like to thank the following institutions for generous grants that enabled this research: the British Academy (SG-34564), the British Academy – Committee for South East Asian Studies, the Centre for Contemporary China Studies at Durham University, the Centre for Chinese Studies at the University of Manchester, the Economics and Social Research Council (RES-580–28–0008), the European Commission (ASI/B7–301/98/679–04), the Rockefeller Foundation, the Universities' China Committee in London, and the Woodrow Wilson International Center for Scholars.

For their warm hospitality during fieldwork and writing, my thanks to Robert Hathaway (Woodrow Wilson Center), Wang Yizhou (Chinese Academy of Social Sciences), Song Xinning (Renmin University), Elizabeth Sinn (University of Hong Kong), Wilt L. Idema (Harvard University), Pilar Palacia (Bellagio Center), Chen Yung-fa (Academia Sinica), and Martha Hickey (Portland State University).

For permission to use images, I thank Ablimit Baki, the British Library, Cai Guo-Qiang, William A. Callahan, Cornell University Library, Hiro Ihara, Liu Gang, Yoshiko Nakano, the *New York Review of Books*, and Somchai Phatharathananund. Every effort has been made to contact all copyright holders. However, if anyone has not been contacted, they should contact the publisher in the first instance.

Finally, I would like to thank Sumalee for everything.

Chapters 3, 5, and 6 are refined versions of:

"History, Identity, and Security: Producing and Consuming Nationalism in China," *Critical Asian Studies* 38:2 (2006): 179–208.

"The Cartography of National Humiliation and the Emergence of China's Geobody," *Public Culture* 21:1 (2009): 141–73.

"Trauma and Community: the Visual Politics of Chinese Identity in Sino-Japanese Relations," *Theory & Event* 10:4 (2007).

I thank the publishers for their permission to use this material.

List of Figures

1.1 Olympics opening ceremony fireworks.   2

1.2 *National Humiliation Gymnastics* (1929).   7

1.3 *Maps of the Century of National Humiliation in Modern
     China* cover.   17

1.4 Patriotic mineral water label.   18

2.1 "Ordinary peasant" hits the talk show circuit.   47

2.2 Lin Zexu statue in New York's Chinatown.   58

3.1 "Never forget national humiliation, strengthen
     our national defense."   64

3.2 September 18th History Museum, Shenyang.   71

3.3 Never forget national humiliation cigarettes (1925).   85

3.4 "May 9th national humiliation commemoration products" ad
     from a consortium of electrical goods producers.   86

3.5 Consuming nationalism with playing cards.   87

3.6 Families enjoying a national humiliation icon.   89

4.1 Map of Zheng He's American voyage (1418).   92

4.2 Back cover of *China's Road* (1999).   93

4.3 Untitled (1743): Map of civilization and barbarism.   97

4.4 First map of the Republic of China (1912).   100

4.5 Map of Chinese national humiliation (1916).   101

4.6 Map of China's national humiliation (1930).   102

4.7 Map of China's national humiliation (1927).   104

4.8 Map of Czarist Russia's occupation of China's
     sovereign territory (1997).   106

4.9 Imperialism's division of China into spheres of power in
     the late nineteenth century (1997).   108

4.10 Map of the Koguryo Kingdom.   115

4.11 Untitled carpet map of Xinjiang (2005).   117

4.12 "Change the Perspective to View Taiwan" (2004).   119

4.13 Map of Tibetan demonstrations (2008).   123

4.14 World map of the hurt feelings of the Chinese people (2008).   124

5.1   The Republic's five-color flag.   135

5.2   Roi-Et businessman becomes an imperial official.   146

6.1   *Painful History of National Humiliation* cover (1919).   163

6.2   Section of panel sculpture at Nanjing massacre memorial.   176

6.3   "Nanjing under construction and development."   184

7.1   "Cleanse the Century of National Humiliation,"
      Guangzhou (1997).   199

7.2   "To wipe out our humiliation with our enemy's blood."   200

7.3   "Project to Extend the Great Wall" (1993).   212

7.4   "The Century with Mushroom Clouds" (1996).   214

7.5   Cai's New York exhibit commemorated on a Chinese stamp.   215

Chapter 1

Introduction: Soft Power, Pessoptimism, and the Rise of China

At 8:08 pm on August 8, 2008 the world's gaze focused on China. What it saw was the birth of a new superpower, which emerged in a novel way through a stunning cultural performance, as opposed to a decisive military victory. For a global television audience, Beijing asserted its power through fireworks rather than firepower, presenting the Chinese nation to the world as young and beautiful, wise and strong. Under film director Zhang Yimou's guidance, China's national interest was defined by this "national aesthetic."[1]

While mainstream international relations scholars see culture and identity issues as a distraction from the real politics of economic strength and military force, I think that the opening ceremony of Beijing's Summer Olympics can tell us much about the political direction of China's rise. The purpose of this book is to trace the links between identity and security in China, especially as they mix positive and negative views of China and the world. Most analyses focus on Beijing's new multilateralism and China's peaceful rise. But I argue that because these themes are not deeply embedded in Chinese society, we also need to look beyond the foreign ministry's official policies to see how Chinese people relate to the world in ways that often go against Beijing's peaceful multilateralism. Foreign affairs thus expands to encompass a range of sovereignty performances; it emerges in social activities where people continually divide friends from enemies, domestic from foreign, East from West, and patriots from traitors in everyday life, as well as in the halls of power. Here, security likewise expands beyond traditional military and national security issues to include the nontraditional issues of nationalist security, regime security, and cultural security.

But first let us take a closer look at how China's identity and security dynamic emerged at the Olympics opening ceremony, because this fantastic performance graphically shows how we need to refocus our analysis from the material measures of hard power to the symbolic politics of soft power.

Just before 8:08 pm, the opening ceremony began with 2008 drummers beating on 2008 drums, while chanting the opening lines of the Confucian *Analects*, "It is glorious to receive friends from afar." Fireworks lit up the skies of the Chinese capital, tracing gigantic footsteps along the sacred north–south axis from the ancient Forbidden City at the center of Beijing out to the futuristic Olympic stadium. Fifty-six children, who represented China's fifty-six official ethnic groups, then carried the Chinese flag across the stadium floor to an honor guard of the People's Liberation Army, while a darling little girl in a red dress sang "Ode to the Motherland." As soldiers raised the national flag, the hometown crowd sang China's national anthem "March of the Volunteers."

After more spectacular fireworks (Figure 1.1), a seventy-five minute show narrated the glories of China's 5,000 years of civilization, presenting achievements ranging from classical calligraphy to Confucian harmony, and from Peking opera to China's four great inventions: paper, printing, gunpowder, and the magnetic compass. Using a mix of traditional culture and high technology, Zhang Yimou's show was both beautiful and awesome. The performance used form as well as content to display China's greatness; many of these images were displayed on a massive LED screen

Figure 1.1 Olympics opening ceremony fireworks. Eunice Khong.

that first unrolled before our eyes like a classical scroll, and later flew through the air.

The Tang dynasty (618–907), which many Chinese see as the apex of their civilization, was celebrated with hundreds of women dancing in elaborate costumes. This cosmopolitan empire was open to the world, spreading both silk and Chinese values across the globe. Zhang Yimou's extravaganza then celebrated the accomplishments of Ming dynasty (1368–1644) Admiral Zheng He, who sailed halfway around the world on friendly missions to Asia and Africa. The message was clear: open doors lead to prosperity, and the inner harmony of Confucian values leads to the external peace of mutually beneficial foreign relations; now that China is once again open and harmonious, nothing can stop its "peaceful rise."

After another short interlude of fantastic fireworks, the program jumped a few centuries to look at the future. World-famous Chinese pianist Lang Lang (along with a young acolyte) serenaded the global audience, while 2008 men in glowing green costumes formed a massive dove with flapping wings. Finally, 2008 Tai Chi masters performed a jazzed-up version of their martial art, while images of waterfalls flashed on the stadium ceiling's LED membrane. This vision of the future stressed on ecological harmony: the world needs a more positive engagement with the natural environment, in the spirit of another oft-quoted Confucian aphorism "Nature and humanity are one." To further illustrate this ideal, a huge globe burst out of the stadium floor. Dozens of men defied gravity to harmoniously tumble around the latitudes in a spectacle worthy of Cirque du Soleil, while a Chinese and an English pop star together sang "You and Me" from the top of the world. The extravaganza ended on this hopeful note with the official Olympic slogan, "One World, One Dream" reiterating the main themes of the show: harmony, peace, and strength.

Although both the People's Republic of China (PRC) and the International-al Olympic Committee (IOC) labored to present the games as an apolitical event, the 2008 Olympics are a very public example of how international relations is a performance that intertwines identity with security. Hosting the Summer Olympics has been a central goal of Beijing's foreign policy for the past twenty years, if not for the past century: For many Chinese, the Beijing Olympics fulfilled their "100-year-dream." This book aims to show how China's performative foreign policy goes far beyond Olympics cere-monies. China's main successes on the world stage increasingly come from the soft power of cultural diplomacy, rather than simply the hard power of military might and economic strength. Indeed, the director of Beijing's new

National Theater, better known as "the Egg," declared that his new building was a "concrete example of China's rising soft power and comprehensive national strength."[2] Beijing is also gaining international influence through its prominent role in regional institutions like the Shanghai Cooperation Organization and the East Asia Summit, and by spreading Chinese values around the world through its network of Confucian Institutes and collaborative development programs for Africa.[3]

Rather than take for granted that we understand what these "Chinese values" are, it is important to see how they are produced in an international context. Soft power thus is about more than the export of existing values – it also involves the production of values both at home and abroad. Like with America's soft power, China's soft power actually takes shape through the romanticization of a particular national culture into "universally desirable values." Following this line of argument for the Japanese case, David Leheny feels that the concept of soft power "has less value as a tool for evaluating Japan's regional importance than it does as a heuristic device for grasping how Japanese policymakers now see their regional role."[4]

This view of soft power helps us make sense of how China sees itself and the world. As it shifts from being a rule-follower to a rule-maker, China presents a set of theoretical and policy challenges along a range of traditional and nontraditional security issues. Part of this "rule-making" involves producing and distributing new norms and values, which Beijing then promotes as "ancient Chinese wisdom" on the world stage. China thus needs to excel not only in economic production, but also in "knowledge production" that "creates new world concepts and new world structures."[5] Since there is much talk about the "Chinese Dream" replacing the "American Dream,"[6] it is necessary to examine the soft power of China's national aesthetic.

The Opening Ceremony of the 2008 Olympics can tell us much about how Chinese see themselves, and how they see the world. Certainly, Zhang Yimou's song and dance of ancient civilization and ultramodern technology very clearly was aimed at a foreign audience: the day before the Olympics a senior Chinese diplomat told the *Wall Street Journal*, "I hope [foreigners] will see a peaceful China, a civilized China and a China that is progressing."[7] The opening ceremony's deputy director elaborated:

> I really hope that the people of the world can get to know the Chinese culture through [the Opening Ceremony], to get to know China, to understand China, to love China, and to desire China. This Olympics is the best opportunity.... What will they see about China? I think the most important thing is to see that Chinese people are happy.[8]

The Opening Ceremony certainly gave "the Communist Party its most uninterrupted, unfiltered chance to reach a gargantuan global audience," and did a much better job of presenting China as a happy and friendly place than stuffy slogans uttered by Beijing's "dour-faced leaders."[9] Successfully hosting the Olympics thus fulfilled China's 100-year-dream of being recognized as a great power on the international stage.

The Opening Ceremony presented a seamless narrative of Chinese history and civilization; but conveying these positive messages was not easy. Zhang Yimou had to work hard – and up to the last minute – to get across this unthreatening message of a civilized China: In a final rehearsal, the 2008 chanting drummers were ordered to smile in order to take the edge off. A week before the show, the glowing costumes of the 2008 people who formed the flying dove around pianist Lang Lang were changed from an ominous black to an ecological green. Yet, these were not simply artistic decisions. The politics of the ceremony became crystal clear when the scandal broke out that the girl in the red dress was actually lip-synching "Ode to the Motherland." Chen Qigang, the ceremony's director of music, explained that the Politburo decided that the real singer needed to be replaced to protect China's "national interest" because she wasn't cute enough: "Everyone should understand it in this way: this is in the national interest. It is the image of our national music, national culture. Especially the entrance of our national flag, this is an extremely important, extremely serious matter."[10] Zhang Yimou later confirmed that members of the Central Committee of the Chinese Communist Party (CCP) regularly attended rehearsals, and gave detailed criticisms.[11] After this "political review," Zhang cut some of the more muscular dances from the program, and made sure that China's national flag and the lighting of the Olympic torch were associated with the heartwarming images and cute voices of children. The goal, once again, was to craft China's image as a civilized and modern superpower. As a young woman in Beijing explained, "For a lot of foreigners, the only image of China comes from old movies that make us look poor and pathetic. Now look at us. We showed the world we can build new subways and beautiful modern buildings. The Olympics will redefine the way people see us."[12]

But we shouldn't forget China's domestic audience, which actually was much larger than the global television audience. At first glance, the internal message was largely the same as the external one: take pride in the grandeur of ancient civilization and the achievements of modern China. However, the meaning of the opening ceremony had a special twist for the domestic audience: "[S]ee how great we have been, and how great we have now become again. Relish it. Seize the day." While Chinese athletes won the gold medal tally, the main Olympic victory went to China's party-state, which took credit for a very successful Olympic Games. As a prominent Chinese blogger reasons, "For ordinary Chinese, even if they can't really articulate it, they feel the Olympics are a very important opportunity for China to demonstrate state power."[13]

China's leaders chose Zhang Yimou to promote this national aesthetic of state power because he was already famous; like the Opening Ceremony, Zhang's big-budget epic films *Hero* and *Curse of the Golden Flower* celebrate state power through elaborate military maneuvers that regiment a cast of thousands. In an interview after the opening ceremony, Zhang explained that only China could produce such an extravaganza; only in China could the central government mobilize tens of thousands of actors (most of whom were from the military and the police), along with the logistics of high technology (most of which also came from the military).[14] Zhang's epic film aesthetic resonated with China's "national aesthetic" in ways that integrate soft power and hard power. The central message of the opening ceremony, which beautifully synchronized thousands of people in collective precision, was the glory of state power in China's harmonious society.

Finally, the domestic message stressed that the party-state was successful because it organized the Games on China's own terms as a Chinese model of governance, rather than according to the wishes of outsiders in the IOC or the West. After the Games, a Chinese think-tank scholar declared:

> The Games proved not only the existence of the China model, but also its success.... At the opening and closing ceremonies of the Beijing Olympics, athletes, volunteers, the audience and even local residents all sent one clear message that the Chinese people act according to their own mode of conduct and will not succumb to any allegedly superior Western values.[15]

The Opening Ceremony's singing and dancing performance of the "Chinese nation" stressed the historical and moral continuity between ancient glories and current prosperity in a way that appealed to popular feelings: "The splendor of the show presented to the world the rich and beautiful history of our culture. If asked to name only one thing to be proud of, many Chinese would say it is the long history of our nation."[16]

Even so, we have to ask, which history? Zhang's positive storyline bypassed China's tragic modern history, when the country was known as the "Sick Man of East Asia." As Figure 1.2 graphically shows, in China's popular imagination the political health of the Chinese nation was closely linked to

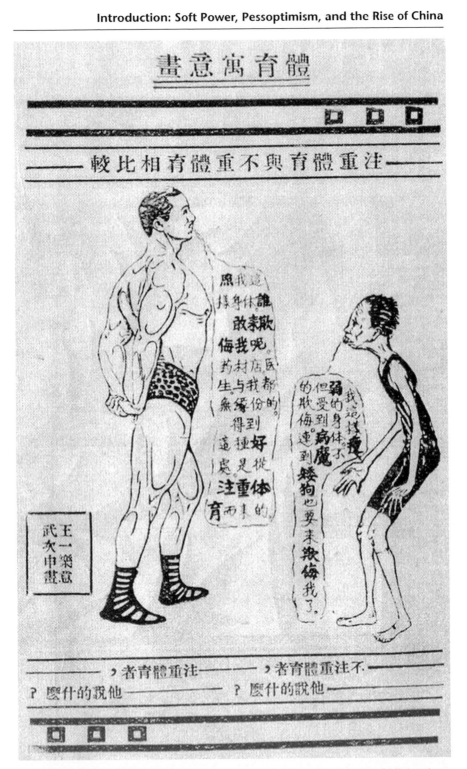

Figure 1.2 *National Humiliation Gymnastics* (1929). Wang Huaiqi, *Guochi jinian ticao*.

the physical health of the Chinese people. The robust Western man says, "Model yourself on my body and who will dare bully or humiliate you? My pharmacist, my physician and I tirelessly worked together to achieve this body, which is the result of vigorous physical training." The scrawny Chinese man replies: "I not only get sick from having a weak body; I also suffer bullying and humiliation. Even little dogs can bully and humiliate me."[17]

China's 100-year-dream of hosting the Olympics emerged in 1908 as a way of curing China's national weakness in international affairs. Many felt that the Chinese body politic, which was disintegrating in the face of foreign aggression and domestic corruption, could only be strengthened through the robust health of many individual Chinese bodies. "Rejuvenate China" therefore means both strengthening Chinese people individually and strengthening China's state power. Joining the Olympic movement thus was seen as a way of joining international society more generally; now, a century later, successfully hosting the Olympics is seen by most Chinese as a confirmation of the PRC's great power status.[18]

But the positive reports of the fulfillment of China's 100-year-dream of Olympic success tell only part of the story. Alongside China's Olympic Dream, there has always been a nightmare: China's "Century of National Humiliation" [bainian guochi] of invasions, massacres, and occupations at the hands of Western and Japanese imperialists. This long century of national humiliation, starting with the Opium War in 1840 and finishing with communist liberation in 1949, is actually an integral part of Chinese understandings of the 2008 Olympics. As Zhang Jigang, the deputy director of the opening ceremony who worked to present "happy Chinese," explains:

> We often said, we cannot remember every year or month, even as a nation. But some years and some months we will always remember, such as the Opium War in 1840; such as the first time the Old Summer Palace was burned in 1860; the Chinese Communist Party's founding in 1921; the People's Republic of China's birth in 1949; the beginning of the reform and open door policy in 1978; and the Beijing Olympics in 2008. These dates are the humiliations and the glories of Chinese history.[19]

My argument in this book is that to understand the success of China's current rise, we need to understand the failures of China's "Century of National Humiliation." Much analysis of the rise of China promotes either optimistic views of the country as a peacefully rising opportunity for the world, or pessimistic views of China as a military and economic threat to the West that needs to be contained. However, such analyses present only part of what is going on: We need to see how the positive and negative are intimately intertwined in Chinese understandings of China's politics.

To put it simply, China is a pessoptimist nation. To understand China's glowing optimism, we need to understand its enduring pessimism, and vice versa. To understand China's dreams, we also need to understand its night-mares. China's national aesthetic entails the combination of a superiority complex, and an inferiority complex. Rather than being opposites, in China, pride and humiliation are "interwoven, separated only by a fine line and can easily trade places."[20] As we saw with the anti-West protests in the run-up to the 2008 Olympics, the country can shift very quickly from positive optimistic actions to negative pessimistic ones – and back again.

This curious mix of positive and negative feelings comes out in the general attitudes of the Chinese public. On the one hand, China is the most optimistic nation in the world. According to the 2008 Pew Global Attitudes survey, 86 percent think that their country is headed in the right direction, up from 48 percent in 2002.[21] Chinese people have good reason to be hopeful. In addition to hosting a fabulous Olympics, they are celebrating the success of thirty years of Deng Xiaoping's economic reform and opening policy. In a story that is now familiar, China's mix of free-market capitalism and state-develop-ment policy has produced high economic growth rates for decades. This economic strategy has lifted hundreds of millions out of poverty, and created a new middle class that is larger in most European countries.

However, China's rapid changes, which have created huge opportunities, also have a dark side: alongside being the most optimistic nation in the world, China has one of the highest suicide rates in the world.[22] Just ten months after the Olympics presented a "happy China" to the world, a hypernationalist book called *China is Unhappy* became a runaway bestseller in the PRC.[23] Hence, even China's pride takes pessimistic forms; bumps in the road of China's rise often produce a fierce response from Chinese people. Xenophobic reactions to March 2008's unrest in Tibet during the Olympic Torch Relay's "Journey of Harmony" are indicative of broader trends of China's "harmonious society." Rather than wondering why Tibetans would protest Beijing's rule, many Han Chinese around the world rallied against the "bias" of Westerners, who they felt had unfairly criticized their homeland. The Tibetan unrest was thus transformed from being a serious domestic issue of racial politics, into an international issue of pride and humiliation that pits China against the West. Historian Xu Guoqi's appeal to this pride/humilia-tion, China/West logic is characteristic of the debate in China that switches the critical focus from domestic politics to international politics:

> For both Chinese and Westerners, the Beijing Olympics present a great opportunity to carry out their respective political goals. While it is clear that Beijing wants to use the Games to convey its best face to the world, it is not surprising that many external groups or organizations would like to use the Games to shame and humiliate China to achieve their own political agendas.[24]

Yet, Chinese public opinion targets not only foreigners; it also increasingly attacks other Chinese. Grace Wang, a freshman at Duke University in the United States, was physically threatened when she tried to mediate between pro-China and pro-Tibet groups. Wang's family back home in China was forced into hiding, and her high school revoked her diploma because she was a "race traitor" [*Hanjian*] to the motherland. Wheelchair-bound Jin Jing became a hero in China when she defended the "Sacred Flame" from protestors during the torch relay in Paris; but a few weeks later this "Smiling Angel" was vilified when she refused to support a popular boycott against the French hypermarket Carrefour: "First she's missing a leg, now she's missing a brain," reasoned one netizen. By going against China's raging Internet opinion, these two women were both denounced as traitors to the Han race. As the Olympic celebration approached in 2008, violence against foreign critics and Chinese "traitors" increased, moving from denunciations on the Web to bullying on the streets.

How can we understand these radical shifts between positive and negative, and between celebrations and demonstrations? What impact do they have on China's domestic politics and foreign policy? Rather than simply being "a land of contradictions" that suffers from "national schizophrenia,"[25] I think it is necessary to see how China's sense of pride and sense of humiliation are actually intimately interwoven in a "structure of feeling" that informs China's national aesthetic.[26] "Structure of feeling" is a useful concept because it allows us to talk about the interdependence of knowledge and emotion, and the interpenetration of institutional structures and very personal experiences.

While opinion in Western countries typically is polarized between left and right, in China it is usually the same people who are wildly optimistic one day, and deeply pessimistic the next. China's "indignant youth" [*fenqing*] who flare up against foreign and domestic critics are also among the most prosperous segment of Chinese society.[27]

While many dismiss such popular pessoptimism as a crude propaganda by the party-state or the rantings of an unrepresentative group of netizens, I think that to understand the direction of China's rise, it is crucial to understand the workings of China's "national aesthetic." While most analysts in China and abroad try to distinguish between a "bad" emotional nationalism and a "good" rational nationalism, I think that it is a mistake to divide Chinese identity in this way; analysis of China's "structure of feeling" allows us to understand the actions and events that emerge from different combinations of reason and emotion, and thus from various combinations of optimism and pessimism. Rather than being a distraction from the real power games of the elite, this book shows how pessoptimism emerges not as the exception of fleeting public outbursts, but is deeply embedded in Chinese society in ways that continue to inform economic and military policy.

The Pessoptimist Nation

China's experience lends itself to hyperbole – both positive and negative. The People's Republic of China has the world's largest population, fastest-growing economy, largest portfolio of foreign exchange reserves, largest army, largest middle class, and the largest diaspora. It has a permanent seat on the Security Council, a nuclear arsenal, and a space program that plans a manned lunar mission by 2024. China's Communist Party is the world's largest political organization, but its excesses during the Great Leap Forward led to one of humanity's worst famines. The PRC now is the world's largest producer of greenhouse gases, biggest source of counterfeit goods, a main source of spam, and the site of the most executions. It belongs to a host of multilateral organizations, and led the formation of the Shanghai Cooperation Organization; it also skirmishes with Japan and Vietnam in the East and South China Seas, and aims 1,300 missiles at Taiwan. The economic crisis has only exaggerated the China hyperbole: according to many commentators, the PRC is either preparing to take over the world, or is about to collapse. To grasp the nuances of how this positive/negative dynamic shapes China's rise, we need to go beyond the statistics to examine how Chinese people understand their rise and how they present it to the outside world. China's pessoptimistic experience shows how its goals are not merely material – a matter of catching up to the West economically and militarily – but social and symbolic. As the aforementioned discussion of the Olympics's national aesthetic graphically shows, China's leaders and the Chinese people are looking for respect (and love); one of the key goals of Chinese foreign policy is to "cleanse national humiliation" [xixue guochi]. "International status" thus is an "overriding policy objective" in Beijing.[28] Yet, as China's search for international respect and status shows, it is often very difficult to determine just what these elusive concepts mean, and pinpoint when they have been attained. Chinese scholars and officials thus often measure respect in terms of its opposite – disrespect.[29]

An examination of China's pessoptimist "structure of feeling" is important because English-language and Chinese-language sources often present very different views of China – and of the world. On the one hand, China has emerged in the past decade as a confident power within the international system in the early twenty-first century.[30] It is presenting itself to the world as a "peacefully rising" power through a charm offensive of public diplomacy: in addition to the Olympics and Confucius Institutes, Beijing has been busy setting up a "strategic partnership" with the European Union and the East Asia Summit with neighboring countries. To complement Beijing's 2008 Olympics, Shanghai will host the 2010 World Expo.

While this optimistic view of China's positive global role is presented at home and abroad, a more negative view of national identity and the international environment is also circulated in China for the domestic audience. Although the scattered references to national humiliation mentioned thus far may seem arbitrary or insignificant, they actually are a part of Beijing's official curriculum of "national humiliation education" that teaches students that the PRC needs to defend itself against a hostile world. While many experts confidently state that China has outgrown its "victimhood complex" that highlights the Century of National Humiliation,[31] this book shows how national humiliation education is actually expanding. This more pessimistic view of China's role in the world helps explain the PRC's "Anti-Secession Law" (2005), which legally sanctions a military invasion of Taiwan, the anti-Japanese riots that rocked urban China in April 2005, and anti-West demonstrations by Chinese around the globe in spring 2008.

While many experts understand these mixed messages in terms of China's gradual – but as yet incomplete – transition from revolutionary power to responsible status quo power,[32] it is necessary to explore how these positive and negative expressions of China's role in the world are linked: the Anti-Secession Law passed just as China's "Strategic Partnership" with EU was taking shape, and national humiliation education is part of Beijing's broader patriotic education curriculum. Indeed, the Olympic torch's global "Journey of Harmony" showed the complexities of China's engagement with the world: friendly "pro-China" events often included hostile "anti-West" and "anti-Tibet" demonstrations. While it is important to recognize how diplomats used a mixture of positive and negative reinforcement to socialize China into the international system, we also need to understand how Beijing employs positive and negative images to understand itself and its role in the world.[33]

China's positive/negative strategy thus is more than an example of factional struggles in the CCP or institutional politics where China's Ministry of Foreign Affairs pursues multilateral diplomacy, as the Ministry of Defense prepares for war.[34] Rather, it is necessary to explore how these different policy strategies are the outcome of different – and complementary – ways of understanding Chinese identity. In this way, we can see how the security issues of China's emergence as a superpower are linked to the identity issues that frame China's domestic and foreign policy. It is popular to probe this overlap of domestic and international politics through an analysis of "Chinese nationalism," with some scholars showing how Chinese identity politics are instrumentally guided by a top-down policy from the party-state, while others provide compelling evidence of genuine grass-roots nationalism.[35] Many thus analyze China by distinguishing between binaries of politics and economics, domestic and foreign, hard and soft power, and elite and grass roots to argue that one factor can explain the other. Yet it is important to see how these often contradictory elements are interwoven: the PRC's national security is closely tied to its nationalist insecurities, domestic politics and foreign policy overlap, soft and hard power produce each other, and elite and mass are intertwined.

In the West, we usually think of the rise of China in terms of its convergence to, or divergence from, international norms of free trade, nuclear arms nonproliferation, human rights, environmental protection, and so on. As Robert Zoellick asked when he was Deputy Secretary of State in 2005, will China be a "responsible stakeholder" in the international system?[36] Yet increasingly, China's elite are asking a different set of questions about their country's proper role in the world. Qin Yaqing, the vice president of China's Foreign Affairs College, put it simply when he stated that the main issue for the PRC's engagement with the world is not the institutional politics of how China will fit into international organizations like the World Trade Organization or the United Nations, but the identity politics of answering the question "Who is China?" The heart of Chinese foreign policy thus is not a security dilemma, but an "identity dilemma": Who is China and how does it fit into the world?[37]

Identity thus shifts from being a distraction to being the central issue that frames economic, political, and military security in China. To understand the important links between identity and security in the PRC, we need to look beyond geopolitics and geoeconomics to consider the furious debates about identity, culture, and strategy that rage within China itself. To probe these issues, this book aims to change the way we analyze China by shifting from "what questions" that seek the "true facts" of the PRC's hard power, to a series of "who, when, where, and how questions" that explore how identity and security are produced and consumed in China and beyond.

Producing and Consuming Pessoptimism

"Never Forget National Humiliation, Rejuvenate China" is a slogan that appears in Chinese discourses ranging from official textbook titles to graffiti in public parks. This negative/positive formula can tell us much about China's pessoptimistic structure of feeling because it is both very official and very popular, emerging through a combination of state institutions and local gossip networks. Exploring the discourse of national pride and national humiliation thus is a good way of answering the question "Who is China?," especially since this pessoptimist dynamic continues to frame how Chinese people understand their role in the world.

Such mixed feelings are encouraged by the party-state's official patriotic education campaign that tells a combination of positive and negative stories. On the one hand, Chinese textbooks are not strange: like history books in other countries, they seek to legitimize their modern nation by linking it to the achievements of an ancient civilization. The prefaces of many modern history textbooks thus begin with a summary description of China's glorious past: "Our great motherland with its long history, vast territory, cultural riches, was founded long ago, and created the most glorious culture in human history, which contributed to the advancement of human civilization."[38]

But patriotic education does more than celebrate the glories of Chinese civilization; it also includes a heavy dose of "national humiliation education" that commemorates China's defeats. This moral tale, however, does not mention recent tragedies that have rocked the PRC since 1949: the famine of the Great Leap Forward, the ten lost years of the Cultural Revolution, or the June 4, 1989 massacre. Rather than focus on the party-state's problems, the discourse of "Century of National Humiliation" (1840–1949) knits together all the negative events – invasions, massacres, military occupations, unequal treaties, and economic extractions – of prerevolutionary history that can be blamed on outsiders. As a result of a combination of foreign invasions and corrupt Chinese regimes, patriotic education texts tell us how sovereignty was lost, territory dismembered, and the Chinese people thus humiliated. Such books narrate how China went from being at the center of the world, to the "Sick Man of East Asia" after the Opium War, only to rise again with the triumphant foundation of the PRC.[39] To understand the workings of China's pessoptimist national aesthetic, we need to reverse Paul Kennedy's famous thesis about "the rise and fall of the great powers," to examine the "fall and rise" of China: many national humiliation book titles include the phrase "from humiliation to glory."[40]

National humiliation seems to be a purely domestic discourse, but its notions of "China's rightful place on the world stage" continually inform Chinese foreign policy in both elite and popular discussions. Although national humiliation occasionally is considered in Western analysis of Chinese foreign policy, it is only mentioned in passing, usually as evidence of a psychological problem of victimization that Beijing needs to overcome for the PRC to be a responsible member of international society. Chinese sources, on the other hand, stress how the outside world, particularly the prosperous West, needs to understand China's unique suffering and their role in it. Rather than take national humiliation as a natural part of China's sad modern history, I think we need to question the logic of national humiliation discourse itself. We thus need to reframe our understanding of humiliation from an irrational emotion which needs to be cured via (social) psychology, to a social practice which needs to be understood in terms of political, historical, and cultural narratives.

We must recognize, therefore, that the Century of National Humiliation is not a standard linear history that would link China's humiliating past to its glorious present and future in a narrative of progress. Long after the Century of National Humiliation ended in 1949, national pride and national humiliation still work together as a guiding historical template that frames political crises in the present and future. Representations of the collision of a Chinese fighter jet and an American reconnaissance plane over the South China Sea in 2001 are a case in point. To Beijing, it was much more than a simple legal issue of the violation of Chinese sovereignty; it was seen as a moral problem, another in a long line of humiliations that China has suffered since the Opium War. Resolving this problem did not involve military retaliation or economic sanctions, as much as symbolic recognition: China demanded a public apology from the United States. Recalling the "Vietnam Syndrome," neoconservative American commentators told President George W. Bush that any apology would be a "profound national humiliation."[41] A few weeks later, China's National People's Congress declared a new national holiday – National Humiliation Day – as part of its new "National Defense Education Law." Although Washington and Beijing were very much on opposite sides of this dispute militarily, the way each framed the issue revealed striking similarities that transformed the goal of international politics from "conquer or be conquered" into "humiliate or be humiliated."

This odd episode shows how identity issues are closely tied to security issues even among political elites; it is part of the expansion of security concerns from traditional measures of military capability to nontraditional issues of identity, history, and culture. International affairs pundits hence increasingly see identity and history as "strategic issues," especially as they inform the dynamics between nationalism and foreign policy.[42] The military is also quite interested in the national aesthetic of both adversaries and allies. The Pentagon is recruiting anthropologists and historians, while the US Army War College recently added the study of culture and identity to its Masters in Strategic Studies curriculum.[43] Humiliation thus has joined guilt, victimhood, and apology as a topic of analytical interest in international studies.[44]

Humiliation may still seem odd for China's national aesthetic; common sense tells us that humiliation is something that is suffered in silence, rather than publicly celebrated. However, in China, humiliation is not just about passive "victimization." National humiliation discourse actually involves a very active notion of history and redemption: The ancient Book of Rites [Liji] tells us that "A thing's humiliation can stimulate it; a country's humiliation can rejuvenate it."[45] As Mao Zedong declared at the founding of the People's Republic of China in 1949, "Ours will no longer be a nation subject to insult and humiliation. We have stood up."[46]

China's patriotic education campaign is not limited to textbooks or classrooms. National humiliation is a popular theme in feature films, museum exhibits, romance novels, pop songs, patriotic poems, specialist dictionaries, pictorials, commemorative stamps, and YouTube videos. Since 2001, the PRC has had its own official National Humiliation Day, which it celebrates each September. A popular historical atlas, Maps of the Century of National Humiliation of Modern China, went into its second edition in 2005[47] (see Figure 1.3). Beijing's Garden of Perfect Brilliance imperial palace [Yuanming yuan], which was looted and burned by British and French troops during the Second Opium War (1860), has become an icon of national humiliation that is testament to both Chinese civilization and foreign barbarism: pictures of the palace ruins grace book covers, commercial brands, posters, calendars, and t-shirts (see Figure 1.4). The CCP's Central Propaganda Department thus has honed patriotic education into a multimedia campaign that ties patriotism very firmly to the party-state.

近代中国

百年国耻地图

人民出版社地图室编

Figure 1.3 *Maps of the Century of National Humiliation in Modern China* cover. *Jindai Zhongguo bainian guochi ditu*, 1997/2005.

Figure 1.4 Patriotic mineral water label. Beijingshi Jiulong shan kuangchuan yinliao gongse.

Conversations with Chinese students confirm that national humiliation, with its list of foreign aggressors and domestic traitors, is now the common-sense way of understanding China's modern history, and thus sets the paradigm for contentious international politics.

But it would be a mistake to conclude that patriotic education is merely propaganda that is instrumentally used by the party elite to manipulate the people. The "Century of National Humiliation" certainly is the official view of modern Chinese history in the PRC; but this discourse is not just "the standard view of Chinese Communist historiography," a "Marxist–Leninist mind-trap," or "stale Maoist ideology" as many scholars presume.[48] It is a recurring theme in both pre-1949 Republican writings and post-1949 Taiwanese discourses. National humiliation thus is one of the few discourses to transcend the communist/nationalist ideological divide. Mao's nemesis, Chiang Kai-shek, discusses it at length in *China's Destiny*.[49] More than a decade before Chiang came to power, an education professor designed a patriotic curriculum in 1915 around the principles of "national studies, national humiliation, and hard work."[50]

Beijing's current positive/negative patriotic education campaign is so successful because it builds on a structure of feeling that actually precedes this particular propaganda policy, and predates the PRC. This mix of entitlement and righteous rage continues to be very strong in China because it draws on self-understandings that are both very ancient and very modern. Chinese identity emerges through a curious combination of modern victimization and ancient civilization.

Civilization, Barbarism, and China's Structure of Feeling

Many credit (or blame) Samuel P. Huntington for making us think about the international role of civilizations in the post-Cold War era. But civilization has been an enduring theme in Chinese discussions of foreign policy and world order for millennia. As we saw at the opening ceremony of the 2008 Olympics, China's concept of civilization provides a national aesthetic that unites elite and mass views of identity and security in the PRC. This book will show how China's current structure of feeling that looks to national pride and national humiliation is an outgrowth of China's "civilization/barbarian distinction" [*Huayi zhi bian*]. Both these structures of feeling work to integrate the party-state's propaganda policy with grassroots popular feelings.

China's domestic policy of "harmonious society" and its foreign policy of "peacefully rising" in a "harmonious world" are both based on the idealized view of Chinese civilization as open to the world, and tolerant of outsiders. *Hua*, which has come to mean both "civilization" and "Chinese," more literally means "magnificent" and "flourishing," and is a homonym for "transformation." Rather than seeking to conquer those who violently challenged it, we are often told how China's magnanimous civilization inclusively embraced difference.[51] Even when China itself was conquered by outsiders, the attractiveness of Chinese civilization was able to assimilate non-Han groups: nomadic Mongolians were transformed into the Yuan dynasty that built Beijing's Forbidden City. Premodern China thus utilized the soft power of Confucian rituals to unify All-under-Heaven [*Tianxia*] through attraction rather than conquest. The PRC's current foreign policy, we are told, is likewise based on the "Peaceful Orientation of Chinese Civilization."[52]

The story of Zheng He is presented as a prime example of how China's peaceful rise will, to quote Zheng Bijian, "transcend the traditional ways for great powers to emerge."[53] While European imperial fleets smuggled opium and established colonies, Ming dynasty admiral Zheng He's massive fleet explored Asia and Africa on seven voyages of peace and friendship. Beijing now promotes this positive view of Chinese power both at home and abroad: to celebrate the 600th anniversary of Zheng He's first voyage, in 2005, China's State Council designated the day Zheng began his first voyage as a new national holiday: July 11th is now "Navigation Day." China Central Television celebrated the first Navigation Day with an eight-episode documentary, and China's post office issued a special commemorative stamp. Vice-Foreign Minister Zhang Yesui explains the contemporary significance of Zheng He's voyages by stressing how they "promoted the peaceful co-existence of various civilizations, demonstrating China's cultural tradition of friendship in international relations."[54]

Southeast Asian countries actually remember Zheng He's voyages quite differently. These trips, which typically included over 300 ships and 27,000 sailors, were seen as means of reestablishing and then maintaining China's tributary empire. Rather than friendship diplomacy, the voyages were an exercise of hard power that employed shock and awe tactics for gunboat diplomacy.[55] China's expansionist policies reemerged in the Qing dynasty, which doubled imperial territory through conquest; while China complains about Western and Japanese imperialist crimes in the Century of National Humiliation, in the last decades of the nineteenth century Beijing invaded, occupied, and exploited Korea in ways that should be described as national humiliations.[56]

But using counterevidence to "falsify" this interpretation of China's modern history would miss the point. Although textbooks use "undeniable evidence" to empirically prove foreign crimes, national humiliation is better understood as a moral discourse that figures China as a magnanimous civilization that was uniquely threatened by immoral barbarians. While Chinese history – like most countries' histories – has involved much violent expansion and contraction, Chinese civilization is presented as "inherently peaceful." China thus sees itself as an innocent victim of immoral international bullying in part because official history tells people that China has never invaded any country – and never will.

As we saw in the opening ceremony of the Olympics, Beijing's idealized view of imperial China is constantly repeated as a way of explaining how China's peaceful rise is not a threat, but an opportunity for all to prosper in a harmonious world. These twin themes of victimization and civilization have been quite successful in shaping China's image at home and abroad: American military analysts not only recognize the allure of this soft power strategy, but even uncritically repeat China's idealized history.[57]

China's concept of civilization differs from the inter-civilizational discourse that frames both the UN's "dialogue of civilizations" and Huntington's "clash of civilizations." In China, discussion of civilization always includes a discussion of "barbarism." This is not just a debate about ancient history: many Chinese writers now are employing the "civilization/barbarism distinction" as a model for domestic politics and international affairs.[58] It is common for Chinese authors to refer to outsiders – either historical neighbors or modern Westerners – as "barbarians."

These discussions of civilization and barbarism show how Chinese politics is understood in terms of cultural and moral categories. Here civilization is more than the Confucian aphorisms and Tang dynasty costumes that we saw in the opening ceremony of the Olympics. Rather than a set of "artifacts," civilization is better understood as a discourse that takes shape in relation to its opposite: barbarism. Whenever we declare something civilized, we are simultaneously declaring something else barbaric. Here I am building on the analysis of China's civilization/barbarism relation that I developed in *Contingent States: Greater China and Transnational Relations*.[59] It is important to highlight how civilization discourse involves drawing distinctions that are not only cultural, but also political and moral. As a structure of feeling, the civilization/barbarism distinction governs how other important political distinctions are made: inside/outside, domestic/foreign, China/West, and pride/humiliation.[60]

Domestic politics thus are tied to foreign relations through this distinction: a positive, civilized inside takes shape only when it is distinguished from a negative barbaric outside. Civilization can engage with barbarism in one of two ways: conquest or conversion.[61] The title of the first chapter of Jiang Tingfu's popular *Modern History of China* (2005), says it all: "Exterminate the Barbarians or Assimilate the Barbarians."[62] While the idealized view of Chinese civilization stresses how barbarians were transformed into civilized Chinese through assimilation, it is also necessary to remember that "exterminate the barbarians" was the other option. Either way, different peoples were not allowed to coexist with Chinese civilization on their own terms. The analytical task, then, is not to search for the core of Chinese civilization, but to trace how power is produced when such inside/outside distinctions are made in sovereignty performances. Indeed, one of the current objectives of this strategy is to limit identity politics to stereotypes of "China" versus "the West."

While the difference between civilization and barbarism seems obvious, historian Arthur Waldron points out that answering the questions "Who is China?" and "Where is China?" has never been easy. Foreign policy elites in imperial China constantly debated where to draw the border between inside and outside as they defined their "civilization" with and against the barbarian:

> At root [the debates] were about how culturally exclusive China must be in order to remain Chinese; about the nature and authority of the Chinese ruler; about where – and whether – to draw a line between the [barbarian] steppe and China proper. They were, in other words, arguments in which fundamentally different images of the polity collided. ... [I]n fact the problem facing successive dynasties has not been conquering "China," or recovering it, or even ruling it. The first problem has always been defining it, and that is as true today as it ever was.[63]

Because these borders of identity and territory are contingent, the "civilization/barbarism distinction" [*Huayi zhi bian*] developed to be a central concept of imperial governance across China's many kingdoms and dynasties.[64] Imperial philosophers, historians, and officials continually employed this inside/outside distinction to draw (and redraw) China's cultural, political, and territorial boundaries. The ultimate goal of the civilization/barbarian distinction was to support and promote China's "Great Unity" [*da yitong*], another key imperial governance concept that still resonates today.

As the phrase suggests, civilization/barbarian relations involve a moral hierarchy that divides the Chinese self from the barbaric Other, with "China being internal, large, and high and barbarians being external, small, and low."[65] Imperial China thus employed a "very clear ideology of civilization/barbarism, honor/dishonor, noble/ignoble" to define political space.[66] Barbarians here not only lack culture – they lack humanity: "the Di and Rong are wolves."[67] Although there is now a debate about whether we should translate ancient terms like "*Yi*" as "foreigner" rather than "barbarian,"[68] this argument misses the point that in such a hierarchical world order, foreigners are by definition barbarians.

Since the division between civilization and barbarism was contingent, political power in China has always involved making clear distinctions between these unstable concepts. While the idealized view of Chinese civilization stresses how Han Chinese embraced their neighbors, classical Chinese texts are also full of passages that stress violent conflict: "honor the king by expelling the barbarians" [*zunwang rangyi*] was a popular classical idiom. A passage from the *Spring and Autumn Annals* (656 BC) elaborates how leadership in China is measured in this negative way: "The Yi and Di barbarians repeatedly harm China, and when the Yi in the South cooperate with the Di in the North, then China is left hanging by a thread. Duke Huan expelled Yi and Di ... and thus saved China. These are the actions of a King."[69]

The notion that the task of leaders is to save China by expelling barbarians is popular throughout Chinese history. "Expel the Northern Barbarians and Restore China" was a prominent Han slogan protesting Mongolian rule during the Yuan dynasty, and "Expel the Tartar Enemy and Restore China" was the revolutionary slogan of Sun Yatsen's anti-Manchu nationalism.[70] A military banner used during the Boxer Uprising (1900) shows how the classical notion of "barbarian" was extended to include Europeans and Americans: "Support the Qing, Exterminate the Westerners."[71]

My argument is that the civilization/barbarism distinction continues to be the structure of feeling that frames Chinese understandings of identity and security. In classical Chinese texts, "humiliation" is commonly deployed for building and guarding social boundaries: male/female, proper/improper, inside/outside.[72] Whereas before the twentieth century humiliation marked the boundary between civilization and barbarism, it is not surprising that the modern discourse is involved in building and guarding national identity through national pride/humiliation. This book explores how current Chinese texts employ a similar pessoptimistic logic in order to assert the unity of the Chinese nation: "Never Forget National Humiliation, Rejuvenate China" thus resonates with "Expel the Barbarian, Save China" as the latest form of China's "ideology of civilization/barbarism, honor/ dishonor, noble/ignoble."[73]

Other contemporary examples of the parallel between civilization/barbarism and national pride/humiliation are not hard to find. In the early 1990s, Deng Xiaoping told party members that they needed to "seize with two hands" to develop both the material civilization of economic prosperity and the spiritual civilization of political loyalty to the party-state against foreign barbaric forces. In the late 1990s, Jiang Zemin's spiritual civilization campaign produced ethical guides for teenagers such as *Civilization and Barbarism*, and *Honor and Shame*. As part of his harmonious society policy, Hu Jintao has promoted the "Eight Honors and Eight Shames" campaign since 2006. This campaign relies on moral distinctions to separate a positive inside from a negative outside for both national identity and foreign policy; the first honor/shame pair is "the highest honor is loving the motherland, worst shame is harming the motherland."[74]

In a more negative light, political leaders and anonymous netizens both continue to employ the concept of Chinese civilization to see outsiders not only as barbarians, but as fierce animals in ways that echo the classical judgment: "The Di and Rong are wolves." During the Tibetan unrest of 2008, the head of the CCP in Tibet called the Dalai Lama a "wolf with a human face and the heart of a beast"; when the value of China's sovereign wealth fund plummeted in 2007 as an American IPO tanked, a prominent blogger warned China's leaders "not be fooled by these sweet-talking wolves dressed in human skin."[75]

Although it appeals to history and culture, my analysis is not culturalist in the sense of positing an essential, exotic, and unique Chinese way that is totally different from the West.[76] Actually, in their heyday, European empires employed similar civilization/barbarism distinctions to govern both the colonies and the homeland: the French had their *mission civilatrice* and the British the "White Man's Burden." European pundits commonly use the language of civilization and barbarism to frame their love/hate relationship with America, as they have since the sixteenth century. During the Cold War and again in the "war on terror," the United States has looked to this distinction to order international relations. Political theorist Walter Benjamin thus presciently concluded that, "There is no document of civilization which is not at the same time a document of barbarism."[77]

Hence, the rise of pessoptimism in China is important, not because China is exotic or unique, but because it is big – and getting bigger all the time economically, politically, and culturally. Because China is important to people around the world, it behooves us to critically understand how

Chinese people see their country's recent rise to prominence, as well as its current economic problems. The PRC demands scrutiny because its policies and perspectives now have an impact far beyond China's shores.

This brings us back to recent analyses that understand Chinese identity as either a top-down state nationalism or a bottom-up grassroots nationalism. On the one hand, the discussion of the "civilization/barbarism distinction" shows how this form of identity politics precedes the Chinese state, and thus is more than simply a campaign of the CCP's Central Propaganda Department. On the other hand, this cultural nationalism could be a continuation of previous policies since the imperial state was strong in premodern China, and it actively engaged in cultural governance to civilize its subjects. But Chinese nationalism is more than a simple extension of either Chinese tradition or the top-down civilizing policies of imperial dynasties. I think that pessoptimism flourishes in China because it grows out of a dynamism of reciprocal influence that integrates official policy and popular culture.

China's identity politics is neither the party-state instrumentally brainwashing the populace, nor the spontaneous actions of an authentic grassroots community. While it is popular to see the state as the actor and the masses as the audience, here the actor is the audience, and the audience is the actor,[78] as Chinese nationalism is produced and consumed in an interactive and intersubjective process. The party-state's campaigns are so successful because they draw on ideas that preceded the state – civilization and barbarism, national pride and national humiliation – that resonate with popular feelings. Although national humiliation discourse was produced by the party-state after 1989, it actually gained popularity in the early twentieth century in the nonstate arenas of teachers' organizations and the popular press. The theme of national humiliation was thus taken up by Chiang Kai-shek in the 1920s and the PRC in the 1990s as a *response* to address popular criticism.

Leaders are successful in China because they become spokespeople for an ideology in ways that should be familiar: as Daniel Bertrand Monk argues, George W. Bush didn't create the religious right, but mobilized them by representing their values. The legitimacy of the Chinese party-state relies on much more than the negative power of censorship and control; rather than see the PRC as a police state, it is better to understand China as a mobilization state that both encourages and feeds off of the positive productive power of popular feelings and mass action.[79]

Pessoptimist nationalism is thus continually produced and consumed in a circular process that knits together urban elites and rural peasants, northerners and southerners, and government officials and the new middle class. In this way the party-state gains legitimacy not only through economic prosperity, but also through a form of nationalism that unites these diverse groups as "Chinese" – and often against "the West." State policy thus both feeds into, and grows out of, the pessoptimist feelings of ordinary Chinese. Patriotic education and popular opinion are intertwined, just as pride and humiliation are interwoven. China's domestic politics are inseparable from its foreign relations in a way that intimately binds together national security with nationalist insecurities.

Here China is not alone. The boundary between domestic and international politics is blurring in most places. Similar to Mao's founding proclamation, other countries' key texts also link national salvation and national humiliation. During the American Civil War, Abraham Lincoln declared April 30, 1863 a "Day of National Humiliation" in order to encourage "the restoration of our now divided and suffering country, to its former happy condition of unity and peace." In a similar vein, Gandhi declared a "National Humiliation Day" of mass demonstrations in April 1919 to unite the Indian nation in its fight against British imperialism. While Serbians tell us that they have been suffering the national humiliation of the Battle of Kosovo for over 600 years, in South Korea national humiliation is used to describe economic crises in the recent past: "Today's agreement [with the IMF] will open up a new door for the South Korean economy to enter into a new era. To many South Koreans, the agreement was 'National Humiliation Day.'"[80]

National humiliation is a useful way to understand China's identity/security dynamics because the discourse has particularly deep institutional foundations both in the party-state and local gossip networks. It is a good entry point for understanding the global politics of China because while "national humiliation" now seems like the natural way to understand history to many Chinese, the discourse itself has a curious history. Although there are classical examples of the politics of humiliation, national humiliation discourse is very modern, arising along with Chinese nationalism itself as a response to a shocking defeat in the Sino-Japanese War (1894–5). National humiliation was a popular topic in the 1910s and 1920s, but between the 1940s and 1990, it was uncommon; other ways of understanding China's modern history were more popular.

It is important to note that pessoptimism doesn't just criticize outsiders; it can involve a thorough self-criticism. In other words, we need to understand how national humiliation comes not just from "foreign invasion," but also from China's "domestic corruption." Because China was never completely conquered, postcolonial criticism is not merely of the Europe-an, Japanese, or American empires, but of the "Chinese character" that allowed such atrocities to happen – again and again. A character in the cult novel *Trainspotting* describes an analogous situation in modern Scot-land: "Ah don't hate the English. They're just wankers. We are colonized by wankers. We can't even pick a decent vibrant, healthy culture to be colo-nized by. No. We're ruled by effete arseholes. What does that make us? The lowest of the fuckin low, the scum of the earth."[81] Because colonialism in China was not territorial so much as ideological, criticism characteristically involves even more robust self-criticism, described by some as "self-loathing."[82] It is common for Chinese critics to vent their anger not just at foreigners, but also at Chinese leaders (and other "traitors") for being weak in the face of foreign provocation.

The most important thing to understand about China's pessoptimism is that it is fundamentally unstable, producing shifting feelings, which at any time can spill over into mass movements that target domestic critics, foreigners, and even the party-state itself. While it is necessary to welcome China into the international community and encourage more moderate voices in Beijing, the most important thing to recognize is that China's pessoptimist nationalism is out of anyone's control. Even mundane eco-nomic twists can provoke extreme reactions: When the value of China's foreign investment in the Blackstone Group tanked in 2007, the influential Chinese blogger mentioned earlier understood the problem not just in terms of the civilization/barbarism distinction. He also sensationally blamed greedy Westerners for looting China as much as their ancestors had during the Century of National Humiliation: "These fierce wolves are similar to the foreign thieves who pillaged our forefathers, only they are all the more cunning and manipulative, but their goal of pillaging China does not change with the centuries."[83]

As the Olympics showed, China's leaders are able to control many aspects of Chinese society – and even the weather. But beyond long-term education and media reform (neither of which is forthcoming), China's leaders can't control popular feelings. This is important because if history serves as a guide, China is overdue for a major political crisis.[84] Even without a major political challenge, Beijing is facing a range of time bombs, such as a deepening environmental crisis, and a looming demographic crisis. Indeed, as well as being the year China celebrated hosting the Olympics and thirty years of economic reforms, in 2008 it experienced a series of crises: a huge snowstorm shut down much of the country in February, demonstrations rocked the Tibetan plateau in March, a major earthquake devastated

Sichuan in May, a widening tainted milk scandal spread from China to the world in September, and in November the global economic crisis came to China. China is a "fragile superpower,"[85] whose unstable identity grows out of a particular combination of victimization and civilization, which presents the country as a benevolent force in an immoral and hostile world.

During the Olympics we certainly saw much genuine happiness and gracious hospitality from the Chinese people. But since China also has a huge chip on its shoulder, we need to be prepared for a harsh popular reaction whenever China hits a bump on its rocky road of political and economic change. Perhaps Stephen Colbert said it best when he satirically described China as a "frenemy" – at least that's how pessoptimistic Chinese see the rest of the world, and themselves.

Contents

This book elaborates on many of the themes raised in this Introduction; the aim is to examine China's pessoptimistic structure of feeling through a close analysis of Chinese understandings of their country's current successes – and past failures. It traces the impact of China's soft power not only by listing the PRC's cultural and diplomatic assets, but also by examining how Chinese identity is produced and consumed both at home and abroad. Here soft power doesn't just take the expected positive form as the values of China's glorious civilization, but the positive/negative dynamic of civilization/barbarism and national pride/humiliation. It frames certain groups as friends and others as enemies: especially in Chinese understandings of Taiwan, Japan, the United States, and the West.

At the risk of making a pun at the expense of China's current Hu-Wen regime, the next five chapters answer China's "who, when, and where questions" through an analysis of current Chinese understandings of history, territory, ethnicity, and gender. Collectively, the chapters demonstrate how the identity politics of Chinese nationalism produces the security politics of Chinese foreign policy. The conclusion examines "how" to be Chinese by looking at how official and nonofficial intellectuals try to end the Century of National Humiliation and dream about China's future. In a way, these chapters follow the usual contours of mainstream analyses of cultural nationalism. But this book is different because it seeks to question the borders that we commonly draw between domestic and international politics, and thus see how "China" only makes sense when seen in its relations with "the World."

In addition to using a new analytical framework, this book looks to a new range of sources. In particular, I am looking beyond the familiar sources that inform most foreign policy studies to see how China's national aesthetic takes shape in official, academic, and popular texts. My aim is to give "voice" to different segments of Chinese society. On one hand, the party-state promotes "correct theories and unified thinking"[86] to guide the official understanding of "the real China" [zhenshi de Zhongguo], which then is reproduced through constant pronouncements of what "the Chinese people think," and what "the Chinese people feel." This book, on the other hand, offers a sample of different views of official and nonofficial China, which underline how it is impossible to speak about "the real China" in the singular because new voices are always emerging in unexpected places. The following chapters thus look to Chinese films, television, novels, photos, blogs, and online videos to analyze the interplay of state policy and popular culture.

Chinese sources are important, but not because they give us "the real China." As New Yorker correspondent Peter Hessler notes, the problem of "how to understand China" challenges not only outsiders, but Chinese people as well:

> When you live in China as a foreigner, there are two critical moments of recognition. The first occurs immediately upon arrival, when you are confronted with your own ignorance. . . . Then, just as you begin to catch on, you realize that everybody else feels pretty much the same way. The place changes too fast; nobody in China has the luxury of being confident in his knowledge. . . . This second moment of recognition is even more frightening than the first. Awareness of your own ignorance is a lonely feeling, but there's little consolation in sharing it with 1.3 billion neighbors.[87]

I look to Chinese voices not only because they provide "the facts," but more importantly because they can tell us how certain groups of Chinese elites and nonelites understand important problems – and thus how they understand possible solutions.

This book's pessoptimist approach could be criticized for taking an overly negative approach to China, which does not give a balanced "objective" view that highlights the country's many positive developments. In a way, this book follows Deng Xiaoping's dictum of "seizing with both hands" to examine both the generally positive aspects of economic reform and the often negative impact of national humiliation discourse. They are interrelated, and I focus more on humiliation than on pride for two reasons. National humiliation provides a good entry point into China's identity politics simply because it has produced so many strange Chinese-language texts that demand explanation. Second, as noted earlier, national humiliation discourse is common, but not constant. Rather than disappearing as China takes its place as a responsible power in the twenty-first century, national humiliation keeps reappearing. For example, to celebrate the eightieth anniversary of the founding of the CCP on 1 July 2001, Jiang Zemin declared that after much struggle, China had finally "put an end to the history of national humiliation once and for all."[88] But just a few months earlier in April 2001 and a few months later in September 2001, China defined its national defense in terms of national humiliation by creating and then celebrating the PRC's first National Humiliation Day. Others have pointed to the return of Hong Kong in 1997 and the successful Olympics in 2008 as positive turning points that finally cleansed China's national humiliation. As we will see, to paraphrase Mark Twain, these various obituaries for national humiliation discourse have all turned out to be premature.

Of course, it is common for sinologists to say that governments need to understand the cultural and historical background of China in forming the policy toward the PRC. This book aims to show how culture and history are more than background: they very directly animate China's encounter with the world (and with itself).

Chapter 2

When Is China? (1): Patriotic Education and the Century of National Humiliation

Mao's dictum, "Make the past serve the present, and make foreign things serve China," aptly describes how modern history is an important security issue in the People's Republic of China (PRC). This chapter and Chapter 3 examine how history is used to answer the question "Who is China?" In other words, we need to see how both official propaganda and popular culture answer the admittedly awkward question "When is China?" In this chapter, we consider how the Central Propaganda Department of the Chinese Communist Party (CCP) uses the grand narrative of the Century of National Humiliation to socialize Chinese people into patriots who must continuously struggle against hostile foreign forces. Chapter 3 discusses how Chinese nationalism is produced and consumed through patriotic activities on a special day: National Humiliation Day. Together these Centuries and Days of National Humiliation will show how historical narratives are employed to unite moral, patriotic, and civilized Chinese against corrupt, hostile, and barbaric foreigners. Chapters 2 and 3 thus examine how history comes alive as a political activity in China, on both a very grand and a very local scale, through a combination of party-state policy and movements in popular culture.

Seeing how particular historical narratives answer the question "When is China?" is important because China's pessoptimist historiography of national pride and national humiliation does more than guide how people understand the past. Long after the Century of National Humiliation ended in 1949, the pessoptimist historical narrative still provides the template that encourages militant Chinese reactions to conflicts in the present and the future. This is especially true for China's controversial relationships with the United States, Japan, and Taiwan. The bombing of China's Belgrade embassy (1999) and the EP-3 reconnaissance plane incident (2001) were explained in China as "new national humiliations"; the unclear status of Taiwan and international criticism of China's Tibet policy are seen as historical legacies of the Century of National Humiliation. In other words, China's campaign to be recognized as a great power has a reverse image: it wants to make sure that it is not humiliated (again) on the world stage.

This chapter thus elaborates on themes raised in Chapter 1 to show how China's pessoptimist structure of feeling frames historical memory, and primes China's angry youth to explode into popular protests when they feel that China is being bullied or humiliated.

Patriotic Education Policy Since 1989

While many saw the 1989 mass movement in Tiananmen Square as a possible solution to the problem of the brutality of the Chinese state, Deng Xiaoping felt that this "counter-revolutionary rebellion" was best explained as a catastrophic failure of the CCP propaganda system. In a speech to top generals on June 9, 1989, Deng concluded that "during the last ten years our biggest mistake was made in the field of education, primarily in ideological and political education – not just of students but of the people in general."[1] In September 1989, he elaborated: "Our gravest failure has been in education. We did not provide enough education to young people, including students. For many who participated in the demonstrations and hunger strikes it will take years, not just a couple of months, of education to change their thinking."[2] Deng realized that loyalty to the party-state was not natural; China's youth needed to be taught how to be patriotic. His dictum "Seize with both hands, with both hands holding tight" thus describes how China needs to develop both the material civilization of economic prosperity and the spiritual civilization of political loyalty.

Although it has faced challenges from a commercialization of the media, the impact of new information and communication technologies (including the Internet), and a globalization of ideas, China still has a formidable propaganda system. To regulate what people can and cannot know, and thus who they can and cannot be, the party-state has been adept at utilizing the market and new technologies to "enhance and strengthen the propaganda apparatus."[3] Rather than being degraded by Deng's economic reforms, which have opened up Chinese society, "the Central Propaganda Department and the system it oversees has expanded and modernized to keep up with these changes."[4] While many hoped that Hu Jintao would bring political reform to China, his regime actually has tightened control over the discussion of key political topics through both negative censorship of dissenting views and a positive socialization of the Chinese public through education and propaganda.

As the CCP's propaganda system has exploited new technologies, the content of its messages still maintains the same fundamental goal: to present a singular correct view of "the real China" to both foreigners and Chinese citizens. While the country we now call "China" has a contingent history that includes different peoples and different territories at different times, the party-state works hard to assert an essentialized primordial view of Chinese civilization, identity, and territory. In this way Beijing's "One China Policy" seems to apply beyond Cross-Straits Relations; unification with Taiwan is part of the propaganda system's very careful promotion of a unified view of China and the world: One China, One Truth, One World, One Dream.

To accomplish this singular correct view of "the real China," Jiang Zemin instructed propaganda workers to regulate the production and the distribution of information about the PRC by promoting "correct theories and unified thinking."[5] To guide political understanding and action, the propaganda system employs a set of official phrases [tifa] – such as "Never Forget National Humiliation, Rejuvenate China." As Michael Schoenhals explains, "By proscribing some formulations and prescribing others, they set out to regulate what is being said and what is being written – and by extension what is being done."[6] While this language politics is common in China's domestic sphere, recently Beijing has been deploying it in a more sophisticated way for foreign audiences.[7] "Peaceful rising-heping jueqi" is another good example of a tifa "official phrase" that shapes Chinese understandings of domestic and foreign politics. It appeared in 2003, and has been popular in China's explanations of its global role since early 2004.[8] The import of "peaceful rising" comes less from its deep meaning, than from the role it plays in official language games, which is reinforced through persistent and continuous repetition in the mass media. Indeed, Chinese texts do not argue that "peaceful rising" is more persuasive than "China threat" for understanding the rise of China; rather, peaceful rising is presented as an "indisputable fact," while China threat is dismissed as a "malicious fallacy."[9]

Any arguments that offer a more complex view of Chinese history, identity, and by extension China's current foreign policy are dismissed as "unobjective" examples of "Western bias." As the deputy director of the

2008 Olympics' opening ceremony informed us, critical understanding that deviates from the party-state's view of "the real China" is unthinkable because "to know China" is "to love China, to desire China."[10] This unified understanding of China leads to a proliferation of pronouncements in the official media about what "the Chinese people think," and what "the Chinese people feel."

The Central Propaganda Department promotes this singular view of the real China through its control over the production and distribution of all types of media and information;[11] while it cannot effectively control the content of the massive amount of information and culture now available in China, it is able to effectively control specific areas of political interest. One of the Central Propaganda Department's key areas of interest is education, where it maintains joint responsibility with the Ministry of Education for curricula and textbooks at all levels of the system.[12]

"History" is a particularly important security issue in China: the legitimacy of the CCP regime grows out of the history of its revolution against foreign imperialism and domestic corruption, rather than from democratic elections, effectiveness, or public opinion. But history can be subversive as well; it records the memories not just of regimes, but of the revolutionary history of mass movements as well. Much of the power of China's mass demonstrations in 1989 came from the fact that they presented an alternative to the official commemoration of a key revolutionary holiday – the seventieth anniversary of the May 4th movement of 1919.

Because of these legitimacy issues, the CCP is very attentive to history education.[13] In the wake of the 1989 mass movement that had shocked the party-state, President Jiang Zemin refocused political education to stress the importance of modern and contemporary Chinese history, which the Central Propaganda Department then targeted as a "meaningful security issue."[14] Hence, rather than China's new nationalism being an expression of popular feeling, we need to understand this nationalism in the context of the state's patriotic education policy that emerged in the 1990s, and which continues to guide education and propaganda today. This is not a new policy: patriotism and national humiliation also were closely linked in newspaper commentaries and history textbooks in the early twentieth century: *History of National Humiliation* is the title of numerous state-approved textbooks from the 1920s and 1930s.[15] Indeed, it would not be an exaggeration to say that when the idea of "modern history" took shape in China in the 1920s, it was guided by the history of national humiliation. Top historian Lü Simian, for example, published a popular history of modern China at the same time that he published a history of China's national humiliation.[16] President Chiang Kai-shek himself appealed to the history of national humiliation as part of the construction of citizenship and national identity in the Republic of China.[17]

With the communist victory in 1949, official history curriculum and patriotic education policy shifted to focus on the more positive Marxist themes of class struggle and revolutionary victory.[18] According to the records of the National Library of China in Beijing, no national humiliation history textbooks were published between 1937 and 1990. Yet, national humiliation history education was suddenly revived in the late twentieth century as a response to the Tiananmen movement in 1989.

To the outside world, the Tiananmen Square movement was seen as a pro-democracy movement, where for the first time in generations popular protest was not directed against foreign imperialism. Indeed, the focus of students' ire was internal: official corruption and the lack of domestic political reform. Hence this presented a security crisis to the Chinese leadership; but not a crisis of traditional national security, so much as nontraditional security of the party-state: the ideological security, regime security, and cultural security of the CCP.

The solution to this problem, China's leaders decided, was to shift the focus of youthful energies away from domestic issues to foreign problems. The CCP thus formulated a patriotic education policy, not so much to reeducate the youth (as in the past), as to *redirect* protest toward the foreigner as the primary enemy. The Central Propaganda Department's "Outline for Implementing Patriotic Education" (1994) states that the policy's objective is to boost the nation's spirit, enhance national cohesion, foster national pride, consolidate and develop a patriotic united front, and rally the masses' patriotic passions to "build socialism with Chinese characteristics." Not surprisingly, the study of history is an important part of this patriotic education policy, especially the study of China's modern history of being invaded by imperialists, and the study of China's national characteristics, especially as they are incompatible with democratic values that are defined as "Western" – and thus foreign.[19] The Central Propaganda Department's "Outline" proposed a multimedia campaign of patriotic education activities that would take place not just in schools but in museums, film, television, popular magazines, newspapers, and on official holidays.

Patriotic education history textbooks thus go beyond the positive narrative of China's ancient civilization and modern revolutionary victories. Although it is not usually recognized outside China, national humiliation education has become an important part of the patriotic education curriculum: the encyclopedic *Practical Dictionary of Patriotic Education* includes a

355-page section recording China's national humiliations in detail.[20] As the patriotic education policy was taking shape in the early 1990s, the national humiliation theme dramatically reappeared in China, perhaps as the result of a caustic remark from Deng Xiaoping. Responding to the Group of Seven's sanctions imposed on China after the June 4th massacre, Deng revived national humiliation themes when he quipped that the Group of Seven was basically the same bunch of imperialists that had invaded China in 1900 to put down the Boxer Uprising and divide up the country:

> I am a Chinese, and I am familiar with the history of foreign aggression against China. When I heard that the seven Western countries, at their summit meeting, had decided to impose sanctions on China, my immediate association was to 1900, when the allied forces of the eight powers invaded China.

Deng thus concluded that in order to properly understand the world "Our people should study Chinese history; it will inspire us to develop the country."[21]

Following Deng's lead, the first National Humiliation history textbook since 1937 was published in 1990 as part of a "history, patriotism, and socialism" book series. The aim was to promote the singular correct history that would persuade China's youth that the CCP's rule was legitimate. By recounting China's humiliating diplomatic and military defeats at the hands of European, Japanese, and American forces, *The Indignation of National Humiliation* follows many of the same themes and rhetorical style as textbooks from the early twentieth century. The author confirms that the timing of the book was very political: it was published in April 1990 on the eve of the 150th anniversary of The Opium War.[22] Patriotic education thus served to redirect students' emotions and energies away from commemorating the first anniversary of the Tiananmen movement, which started in April 1989.

Other national humiliation textbooks were more direct in linking national humiliation and the Tiananmen movement. In June 1990, for the first anniversary of the crackdown an education journal article, "How Can We Conduct National Humiliation Education?," attacked the question head on:

> How can we make national humiliation education the guiding line of patriotic education, in order to make students understand the crimes of the imperialist invasion of China, the suffering of the Chinese nation, and thus grasp class exploitation and oppression in today's world? How can we use the perspective of class struggle to clearly understand the general international political climate and the specific domestic political climate so as to build an ideological Great Wall to oppose the "peaceful evolution" policy of the reactionary international powers?[23]

The article answers this set of questions with a set of suggestions on how to integrate national humiliation education into Chinese, English, and French language instruction; chemistry, biology, and geography curricula; thematic extracurricular activities including political study groups, movie dates, poetry readings, and even public-speaking contests. The aim was to instruct teachers about how to answer questions raised by students in the Tiananmen movement – specifically about the reasons for China's backwardness and political corruption – in the correct way. The answers, according to this article, are simple: China is backward because the West has obstructed its rise, and corruption in China comes from foreign capitalist ideology. Chinese critics are seen as counterrevolutionary liberal elites who wanted "total Westernization," while foreign critics – especially from the United States – are simply the latest generation of reactionary hostile foreign imperialist invaders.

The preface by China's vice-minister of education to a history textbook edited by the National Education Committee thus explains how patriotic education can protect the Chinese nation from threats, both foreign and domestic: "Today we are confronted with foreign and domestic enemies who are plotting to force 'peaceful evolution' on our country. We need to make the youth understand [the history of national humiliation]. . . . I hope that patriotic education will end the turmoil and counter-revolutionary tendencies among primary and secondary school students."[24]

While this anxiety about the patriotism of China's youth initially was a knee-jerk reaction to challenges faced by the party-state after 1989 (which included the fall of fraternal communist parties in the Soviet Union and Eastern Europe), this short-term propaganda tactic eventually became Beijing's long-term propaganda strategy. Throughout the 1990s, patriotic education policy continued to develop and become more institutionalized. While the PRC was embracing the world in the twenty-first century through its foreign policy narratives of "peaceful rising" and "harmonious world," the number of articles in education journals about the importance of national humiliation education was actually increasing. After scores of textbooks and hundreds of academic articles were published, in 2004 the PRC's main newsweekly *Outlook* [*Liaowang*] concluded that national humiliation was an under-researched and under-taught topic. China's "history of suffering" is an "invaluable heritage" because of the "tragedy" of "the lack of understanding among China's youth about national humiliation and national crises." The author thus concluded that national humiliation education is still necessary so that "the youth would feel how their happiness today is the outcome of a time of difficulty. Only then would they work hard in trying to repay the motherland."[25]

This view of China's modern history guides textbooks, university entrance exams, and core university courses.[26] Patriotic education and national humiliation education thus have become an institutionalized part of China's propaganda system because, as Deng Xiaoping reasoned in 1989, the CCP couldn't take loyalty for granted. The Central Propaganda Department had to socialize China's youth and the general public into a particular form of identity that tells people what to remember – and what to forget.

National Humiliation History Textbooks

To understand how historical memory informs both domestic and international politics in China, we need to look at the textbooks and teaching materials produced by the patriotic education policy. Modern history (1840–1949) for China is not the story of the triumph of development and progress; it is a painful record of defeat and loss. Modern history textbooks thus tell us how at the hands of foreign invaders and corrupt Chinese regimes, sovereignty was lost, territory dismembered, and the Chinese people thus humiliated. As *National Humiliation, Hatred and the Soul of China* (2001) summarizes China's painful century: "in modern Chinese history since the Opium War, foreign powers have launched invasion after invasion, act after bloody act of coercive pillage, occupying Chinese sovereign territory, slaughtering the Chinese masses, looting China's wealth, and stealing China's cultural artefacts. All this stained China with blood and tears."[27]

This tale is characteristically written as a chronological diplomatic history: indeed, the librarian at an American university chose to translate the title of *The History of National Humiliation* (1927) as "A History of China's Modern Foreign Relations."[28] This linear narrative records the various invasions, wars, massacres, occupations, lost territories, lootings, and unequal treaties that China suffered at the hands of imperialism. The table of contents of a slick illustrated history textbook, *A Record of National Humiliation* (1998), gives a good idea of the nature of national humiliation historiography:[29]

1. The beginning of national humiliation and the forfeit sovereignty: the First Opium War
2. The expedition of the next generation of pirates: the Second Opium War
3. A disgrace beyond redemption: Franco-British forces burn the Garden of Perfect Brilliance
4. Nation conquered, country smashed: the Sino-Japanese War [1894–5]

5. Ghosts of the Black River: the massacres of Hailanpao and the 64 Jiangdong villages [in Manchuria by the Russians]
6. Deep humiliation of the Boxer Uprising: eight-power allied forces invade China
7. No national boundaries here: the Russo-Japanese War [1905]
8. A heavy "cross" to bear: the humiliation of the missionary courts
9. Dirge of the Songhua River: the events of September 18 [1931: Japanese invasion]
10. Reign of terror in Jinling: the Nanjing Massacre [1937].

This table of contents, which chronologically lists horrible events suffered by China, shows the peculiarities of the historiography of national humiliation. Like other such texts, it is missing the key event of the nineteenth century: the Taiping Rebellion (1851–64), which has been called "the most destructive civil war in the history of the world (at least in terms of lives lost)," and was "the most serious threat to the survival of the last imperial dynasty in China."[30] Likewise, these history textbooks skate over the Republican Revolution of 1911 that ended over two millennia of imperial rule in China. Such pivotal events are not included in national humiliation histories because they do not fit in with the moral narrative of patriotic education: foreign imperialism aided and abetted by domestic corruption and treason.

This chronology of key historical events thus guides China's understanding of threats and solutions in particular ways. Starting at the turn of the twentieth century, the main enemy shifted from European imperialism to Japanese imperialism with the Sino-Japanese War (1894–5). After a series of Japanese invasions of China, the final atrocity is the "Rape of Nanjing" where invading Japanese troops systematically massacred the civilian population of China's capital city in 1937–38. The Century of National Humiliation in these textbooks ends with the national salvation of China in 1949 when Mao and the CCP finally liberated the country and founded the PRC. This narrative is painstakingly reproduced in textbooks, museums, popular history books, virtual exhibits, feature films, as well as in the National Humiliation dictionaries, journals, atlases, pictorials, and commemorative stamps. Like other propaganda campaigns, it has its own set of specialized vocabulary, iconic images, and idioms.

Rhetoric of national humiliation

Although patriotic education is a multidisciplinary and multimedia project, Jiang Zemin instructed educators and students to pay particular attention to

China's modern and contemporary history.[31] The bulk of patriotic education policy's work is done through low-cost history textbooks, which explain how "Chinese history records not only pride, but also humiliation and agony."[32] As we saw earlier, these textbooks are organized chronologically around a series of events starting with the Opium War, and ending with Liberation in 1949. They utilize long lists of atrocities to enumerate crimes against China: invasions, massacres, unequal treaties, war reparations, stolen cultural treasures, foreign occupations, and lost territories. These disjointed numbers and disparate events are joined together into the historical narrative of the Century of National Humiliation, not just through the common theme of loss, but through a common rhetorical style that employs pessoptimist distinctions. As we saw in Chapter 1, this binary positive/negative rhetoric reduces the complexities of political life to a simplistic zero-sum distinction. Yet in practice such stark distinctions quickly break down into a dynamic of complementary opposites where pride is intimately tied with humiliation, and vice versa.

The patriotic education textbooks thus employ China's pessoptimist structure of feeling to join together pride and humiliation: *Never Forget National Humiliation* (1998) explains that when Chinese people "look back at history they see not just the Four Great Inventions, ancient culture, the early heyday, the Silk Road, but also see the Opium War, the Sino-Japanese War [1894–5], and the Nanjing Massacre." The goal, the author tells his "young friends," is to rejuvenate the Chinese nation, which, under the leadership of the CCP must "rise again to be an awesome and gracious great power like in the past that will stand lofty and firm in the Eastern part of the World."[33]

Domestic/foreign

This version of modern Chinese history is not simply a historical record of the facts. It is a moral tale that records China's "fall and rise" rather than its "rise and fall." Most of the textbooks begin by stating how China went from being the highest civilization to be the Sick Man of East Asia:

> Our beautiful and fertile motherland has vast territory and a long history. Our industrious and courageous people utilized these invaluable resources to create the top civilization of the ancient world. However, for more than the last century the world has been in disarray. Japan leapt like a tiger and the West soared like an eagle, energetically advancing forward.
>
> Although we were one of the earliest classical civilizations in the world, we did not eradicate the feudalist chronic disease . . . and we fell behind.[34]

The basic reason for China's backwardness in the nineteenth century, another book tells us, was not China's "feudal conservatism or the inherent stupidity of the Chinese people," but simply because "China was barbarically invaded and pillaged by imperialism.... Capitalist imperialists turned China into semi-colony, and enslaved and slaughtered the Chinese people."[35]

Foreigners thus are written into Chinese history as a wholly *negative* force: invaders, capitalists, imperialists, barbarians, and devils, who are "pirates" when on the sea, and "bandits" when on land. According to humiliation history books, the actions of these "evil imperialists" and "foreign devils" come less from a rational pursuit of international trade or national interest, than from moral and psychological problems: foreigners are characteristically described as greedy, crazy, reckless, shameless, unreasonable, and inhumane; they acted "like beasts" because their "wild desires were insatiable."[36] Thus, the aim of foreigners in China is not international commerce, but smuggling and invasion; foreign governments do not engage in diplomacy with China, but utilize schemes, tricks, and sinister plans to exploit China. Hence, according to *Never Forget National Humiliation* (1998) and other textbooks, Western countries do not have a "China policy" to guide their international relations; rather we are told that "Western colonialist countries" pursue an "invade China policy."[37]

Europe, America, Russia, and Japan certainly were engaged in a scramble for colonies in East Asia in the nineteenth and early twentieth centuries. Yet, these textbooks criticize imperialism not out of solidarity with Vietnamese, Koreans, and Filipinos, but because the textbooks argue that France, Japan, and the United States conquered these territories in order to gain "bases from which to invade China."[38] The Century of National Humiliation discourse thus colonizes the French invasion of Vietnam, for example, as an event in China's modern *national* history. Rather than an empire that has itself invaded, occupied, and exploited Vietnam, Korea, and many other countries,[39] China is presented as an innocent victim that has never invaded another country.

Patriotic education textbooks thus stress how immoral Western and Japanese imperialists did not simply attack China – but how they actually *enjoyed* slaughtering, raping, torching, and looting China. To arouse the righteous indignation of the Chinese people, Cheng Shiwei notes how the British "with a smile" torched the fabulous Garden of Perfect Brilliance imperial palace [*Yuanming yuan*].[40] Liang Zhanjun records how Japanese soldiers laughed when killing Chinese people, while imperialists exploited China with a combination of smiles, laughs, and snickers. Hence the "Heavenly" society that foreigners enjoyed in China was built on the "Hellish" labor of the Chinese people.[41]

41

Civilized/barbaric

In this way, national humiliation textbooks appeal to concepts from China's pre-modern international relations: the hierarchical moral order of the "Civilization/barbarism distinction" that we examined in Chapter 1. Indeed, China's use of "Civilization" to describe itself and "barbarian" to describe Westerners was so pervasive that the British insisted on including a provision forbidding China from calling them "*Yi*-barbaric" in the Treaty of Tianjin (1858).[42] While most countries now organize world history courses around comparative civilizations, in China's history textbooks, there is still much talk of barbarism: "in the eyes of powerful and wealthy Chinese empire, these blue-eyed and big-nosed foreigners were not seen as special people; they were called barbarians. They were barbarians because on the one hand their civilization was inferior to Chinese civilization, ... and on the other, their cruel behavior was no different from barbarians."[43] History textbooks thus instruct China's youth on how to distinguish the positive inside from the negative outside, domestic patriots from evil foreign invaders, and thus civilized Chinese from barbaric Europeans, Japanese, and Americans.

Hero/traitor

Patriotic education textbooks also make stark moral distinctions *within* China between patriotic heroes and treacherous traitors to the Han race [*Hanjian*]. Indeed, the inscription on the Monument to People's Heroes in Tiananmen Square targets both foreign and domestic enemies in the Century of National Humiliation: "Eternal glory to the people's heroes who sacrificed themselves in the struggle against domestic and foreign enemies and for national independence and the people's freedom and happiness since 1840."[44] A book about historical traitors (which was co-published with a book about patriotic heroes) explains:

> In the history of the Chinese nation, there are many heroes like those who sacrificed their lives on the battlefield. ... But, there is a tiny minority of people who are the scum of the nation, ... who wouldn't hesitate to betray the country's and the nation's interests to become confederates of those who sell their soul for personal gain, and shamelessly bow [to foreigners] as slaves.[45]

The top hero in modern Chinese history is Lin Zexu, the honest government official who persuaded the Qing emperor to ban the Opium trade in 1839.[46]

The key traitor is Li Hongzhang, the Qing diplomat who signed away many Chinese territories (including Taiwan, Hong Kong's New Territories, Vietnam, and Korea) in unequal treaties that also burdened China with huge war reparations. While Lin Zexu was willing to use the military to defend China's sovereignty, we are told that Li Hongzhang's diplomatic compromises betrayed the nation for Li's own personal gain. As Liang summarizes, "these traitors lacked national spirit, they were a major factor that weakened us and strengthened our enemies" during the Century of National Humiliation.[47]

Like with Chinese civilization and foreign barbarism, the distinction among Han Chinese is clear: patriotic heroes sacrifice themselves for the nation, while traitors sell out the nation for their own personal gain. *A Record of a Shameful Legacy* (1990) underlines how the problem of Chinese traitors is not simply historical, but persists in the present: while China has experienced fantastic economic growth due to the selfless sacrifices of its contemporary heroes, the book warns that "there are also individuals who prostrate themselves to others, don't hesitate to sell their own soul to betray the nation's and the state's interests. . . . Their fate will be worse than that of the historical scum of the nation."[48]

While these textbooks present the division between hero and traitor as self-evident, these distinctions are actually very slippery. In the 1990s, some of the modern Chinese history's key historical figures, like Zeng Guofan, who previously were denounced as "traitors to the Han race" and "traitors to the country," were reinterpreted to be "national heroes." This revision of history was based less on new facts coming to light, and more on the rise of the new nationalist historiography promoted by the CCP's patriotic education campaign. Rather than presenting a more nuanced view of China's recent past, the goal is a clear "reversal of verdict."[49]

Through both *content* that graphically lists the horrific crimes of imperialists in excruciating detail, and a *rhetoric* that starkly separates Chinese civilization from foreign barbarism, the lesson that these patriotic education textbooks teach is clear: foreigners – especially Westerners and Japanese – are barbaric imperialist invaders who only seek to exploit the Chinese people and steal Chinese treasures. Chinese people who admire them risk becoming traitors whose dastardly deeds will be criticized not just now, but for generations to come. These are not merely history lessons; the textbooks stress how China still cannot trust foreigners and their running dogs today.

Patriotic education is not new in China; it was popular in the early twentieth century as the country dealt with the transition from empire to nation-state, and also in the transition to a socialist party-state in the Maoist era. But in the Deng era, patriotic education took on a new form to stress nationalist themes over Marxist–Leninist themes. Still, the goal of this propaganda campaign is not loyalty to the nation, but loyalty to party-state.

The Political Economy of National Humiliation

Since the textbooks highlight how Western countries – especially the United States – used an "Open Door" policy at the turn of the twentieth century to invade China not only politically, but economically, it would be easy to conclude that patriotic education is against China's current economic reform policy that has opened up China to the international market. But the long-term aim of the national humiliation narrative is both political and economic, aiming to resolve both foreign challenges and domestic problems. To "cleanse national humiliation," the Chinese government first needs to overcome imperialism by uniting the country and asserting national sovereignty under Beijing's leadership – as it did in 1949. Now the CCP needs to prove that it can develop China's social and economic system better than previous "stupidly corrupt" regimes that were "backward."[50]

Some of the textbooks argue that backwardness of the Qing dynasty and Republican China was not simply the fault of a few "race traitors"; China was weak because of *systemic* problems. In other words, the struggle was not just between countries like China and Britain, but between political and economic systems: capitalist imperialism attacked the feudal system of the Qing dynasty. Here the textbooks employ Mao Zedong's version of Marxism[51] to explain how imperialist expansion transformed China domestically:

> The feudal economy was seriously challenged, transforming China day-by-day into a commercial market and source of raw materials for world capitalism, thus changing China step-by-step into a semi-feudal and semi-colonial society. After the Opium War, China's independence was completely destroyed... with the expansion of foreign control over its politics, economics and culture.[52]

China thus became a target of imperialist aggression because its "closed-door" foreign policy made it weak and backward militarily, politically, economically, and culturally. In the early 1800s, we are told, Britain first conquered India before it targeted China as the most "politically corrupt and scientifically backward country in Asia."[53] The national humiliation textbooks thus repeat, again and again, that the lesson that the Chinese people must take to heart is that "a weak country will be bullied and humiliated, and the backward will be beaten."[54] As another national humiliation textbook concludes: "History indisputably tells us: the backward must be beaten. But history at the same time clearly tells us: if we yield to a stronger enemy's despotic power and don't dare to resist, then we will certainly be beaten."[55]

Here China's narrative of national humiliation, which is highly critical of foreigners and traitors, becomes self-critical. As *Never Forget National Humiliation* (1992) succinctly puts it: "When facing the challenge of the modern world in the nineteenth century, China fell behind."[56] As *Modern Chinese History* (2005) explains, "In the past century the basic question facing us is 'Can the Chinese people modernize?' . . . If we can, our nation's future will be bright. If we can't, our nation will have no future."[57]

IR theorist Qin Yaqing likewise highlights the link between development and identity:

> In the last century China began to experience anxiety regarding its identity with respect to the international system, and China fell into the dilemma of its place in the process of achieving modernity. Chinese people were forced to consider the question 'Who are we?' In the past, China regarded those who had not been civilized by Chinese culture as barbarians; but now, it seems that Chinese themselves become barbarians.[58]

The backward/modern distinction, which works parallel to the civilization/barbarian distinction, thus continues to frame key issues for the Chinese leadership in the twenty-first century.[59]

Patriotic education textbooks therefore stress that Chinese people need to recognize not only the fact that the CCP saved China in 1949, but also that "only reform and opening would allow China to develop" in the twenty-first century.[60] Although China has prospered with the economic reforms, *Never Forget the Century of National Humiliation* underlines how China's level of "development in economy, science and the people's livelihood is still far behind that of economically advanced countries." It argues that this is not just an economic problem, but a problem of national security because China still faces threats like those in the Century of National Humiliation: "we may still face a grave situation where we could be beaten up because we are backward."[61] Chinese people thus need to beware of the ever-present danger of hostile foreign powers.

Hence, while the dominant theme of the narrative of national humiliation that pits Chinese civilization against foreign barbarism can be xenophobic, this modernization sub-theme seeks to engage with the world economy. Its goal is in line with China's stated policy: use the negative lessons of the corrupt and isolationist Qing dynasty to promote the PRC's economic reform project, and use the international system to develop China. Economic reform opens China up to the world; but the party-state still is wary of political reform, foreign influence, and the risk of being "beaten up" in the future. The Chinese thus are instructed to guard the PRC's political, economic, and cultural sovereignty through the curious combination of national defense discourse and economic reform discourse presented in the national humiliation history textbooks. The textbooks reflect this somewhat contradictory policy by employing Marxist vocabulary in a new way. The goal of the propaganda system in the reform era is no longer a "world socialist revolution" that unites the workers of the world, but is safeguarding (and promoting) the Chinese nation: recall the popular slogan "Never Forget National Humiliation, Rejuvenate China." Nationalism in China is not merely antiforeign; it also promotes modernization, just as the modernization of China helps to confirm the patriotic nationalist credentials of the party-state. Deng's dictum to "seize with both hands" thus joins together China's open-door development policy with its xenophobic propaganda policy in order to create a strong and wealthy nation. This politics/economics nexus promotes national strength and party legitimacy in particular ways to stress the politics of the party-state, by the party-state, and for the party-state.

The Popularization of Patriotic Education

Many serious scholars in China and abroad dismiss these mass market textbooks as clumsy propaganda artifacts that have little influence on how people think and act. But the textbooks' importance is confirmed by their celebrity endorsements: the first few pages of many of these books include laudatory inscriptions by top political and military leaders. Moreover, while some analysts dismiss these textbooks as shoddy history written by party hacks, key national humiliation history books have been endorsed by China's top historians and historical research institutes. Dai Yi, a prominent historian of modern China, wrote the preface for the first national humiliation history book, *The Indignation of National Humiliation* (1990), as well as for the *Dictionary of National Humiliation: 1840–1949* (1992).[62] The president of China's World War II History Association, who is a history professor at China's National Defense University, wrote the preface for *Never Forget National Humiliation: Use History to Teach the People* (2003).[63] The director of the elite Modern History Institute of the Chinese Academy of Social Sciences (CASS) co-authored *100 Events of National Humiliation*

(2001).[64] The Modern History Institute edited the *Simple Dictionary of National Humiliation* (1993), and CASS has published other national humiliation books as well.[65]

While political and academic endorsements are important, in the late 1990s and 2000s national humiliation publications have increasingly aimed for a wider non-academic audience. Like with the commercialization of the mass media, there has been an expansion beyond the standard textbook format to a more "fresh and lively" style that engages a broader readership for patriotic education beyond the classroom.[66] Perhaps the best example of this populist mode of national humiliation education is an exhibit called "Never Forget National Humiliation" that was independently organized and funded by an "ordinary peasant."[67] This exhibit of photographs, maps, and artifacts from Japan's World War II invasion of China started as the pet project of Ren Diaoyue, a peasant from a small town in central China. Ren's private collection travelled the country for eight years, gradually building up influence until it was invited to exhibit in major cities

Figure 2.1 "Ordinary peasant" hits the talk show circuit. Liu Xinduan, Peng Xunhou, and Sun Huijun, *Wuwang guochi, Yi shi yu ren: Nongmin Ren Dianjue zifei chuangban Rijun QinHua xuixing zhan jishi*, 2003.

like Beijing and Shanghai. The travelling museum, and the strange story of the success of the "ordinary peasant" in an arena dominated by intellectuals and party officials, ended up generating publicity at the highest levels of Chinese media. National newspapers published articles about the exhibit, while Ren became a popular guest on China's talk-show circuit (see Figure 2.1).

As we saw with the Opening Ceremony of the 2008 Olympics, film directors can effectively guide China's structure of feeling. Hence to see how China's national aesthetic shapes patriotic education at the turn of the twenty-first century, we need to go to the movies. *The Opium War* opened in cinemas all over China in June 1997.[68] This epic is usually described in terms of superlatives. It was China's most expensive film. It literally employed a cast of thousands, including 3,000 foreign extras and dozens of professional foreign actors. It was financed by numerous semiofficial and semiprivate sources, and was publicly endorsed by President Jiang Zemin and other political leaders. Its premier was marked by both a Hollywood-style event at Beijing's Great Hall of the People, and by a somber academic conference. The result was a film that was successful among both the intellectual elite and the masses, wowing the critics and conquering the market: in its first few months *The Opium War* accounted for 37 percent of mainland China's *total* box office receipts, making it the highest-grossing Chinese film.[69]

Its director, Xie Jin, was already well known for his "revolutionary films" that were part of the CCP's propaganda arsenal during the Maoist era. However, *The Opium War* was different. It had private funding, and was much more sophisticated, both technically and aesthetically. Compared with an earlier cinematic treatment of the same historical events, *Lin Zexu* (1959), *The Opium War* was seen by many as much more "balanced." It was the first Chinese film to use foreign actors, and it presented them as more well-rounded characters.[70] Yet, the opposite interpretation can also be true: Xie's technical and aesthetic sophistication actually enables the film to much more persuasively convey the same messages as the patriotic education campaign: the Chinese people need a strong and modern party-state to avoid national humiliation in the twenty-first century.

Xie very quickly locates *The Opium War* in the now familiar pessoptimist structure of feeling. The film shows how China's struggle with Britain over opium relies on cultural distinctions to separate Chinese from foreigners, and sort out enemies from friends. It employs the same binary distinctions as the textbooks we analyzed earlier – foreign/domestic, civilized/barbaric, and hero/traitor – to make a patriotic sense of a war fought nearly two centuries ago. While textbooks simply use words and phrases to define a person as civilized or barbaric, *The Opium War* does it through images, dialogue, musical background, as well as running textual commentaries. For example, the film's protagonist, Lin Zexu, is introduced to the audience as a civilized scholar-official who writes poetry for his teacher. The key antagonist, Denton the British opium smuggler, is introduced shooting a seagull for fun. When his daughter Mary protests, he assures her that "it's only a game" to underline how foreigners take pleasure in being cruel and wasteful. Throughout the film, foreigners are presented as barbaric against Chinese civilization: when reading a letter from the British, Lin complains that their calligraphy is ugly and that they misspell his name.[71] Thus, when the hostilities begin the Chinese emperor can declare, "These foreigners are barbaric and ignorant. I tried peaceful means before resorting to force."

The clearest example of the film's organizing principle of civilization/barbarian is conveyed in the scene where the Chinese envoy Qi Shan goes to the British camp to negotiate a truce over dinner. Viewing his rare steak with distaste, Qi Shan opines that "You are born bellicose because you like to eat bleeding food." The British envoy responds: "I understand that the Chinese cuisine is unrivaled anywhere in the world. I can't say as much about your cannons. If you had applied just a little of your expertise in cooking to the manufacturing of cannon it would be we who today were begging for a truce." Thus, the superior spiritual power of Chinese civilization is vanquished by the superior military power of Western capitalist imperialism; it is important to note that Xie still has foreigners recognizing the wealth of Chinese civilization.

The patriotic meaning of *The Opium War* is likewise built around the hero/traitor distinction. Lin is not just a civilized person, but a national hero. Through various scenes we are shown that Lin is a good, honest, and upright official who respects his elders, and is a filial son. But this upright official is not passive: to save China he actively fights against Chinese merchants who smuggle opium in cahoots with corrupt government officials. These two groups of Chinese people are not simply criminals; the film shows time and again that they are *traitors* who sell out the Chinese nation for their own personal profit.

Curiously, Lin Zexu is not the only hero in *The Opium War*. A sing-song girl, Rong'er, also fights for China against both foreign barbarians and traitors to the Chinese race. Early in the film she is forced to prostitute herself to support a drug habit that was encouraged by a greedy merchant. But when she finds out that her john is Denton, Rong'er recoils in horror: "No, no. I don't sleep with foreigners." She is only saved from this indignity when Lin Zexu's officials raid her club. Later in the film, Rong'er suffers the

49

same fate again: after Qi Shan has sealed the deal with the British, he offers them Chinese food and Chinese women since "now you are our guests." The film presents British soldiers as drunken lechers with insatiable appetites, who paw at defenseless Chinese women. Rong'er, however, is willing to sacrifice herself for the good of the Chinese nation by agreeing to have sex with the British envoy. But once in bed, she fights back, trying to stab him with secreted scissors. In this way, Rong'er is like "China" itself. Both greedy merchants and corrupt officials are willing to sacrifice her body to foreigners – but like the Chinese people in the patriotic education narrative, Rong'er fights back. As the Qing dynasty bows before British gunboat diplomacy, she successfully resists foreign men – only to be martyred by corrupt Chinese officials.

Through its epic story, *The Opium War* clearly distinguishes between a civilized and heroic inside and a corrupt and barbaric outside. It is true that the film is progressive when compared with *Lin Zexu* (1959), because outsiders are not presented as completely evil. But the sympathetic foreigners are typically daughters and priests, not "real men" with political and economic power; and these and other sympathetic foreigners are required to praise Chinese culture to reinforce the civilization/barbarism distinction. Hence, foreigners and foreign ideas are still presented in *The Opium War* as a key moral, economic, military, and political problem.

Like with national humiliation textbooks, the film reminds us that China's fall from grace is not wholly the result of foreign invasion – it also stems from the structural and ideological "backwardness" of the Qing state. While *Lin Zexu* focuses more on the Chinese people and their resistance to imperialism and feudalism, *The Opium War* tells us that the problem in 1839 is as much the weak Qing dynasty as it is the aggressive British Empire. Long scenes emotionally document bloody battles where the heroic Chinese army is brutally destroyed. Another extended scene solemnly records how the British ceremoniously took control of Hong Kong in 1840, complete with British troops singing their national anthem and raising the British flag over China's sovereign territory.

While *The Opium War* was still dominating Chinese cinemas, the official handover ceremony, where Jiang Zemin declared that "the occupation of Hong Kong was the epitome of the humiliation China suffered in modern history,"[72] took place on July 1, 1997. The cinematic spectacle of British forces raising their flag over Hong Kong in 1840 thus formed a counterpart to the real time spectacle of the handover ceremony that focused on the lowering of the British flag and the raising of the Chinese flag. In case the film audience had forgotten, the film ends with white text on a black background: "July 1st, 1997 the Chinese government takes back sovereignty of Hong Kong, 157 years after the Opium War." The lesson is clear: only a strong state can safeguard China's political, economic, and cultural sovereignty. Actually, the state itself was a major segment of the audience behind the blockbuster success of *The Opium War* – most of the tickets were sold as "group purchases" to organs of the party-state.

The Opium War, therefore, is successful because it appeals to the structure of feeling of China's national aesthetic. It is full of facts, many of which are presented in running textual commentaries that explain the war's historical background with important dates and the official titles of Chinese and foreign historical figures. Although this documentary style delivers much important information to the audience, the film actually targets the frustration and indignation of the Chinese people who still suffer the legacies of the Century of National Humiliation. Indeed, the film shows how Lin Zexu doesn't just rationally plan his strategy for curing China's opium habit. Numerous scenes also show him yelling in anger at evil foreigners and corrupt Chinese merchants and officials. This would seem to go against Lin's role as an "upright official," where he is kind and gentle to "victims" who deserve his care. But it graphically shows Lin as a tough guy who uses his righteous rage to stand up for the Chinese people, even though he knows that he is fighting a losing battle against political–economic forces that are beyond his control. Viewers also feel the geopolitical pain of Rong'er, who has to prostitute herself to evil foreigners because she cannot afford to marry her childhood sweetheart. The film ends with long shots of the Chinese emperor weeping in the face of the judgment of history: the camera then pans across official portraits of his more successful predecessors. The ultimate issue here is whether the emperor, and the state he embodies, is strong enough to defend itself – because, as the slogan tells us, the backward will be beaten. The camera finally settles on the stone lions that guard the imperial palace in Beijing: the red glow of the lion's eye shines through the rainy gloom, promising revenge against China's foreign and domestic enemies.

Films like *The Opium War* are successful because they show how modernization in China is both material and spiritual in ways made familiar in national humiliation history textbooks. Patriotic education promotes the material goals of China's economic development project; it also works to achieve spiritual and emotional goals by both guiding and responding to how the Chinese people *feel*. Patriotic education policy documents quote how Deng Xiaoping and Jiang Zemin both stress the importance of "national self-respect, national self-esteem, and national pride."[73] Many patriotic education textbooks dutifully state that students should "Read these books and then be able to *feel* the proper sense of pride for the Chinese people. Read them and then be able to *feel* the mission and duty of the Chinese people."[74] But this pride is always intimately linked to humiliation: the writers of *Never Forget National Humiliation* (2002) feel that their "work as writers will be done" when readers "feel the unforgettable national humiliation and mass hatred, which makes the Chinese nation self-sufficient and self-reliant"[75] in its quest for wealth and power.

Resisting National Humiliation Education

By many measures the patriotic education campaign has been fantastically successful. Yet, some in China are worried that it is shaping their country's "national character" in violent and xenophobic ways, which ultimately work against the rise of China as a responsible member of international society. Historian Yuan Weishi's article, "Modernization and History Textbooks," is the most famous recent critique of patriotic education policy. It was published in *China Youth Daily*'s weekly supplement "Freezing Point" in January 2006.[76] Yuan wrote this article because he "was stunned to find that our youth are continuing to drink the wolf's milk" of harsh history textbooks, which he felt had inspired the violent chaos of the Cultural Revolution. Rather than building patriotism on a distinction between Chinese and foreign, Yuan argues that China would be strengthened if its history education developed "the national character of the Chinese people" in ways that stressed "rationality and tolerance." Yuan's reasonable conclusion actually is in line with the party-state's economic reform policy.

However, the Central Propaganda Department of the China Youth League, which owns the *China Youth Daily*, criticized Yuan and his article. It banned "Modernization and History Textbooks" because the article "seriously contradicted news propaganda discipline," and thus "hurt the feelings of the Chinese nation." The committee felt that this lack of propaganda discipline was endemic in "Freezing Point," so it shut down the magazine and fired its editor. This blatant censorship of academic analysis became a cause célèbre in Greater China and the international community. Yet, if we read the Central Propaganda Committee's judgment closely, we can see that they were enraged not just by *what* Yuan wrote, but with *how* he wrote it. It declared that Yuan himself was "seriously distorting historical facts" in ways that "attempted to vindicate the criminal acts of the imperial powers' invasion of China." Indeed, in "Modernization and

History Textbooks" Yuan plays with the rhetoric of national humiliation, often taking the pessoptimist distinctions examined earlier – inside/outside, civilized/barbaric, hero/traitor, modern/backward, and domestic/foreign – and reversing their logic. This probably is what most incensed the censors – and it also can show us how patriotic education works to promote a singular correct view of "the real China."

While textbooks see China as civilized and foreigners as barbaric, Yuan points to the Boxer Uprising (1900) to argue the opposite: here these Chinese are barbaric, anti-civilization, anti-humanity, xenophobic, ignorant, and backward. Using the same phrase that is commonly employed to describe the barbarity of foreigners, Yuan writes that "The Boxers burned, killed, looted and deliberately destroyed modern civilization." Likewise, Yuan uses the example of the Second Opium War (1858–60) that saw the burning of the Garden of Perfect Brilliance imperial palace to reverse the valence on patriotic hero/evil traitor. He points out that because they violated military discipline, the "irregular" Chinese forces that attacked European troops in 1858 cannot be called patriotic or heroic. Moreover, while diplomats like Li Hongzhang are prominent on lists of Chinese traitors, Yuan lists Li as an "astute official" who was patriotic and heroic.

While the history textbooks generate patriotism by "inflaming nationalistic passions" against foreigners, Yuan criticizes this strategy, saying that "Our thinking is still poisoned by . . . traditional Chinese culture's deeply ingrained idea that 'Chinese and foreigners are different.'" He warns that we "should not underestimate the consequences of this mis-education," and draws a close parallel between the logic of the Boxers' attack on Beijing's diplomatic quarter in 1900 and the Red Guards' torching a British consulate during the Cultural Revolution. Hence, while patriotic education textbooks list the national humiliations of foreigners' barbaric invasion of China, Yuan thinks that Chinese textbooks themselves are a "national humiliation." Speaking of the barbarities of the Boxers, he concludes that "these are all facts that everybody knows, and it is a national humiliation that the Chinese people cannot forget. Yet our children's compulsory textbooks will not speak about it."

Yuan is not the only critic of Beijing's ideological campaigns. In another newspaper article, "China Must Adopt a Great-power Mentality, and Make Psychological Change Part of its Modernization," CASS scholar Jin Xide also argues against patriotic education and national humiliation discourse.[77] While Yuan is mainly concerned with how national humiliation education fans extremism in China's domestic politics, Jin is interested in patriotic education's impact on international relations. While historians like Yuan are interested in how the events of 1840–1949 are presented to Chinese students, Jin is interested in how the dynamic of "glory and humiliation" has shaped the PRC's relation to the world in the past half century. Rather than seeing glory and humiliation as opposites, Jin tells us that these positive and negative "extremes" are "interwoven, separated only by a fine line and can easily trade places." This pessoptimist mentality has led Chinese to "conduct ourselves in the world either arrogantly or with an inferiority complex."

China's unstable foreign policy over the past five decades, Jin tells us, has been fostered by a crisis mentality in education and the media, which exaggerates China's various problems into existential threats to the nation. Yet, Jin feels that in the twenty-first century China is hardly in a crisis – it is stronger and more successful than at any time over the past few centuries. There are still problems with China's international environment, including many hostile "anti-China" critics abroad. But Jin argues that the main challenge is less a "foreign threat" than the domestic identity politics of "how should we look upon ourselves? How should we approach the international community?" Being a great power is not merely an achievement of material success, for Jin tells us that it involves "a need for us to do some soul-searching on the national psychology, national mentality, and strategic thinking in the context of our response to the outside world." Modernization thus needs to target not just the national economy, but China's "national ideology." The real question for Jin is "are we prepared psychologically" to be a great power?

Jin's solution to the problem of China's pessoptimism is to use the media to shift "public opinion and the national psychology" away from "parochial and xenophobic nationalism." He argues that there should be more "good news" about international events: "Those who study and report international affairs must interpret a matter correctly and explain it fully without, however, steering public opinion in the direction of pessimism and xenophobia." Still, Jin is not naïve; he doesn't expect the outside world – especially Europe, Japan, and the United States – to be fair to China. But a strong national consciousness will enable China to resist any "psychological offensive that the world may launch against us." Jin thus concludes that "We should adopt a neither-obsequious-nor-supercilious attitude toward international affairs. We should handle things calmly and keep our cool."

These and other examples of resistance to patriotic education show how there is some space in China to critically comment on orthodox versions of Chinese identity. This broader view of politics that avoids categorizing things as either totally right or wholly wrong, is leading to what Richard

Curt Kraus feels is an "increased toleration for rival points of view" in China's civil society.[78] In this way, commentators can go beyond the Central Propaganda Department's structure of feeling, which sorts statements as either pro- or anti-Chinese, to encourage people to think about different ways of being Chinese.

But new forms of patriotic education and critique also show how the party-state's propaganda apparatus is adapting to the multimedia environment of the twenty-first century. Commercialization of the media has not lead to a meaningful liberalization of discourse because the Central Propaganda Department still maintains ultimate control over mass communications and education. Indeed, even critics like Yuan and Jin follow the party-state's ideology by arguing, on the one hand, that their views are the "correct" way to understand "the real China." On the other, they both feel that propaganda is still important: it just needs to be redirected to promote more positive themes. Hence, we need to both recognize the limits of the Chinese party-state, while not exaggerating the impact of criticisms of China's political system; against the overwhelming din of patriotic education, critics of national humiliation discourse are merely a whisper of dissent.

Conclusion

China's leaders and scholars often tell foreigners that the world should not be worried about the spread of xenophobic nationalism in the PRC. They state that the party-state is actually against any divisive, narrow-minded, or parochial nationalism, and that it works hard to promote a "rational nationalism" that is pragmatic. In Autumn 2006, for example, secondary schools in Shanghai started using new textbooks that downplayed ideology and national humiliation discourse, and had only one brief reference to Mao Zedong.[79]

This chapter has shown that while China's education and propaganda systems certainly do promote a positive image of China and the world that the Chinese people can be proud of, at the same time they also present a very negative view of China's relation with the world based on the history of national humiliation. The Central Propaganda Department has very deliberately developed the pedagogy of national humiliation as an important part of its patriotic education policy. This elaborate policy graphically shows how historical memory is a social phenomenon; as Deng Xiaoping concluded in 1989, China's youth need to be taught how to be patriots:

they need to be taught to remember to "Never Forget National Humiliation."

This chapter has examined Chinese-language sources from official and popular culture – including textbooks, pop histories, exhibitions, and films – to show how patriotic education promotes a particular structure of feeling that draws thick moral distinctions between patriotic Chinese on the one hand, and evil foreigners and their Chinese race-traitors on the other. This harsh division of a civilized domestic sphere from a barbaric outside world helped the party-state survive the regime security challenges it faced after 1989. While the patriotic education policy was initially formulated in the wake of the June 4th massacre, this mass campaign is continually adapting to China's new circumstances in a way that is both flexible (to promote new slogans like Hu Jintao's "harmonious society"), and institutionalized (to not only maintain the power of the Central Propaganda Department, but to spread it beyond traditional education to entertainment and new media products).

The CCP's Central Propaganda Department thus uses a multidisciplinary and multimedia campaign to tie patriotism to the party-state, while critics want to use history education to produce rational citizens rather than rabid wolves. Crucially, all sides talk about China's national character, national psychology, and national mentality – they just have different answers to the question "Who is China?" On the other hand, the propaganda system's sharp distinction between patriotic Chinese and hostile foreigners can help explain how and why the country's indignant youth are so quickly and easily aroused to defend China against enemies both foreign and domestic.

While international security experts like Bates Gill confidently state that China has "abandon[ed its] long-held and reactive 'victimhood' complex, and put the country's 'century of shame' to one side,"[80] the reaction of vocal segments of the Chinese public in spring 2008 to international criticism of Beijing's crackdown in Tibet is instructive. The party-state's official spokespeople and publications quickly labored to turn a domestic issue of interracial relations into an international issue of "the West" attacking China: *Lies and Truth*, the title of a book that was quickly published during the uprising, underlines the pessoptimism of such propaganda campaigns.[81]

Yet, Chinese reaction went far beyond official propaganda products produced and distributed by the party state. China's official anger was accompanied by a firestorm of anti-Western feeling on the Internet, which repeated the themes and vocabulary of national humiliation education. YouTube videos, special Web sites, and e-mailed essays all employed official historiography to defiantly proclaim "Tibet is ours!" The common theme was not simply political, but epistemological in the sense of promoting a single correct view of "the real China": many of these texts instruct foreigners not only in how to correctly understand China, but also in the proper way to criticize China. If you transgress the bounds of respectful commentary, then watch out: "Hopefully the good intention can bring positive result when it's combined with insight. As to those who have other purposes, China has a unique program for them as well, but that's a different thing."[82] A popular YouTube video "Tibet WAS, IS, and ALWAYS WILL BE a part of China" was even more blunt in its harsh division between patriotic Chinese and hostile foreigners: "to all you bandwagon jumpers who know nothing about chinese [sic] history, and to all you bashers, let me give you some solid FACTS why Tibet was, is and always will be, a part of China, so you can f*** right off trying to separate our country."[83] Many of these postings and videos were gathered together on a Web site that highlights the negatively productive nature of the attacks: Anti-CNN.com.

Spring 2008's popular reaction by Chinese netizens, which was both earnest and harsh, to what they saw as foreign provocation is far from unique. It followed the familiar institutional and rhetorical patterns that produced and guided popular Chinese opinion in earlier crises.[84] But there have been new developments in recent years. While the NATO bombing of China's Belgrade embassy (1999) and the EP-3 reconnaissance plane collision (2001) were clearly international issues, national humiliation discourse is increasingly deployed to deal with China's domestic problems. Like with the Tibet controversy in 2008, the party-state and the indignant youth both employed national humiliation discourse to frame the controversy over the health and safety of Chinese exports that arose in summer 2007. In the face of this singular view of China's history, identity, and security that unites Chinese people against a hostile foreign enemy, it is not surprising that Shanghai authorities withdrew their new history textbooks in 2007.

The PRC's patriotic education policy is certainly not unique. It has parallels in many countries in Europe, Asia, and North America.[85] Japan and Russia, for example, have been beefing up their curricula to instill a proper state-centric pride in the youth over the past few years.[86] In Europe many identities, both national and regional, are predicated on being "not American." Debate over China's patriotic education also resonates with struggles in the United States. Understanding the Sino-British conflict in the nineteenth century as the Opium War is very similar to the "war on drugs" that the United States has pursued over the past few decades.[87] Indeed, the

Figure 2.2 Lin Zexu statue in New York's Chinatown. Courtesy of William A. Callahan.

overseas Chinese community put up a statue of Lin Zexu in New York's Chinatown; it faces One Police Plaza and its inscription praises Lin as the first soldier in the "war on drugs" (see Figure 2.2). More importantly, the debate in China about the utility of patriotic education is quite similar to the debate about the "war on terror" in the United States. Yuan and Jin's questioning of how China should understand its modern history is similar to debates over how to understand the September 11 attacks: are they an emotional issue in "the war on terror," or a rational–legal issue where "terrorists are criminals."

The difference between China and the United States here is that while the September 11 attacks are still a recent phenomenon in living memory, China's Century of National Humiliation ended in 1949 and now is largely known through official propaganda. China certainly suffered at the hands of European, American, and Japanese imperialism, but enough time has gone by to allow us to go beyond "the facts" to see how history and memory are being produced and consumed in the PRC. Crucially, both propagandists and their critics trust that education and propaganda can effectively socialize the Chinese public. Indeed, all follow Mao's double injunction to "Make the past serve the present, and foreign things serve China" in order to make the PRC a great power.

Chapter 3 answers the questions "Who is China?" and "When is China?" in a different way. While this chapter has looked at how the party-state's propaganda policies have socialized the Chinese public, Chapter 3 examines how Chinese people produce and consume their national identity through popular practices like National Humiliation Day. Together these two chapters show the interplay of state policy and popular practices in China's identity and security politics.

Chapter 3

When Is China? (2): Producing and Consuming National Humiliation Days

October 1st is China's National Day. It celebrates the success of the communist revolution that established the People's Republic of China (PRC) on October 1, 1949. National Day starts early in Beijing, with the honor guard of the People's Liberation Army marching out through the Gate of Heavenly Peace at 6:10 am to raise China's national flag over Tiananmen Square. Thousands of onlookers, from both Beijing and the provinces, join in to sing the national anthem while waving miniature national flags.[1]

After the flag-raising ceremony, people can gaze at the colorful flower displays set in front of the Forbidden City. In 2007, for example, 400,000 pots of flowers were arranged as "scale models of the Acropolis in Athens, the Great Wall, and a 9.8-meter Olympic torch, which represents the torch relay from Greece to China" on one side of Tiananmen Square, with "models of the Temple of Heaven and major scenes marking key events in the history of the Communist Party of China (CCP) to welcome the Seventeenth National Congress of the CCP which starts on October 15," on the other.[2]

Like on the Fourth of July in the United States, after dark, Chinese citizens can admire elaborate firework displays that light up the sky in cities all around the country. Since its return to China in 1997, Hong Kong has added its own twist to National Day celebrations: its horse race calendar now includes the National Day Cup, which is a deliberate reference to Deng Xiaoping's promise that "the horses would keep on racing, the dancers would keep on dancing" after the handover.

The National Day celebration is even more elaborate in milestone years: a huge military parade marked the fiftieth anniversary of the founding of the PRC in 1999. That morning, the honor guard marched at the more social hour of 10:00 am into a sea of 100,000 people waving paper flowers. When they raised the flag, the flower placards flipped to display the national emblem of China, with "1949" on the left and "1999" on the right.

After Jiang Zemin's speech from the same rostrum where Mao Zedong proclaimed the PRC in 1949, the five-mile long parade began. It included servicemen and women from the army, navy, air force, and militia, as well as China's latest military hardware: tanks, armored personnel carriers, and cruise missiles, and intercontinental ballistic missiles (ICBMs) mounted on launchers. A low-level flyover of fighters, bombers, and refueling planes roared above the city.

This display of military prowess was followed by over ninety floats and civilian marchers that celebrated China's achievements over the past fifty years, and especially since economic reform began in 1978. Floats carried beautiful women dressed in Tang dynasty costumes and China's ethnic minorities in national dress. A division of newlyweds, who were all married on National Day, marched past. Hundreds of participants in wheelchairs, on roller skates, and unicycles rolled by. Dragon dancers, lion dancers, fan dancers, and ring dancers performed. Thousands of balloons and birds were released. Altogether, the parade involved over half a million people who had been practicing for months, in ways similar to the preparations for the 2008 Olympics opening ceremony. Indeed, Beijing's Olympic imagineers have been hired to craft the celebration of the sixtieth anniversary of the PRC in October 2009.

While the party-state's elite and invited foreign guests witnessed this spectacle from the reviewing stands at the foot of the Gate of Heavenly Peace, everyone else watched this fabulous performance on television. The parade was complemented by numerous other National Day activities, including a show at Beijing's national Exhibition Hall that displayed all of the PRC's achievements in one huge space.[3]

October 1 is like National Days in other countries, where independence and revolution are celebrated in a grand style. China's other national holidays, however, are in a period of transition. Starting with the 1999 National Day celebration, the PRC had three main national holidays – Chinese New Year, May Day, and National Day – where people not only had one day off, but a "golden week". Yet in 2008, Beijing demoted its celebration of international socialism's May Day from a golden week to a single day. It also added new daylong public holidays to promote China's own traditional culture: Tomb Sweeping Day (April), the Dragon Boat festival (June), and the Mid-Autumn Festival (September).[4] This follows the general trend of refocusing the party-state's propaganda from international socialism to

Chinese nationalism seen in earlier chapters. Indeed, these national holidays, which tell people when and how to be patriotic Chinese citizens, are a key example of how China's national aesthetic is expanding the concept of security beyond military strength to address other issues: ideological security, regime security, and cultural security.

Another less grand holiday complements the positive pride of National Day with a sense of shame to balance national security with nationalist insecurities. On a neighborhood notice-board in Shanghai in mid-September 2003, I saw a poster of a soldier wielding a bayoneted-rifle against the background of the national flag, fireworks, and missiles. The caption enjoined the public to observe National Defense Education Day because "National defense connects you, me and others in the national borders that peacefully hold together millions and millions of families [in China]." This new holiday, which was declared in 2001, joins together traditional and nontraditional notions of security because on the one hand it clearly refers to the proud tradition of military security of guarding territorial borders for the well-being of the nation now and in the future; and on the other hand, in ways unlike National Day's proud celebration, this new holiday appeals to China's sense of loss and danger because it is informally known as "National Humiliation Day."

This commemoration day was first observed in Beijing by thousands of university students who gathered at the ruins of the Garden of Perfect Brilliance imperial palace [*Yuanming yuan*]. The People's Liberation Army (PLA) explained the National Defense Education Law to these students in the context of this opulent palace that had been destroyed by British and French troops in the Second Opium War (1860).[5] Hence, while America's National Defense Education Act (1958) dealt with the Cold War humiliation of Sputnik by looking outward to the future by promoting math, science, foreign languages, and area studies, China's National Defense Education Law looks inward to the past by directing us to remember the atrocities of China's national humiliations. Indeed, the theme of the 2004 National Defense Education Day was "Never forget national humiliation, strengthen our national defense."[6] (See Figure 3.1.) In this way, National Defense Education Day has become another manifestation of the discourse of national humiliation, especially in 2004 when it fell on September 18th, the day that commemorates Japan's conquest of Manchuria in 1931.

Yet, this recently declared and popularly celebrated military holiday is not completely new; it recalls a structure of feeling popular in the early twentieth century. National Humiliation Day was an unofficial holiday in China from 1915 to 1926, and an official holiday from 1927 to 1940 under

Figure 3.1 "Never forget national humiliation, strengthen our national defense." Poster for National Defense Education Day, 2004.

Chiang Kai-shek's Nationalist (Guomindang) regime. During the Republican period, the holiday commemorated May 9th, the day when the Chinese government succumbed to Japan's Twenty-one Demands in 1915, which seriously compromised China's national sovereignty. As we see, recent National Humiliation Day events closely mirror activities from the early twentieth century.

This chapter thus explores the workings of the curious custom of National Humiliation Day to see how China's pessoptimist structure of feeling answers the question "When is China." While Chapter 2 examined patriotic education's historical construction of the nation, this chapter explores the use of time in nation-building projects: the *national* time scripted by National Humiliation Day, as opposed to temporal events that celebrate regional, gender, or class identity. Rather than assuming the coherence of "the nation" or "security," I examine how national security is an identity issue that takes on coherence through the public performance of national insecurities such as National Humiliation Day. Indeed, strange as it may seem, this holiday is not peculiar to China; there have been similar practices of national insecurity in South Korea, North Korea, Taiwan, Russia, England, America, India, and other countries – indeed, the US Congress declared a "National Day of Humility, Prayer, and Fasting" at the height of the invasion of Iraq in 2003.[7] National security here concerns more than an elite discourse of policy issues, for it addresses the security politics raised in the events of everyday life and popular culture. National security thus takes shape in China through the interplay of state policy and popular movements.

Although it is important to examine what people "think" when they construct the nation, intellectual histories of nation-building tend to universalize elite views of identity. Historian Jeffrey N. Wasserstrom thus argues that the politics of Chinese student demonstrations is best understood not only through analyzing the ideology that they promote, but by tracing the performative techniques that mobilize people for specific political events. In this way, we can better understand the political importance of the activities of different groups, often nonliterate groups and nonelite groups. Wasserstrom thus describes China's political protests as either "political theater" that is subversive, or "political ritual" that reinforces the status quo in a way that stresses the interplay of actor and audience in creating political meaning.[8] Indeed, the party-state's promotion of political ritual is helpful for understanding Chinese nationalism because the state has been intimately involved in setting cultural and moral standards for the populace from imperial times up to the present People's Republic; resistance to the state's propaganda campaigns also has taken cultural forms, often deploying and redeploying the same set of techniques in new and different ways. But while the state's political ritual stresses the themes of national unity and patriotism, the chapter shows how the cultural resistance of political theater undermines the solemnity of commemoration through satire and commercialization that turns serious commemorations into entertainment events. I argue, therefore, that the international politics of national humiliation days, like international politics in general, is best analyzed as a series of sovereignty performances, not just by state actors in official sites like the Foreign Ministry, but also through political performances at less official sites in art, film, literature – and public holidays.

As I argued in Chapter 2, much of the power of China's mass demonstrations in 1989 came from the fact that they presented an alternative to the official commemoration of a key revolutionary holiday – the seventieth anniversary of the May 4th movement of 1919. In the twenty-first century, National Humiliation Day (scheduled for the third Saturday of September) is likewise placed near another key event in Chinese revolutionary history: September 18th, the Mukden Incident, whereby Japan conquered Manchuria in 1931, and which was commemorated in the 1930s as the second National Humiliation Day. Indeed, the cycle of protests that led to Beijing spring in 1989 started in 1985 when Peking University students commemorated "September 18th" as a way to protest a new Japanese economic invasion. When National Defense Education Day fell on September 18th in 2004, the official theme was "Never forget national humiliation, strengthen our national defense." Responding to Japan's quest for a permanent seat on the United Nations Security Council, in 2005 China's "history activists" collected over 22 million signatures in Spring 2005 on an online petition whose URL commemorates September 18th: http://yahoo.1931–9–18.org. National Humiliation days thus continue to integrate state policy and popular feelings in the twenty-first century.

The body of this chapter analyzes the activities that take place on National Humiliation Day to consider *when* and *how* the nation is produced through national time. It explores how identity and security are produced together through sovereignty performances from both state and nonstate actors. By comparing the differing practices of the holiday as it was celebrated in the early twentieth century, and is observed in the early twenty-first century, I argue that in the early twentieth century, popular political performances aimed to *produce* a proper Chinese nation out of the clashes between the Qing dynasty, northern warlords, and foreign empires. The goal was to construct a "China" worthy of being saved. In the early twenty-first century, the party-state's political performances are more focused on *containing* the nation through a commemoration of the various crises of the early twentieth century. Thus, while the early-twentieth-century discourse used nontraditional modes of popular culture to address the dramatically traditional security crisis of foreign invasion, the chapter shows how activities in the twenty-first century use a traditional vocabulary of war and foreign relations to address the nontraditional security issue of the CCP's political legitimacy. I argue that the nation does not just arise from the ideology of its leaders (at either end of the twentieth century), so much as through popular performances such as National Day and National Humiliation Day. Hence, while it is true that economic reforms have dramatically hollowed out socialist ideology, I argue that this is beside the point. In China, we need to look at what people do, as well as what they think. In this way, national humiliation day activities go beyond producing and containing nationalism; Chinese people are also *consuming* nationalism to produce a particular form of identity – and a particular type of security.

Although patriotic education was revived in 1990 as a propaganda campaign that served as the party-state's response to the Tiananmen uprising, by the mid-1990s, national humiliation discourse had spread beyond official control as China's popular media were opened up to market forces. To put it simply, patriotism sells – not just in China, but in most countries. Thus, patriotism is more than the result of an instrumental manipulation of national symbols by the elite; patriotism has generated an active consumer market for its symbolic commodities. Moreover, although many see patriotic education and National Humiliation Day as peculiarly communist activities, sources from popular movements in the early twentieth century confirm that national humiliation is an enduring narrative of modern Chinese history and identity. It is thus necessary to compare how China's nationalism and security are shaped by the historical insecurity of national humiliation in both the early twentieth century and the early twenty-first century.

In the next two sections, I consider the techniques of National Humiliation Day as political performances in the early twentieth century and early twenty-first century. In this way, we go beyond an examination of the ideological question of *what* is being remembered, to see *when* and *how* the past is commemorated as a nationalist performance in international space.

When: Proclaiming National Humiliation Day

In *Festivals and the French Revolution*, Mona Ozouf argues that the French Revolution was more than an ideological project of liberty, equality, and fraternity. It was also a cultural project that revolutionized the everyday life of common people. Indeed, the French were created as citizens of the Republic as much by new practices as by "the Declaration of the Rights of Man and Citizen." An important part of this new Republican lifestyle was the new French calendar, with its list of new revolutionary festivals.[9]

After China's own Republican revolution of 1911, which overthrew not only the Qing dynasty, but also two millennia of imperial governance, the new leadership likewise worked hard not only to found new state institutions and ideologies, but also to fashion republican citizens out of imperial subjects. One marked oneself as a new citizen less by subscribing to the new ideological program, than by following revolutionary fashion. Republican men cut their queues (the mark of imperial submission), and women unbound their feet. Both men and women put on Western-style clothes.[10] One of the first official acts of the Republic of China was the dramatic shift from the imperial Chinese lunar calendar to a Western-style solar calendar; the regime's first official *Almanac* (1912) actively asserted a new time for a new China because it included tables to convert dates from the old imperial lunar calendar to the new Republican solar calendar.[11] Indeed, in much the same way as the French Revolution's new calendar founded a new republican society through its festivals, the solar calendar instituted a new series of positive celebrations that not only added to the legitimacy of the state, but also forged a new society of citizens. National Day was first officially celebrated in 1912 as "10–10 day" (October 10th). The first national protest day came two-and-a-half years later on May 9, 1915, which was named "May 9th National Humiliation Commemoration Day" [*Wujiu guochi jinianri*].

The Century of National Humiliation, many textbooks tell us, started in 1842 with the signing of the Treaty of Nanjing that ended the Opium War with Britain. Indeed, many official and popular history books now declare that date – August 29, 1842 – China's "first National Humiliation Day."[12] But actually National Humiliation Day itself was not proclaimed until 1915 – seventy-three years into what would later be named "the Century of National Humiliation." While European powers were distracted by World War I, Japan made imperial claims on Chinese territory in early 1915. A long process of secret diplomacy culminated on May 7th, when Japan sent its ultimatum of "Twenty-one Demands" to the Chinese government. These included ceding to Japan the Chinese territories formerly occupied by Germany, as well as a host of other lucrative economic concessions. Chinese president Yuan Shikai accepted most of these demands on May 9th.[13]

Nationwide mass protests broke out once this agreement was announced. Both National Salvation Societies and National Humiliation Societies were formed to hold meetings to discuss this insult to China's national honor. In mid-May 1915, May 9th was proclaimed as "National Humiliation Day": a holiday to be celebrated and a humiliation to be commemorated on an annual basis. But this patriotic movement to defend China's national security was not state-led. Rather, it was proclaimed as resistance against the state by the National Teachers' Association. Other corporate associations for national humiliation were also formed, including groups representing chambers of commerce, student unions, female student unions, overseas student associations, labor unions, provincial governors, soldiers, and "common citizens."

To underline how this political protest was political theater – performing nationalism like in the 2008 Olympics opening ceremony – an actors union put on a special play, not just to commemorate the national humiliation of the Twenty-one Demands, but also to raise money for the National Humiliation Fund to buy arms to fight Japan.[14] Thus, after 1915, "May 9th" was commemorated on an annual basis in cities across China. This explosion of resistance activity was necessary because "the events of May [1915] confirmed that the Chinese could not depend on their politicians to preserve China's immediate interests, much less the integrity of the nation."[15]

Moreover, political resistance activities increasingly took on a *national* (as opposed to a regional or class) character in response to China's accepting Japan's Twenty-one Demands. Not only was a nationwide national humiliation day declared, nationwide and cross-class associations were established with the mission of saving China from national humiliation, which they feared would lead to "national extinction" [*mieguo*]. As early as July 1915, a national curriculum for national humiliation education emerged to guide people's understanding of identity and security; national humiliation history and geography textbooks soon followed.[16] As Sun Xiangmei explains, "Through National Humiliation education at school, public debates, and guidance by patriotic organizations, it is not surprising that National Humiliation Day became an unforgettable memory for the vast majority of youth and students" in the Republican era.[17] In this way, Chinese nationalism is one of the products of National Humiliation Day, not just in terms of ideas, but in terms of the institutional practices of nationwide social movements and national curricula.

Once the Nationalists asserted state sovereignty in 1927, they quickly made "May 9th National Humiliation Commemoration Day," an official holiday as an important part of a very deliberate construction of citizenship and national identity in the ROC.[18] Actually, since Japan and the other imperial powers had humiliated China numerous times since 1915, in 1928 the Nationalist Party issued an official calendar of twenty-six National Humiliation Days that were observed throughout the year: government officials lamented that "only December lacks one."[19] The official announcement tells us that this list of twenty-six humiliation holidays was the result of the Department of the Interior's survey of China's various locally observed National Humiliation Days. Rather than relying on ideas, the state thus sought to mirror and contain popular practices by nationalizing these local customs in order to buttress its particular patriotic national identity through national time.

However, since odd days are included and familiar days are excluded, a certain logic of selection seems to have prevailed. The purpose of distributing the National Humiliation Days throughout the year was both political and economic. The concentration of humiliation holidays in May was beginning to cause problems for the government: in 1921 a national humiliation day article proclaimed, "There are commemorations on May 1st, May 4th, May 7th."[20] In 1925, the May 30th Shanghai massacre was added, as was the May 3rd Ji'nan massacre in 1928. It got so bad that one author sarcastically commented, "May has become a sad month. We should follow the English pronunciation of 'May,' which is the same as the Chinese word '*mei* – out of luck.' May is the unlucky month."[21]

The authorities did not have such a sense of irony; after the Nationalists took control of Shanghai in 1927, it instituted "Humiliation Month Precautions," to "suppress communist uprisings and radical movements" during May.[22] Hence, in 1928 the government deployed this new commemorative calendar to control security threats in much the same way as the CCP would after 1989. The aim was to use a calendar of approved humiliation holidays to redirect and contain the political protest and economic disruption produced by mass demonstrations. The temporal politics of national holidays thus was one of the ways that the Nationalists sought to police, and thus control, nationalism by transforming the energy seen in the political theater of resistance into a regularized political ritual performed by the party's corporate groups. The holiday was officially terminated just before its planned celebration in 1940. As the official announcement proclaimed: "Since July 7, 1937, the whole country has been involved in a war of resistance. Therefore, July 7th is now the War of Resistance commemoration day. Thus, the May 9th commemoration is no longer necessary."[23] National Humiliation Day ended in the Republican period not with a victory, but in the face of the even greater crisis of Japan's all-out invasion.

National Humiliation Day reappeared in 2001 as National Defense Education Day. It was proclaimed through an official document, the National

Defense Education Law, which was passed by the National People's Congress. But this nationwide national humiliation day was the upshot of a decade-long process. A regional "National Humiliation Day" had been declared in Shenyang to commemorate the September 18th Mukden Incident;[24] indeed, Shenyang's September 18th History Museum is actually shaped like a calendar to highlight the temporal politics of memory (see Figure 3.2). Many cities, including Hong Kong, annually commemorate July 7th as the national humiliation of Japan's invasion of China proper in 1937, while Nanjing set aside December 13th to commemorate the Nanjing Massacre that followed.[25]

As early as 1995, people were calling for the government to "Please Establish 'National Humiliation Day'" in prominent publications.[26] Chen Yunjie, for example, argued that it was time to institutionalize the increasingly haphazard commemoration of national humiliation:

> Our country has many traditional holidays; many more have been established since New China was founded. Most are celebrations, commemorations, or holidays, so why do I propose a "National Humiliation Day"? ... The shame of history cannot be forgotten, forgetting the past

Figure 3.2 September 18th History Museum, Shenyang. Courtesy of William A. Callahan.

is a betrayal. Establishing a "National Humiliation Day" would make an alarm bell ring out in the heart of every Chinese, and arouse the national spirit.[27]

In a 2002 essay, Liu Jichang agrees: "Now national humiliation activities are courageous and dynamic (and not the heavy burden as some people thought), and can both encourage and warn us." Although many admitted that it was a strange sort of holiday, Liu labors to point out that national humiliation days are not unique to China. Powerful countries like the United States, Japan, South Korea, and Russia already have National Humiliation Days "to promote patriotism among their citizens, and spread an awareness of national shame. For example, America sees the day when Japan attacked Pearl Harbor as National Humiliation Day."[28] Indeed, in commemorating the first National Humiliation Day in 2001, a key article in the prominent *China Youth Daily* newspaper explains that other countries have observed this custom.[29]

Thus, in 2001, the National People's Congress (NPC) decided that China also needed a nationwide national humiliation day. The timing of this holiday was much debated. In early drafts, "the law named September 7, the date when China was forced to sign a humiliating treaty with eleven foreign powers 100 years ago" after the Boxer Uprising. Supporters said "this date is proper because it is not related to any one particular foreign country." But others wanted to be more specific, and hoped to mark dates when Japan invaded China as the holiday: July 7th or September 18th. Even so, there were worries that calling attention to imperial Japan's "historical aggression" would upset Japan in ways familiar to China: "The choice of this date should not be viewed as an offense to the Japanese people, but a reminder of Japanese military imperialism, because it reflects the truth of history," one promoter declared.[30] Finally, the NPC decided that China should avoid targeting any one nation, and thus no specific historical date was chosen. Rather it chose the third Saturday of September, which often lies between September 7th and 18th, to divert attention away from specific historical memories. The first national humiliation day was marked on September 15th, in the shadow of the September 11th attacks on New York and Washington, DC.

More than just positively creating a new holiday, National Defense Education Day is negative because it outlaws competing holidays. The law stipulates that

Once the timing of National Defense Education Day is determined, all the other holidays prescribed by local and provincial governments, such as "Defense Education Day," "Military Activity Day," "National Humiliation Day," "National Defense Education Week," and "National

Defense Education Month," will no longer be legally in effect. Each province and autonomous region must scrap its particular holiday for National Defense Education Day.[31]

In this way, the central authorities are not just using festivals to contain resistance, Beijing also aims to contain the rival bases of power at provincial and municipal levels of government that were asserting regional identity through the regional time of their own holidays. Like with the Nationalist Party's 1928 National Humiliation calendar, this official holiday seeks to construct a particular national time; a nonhistorical date (the third Saturday of September) is helpful because its national abstraction outlaws the regional times of September 18th (for Manchuria) and December 13th (for Nanjing). Much like the Chinese party-state's recentralization of fiscal governance in the mid-1990s, this law shows how the PRC works to centralize and thus nationalize identity. It very forcefully tells patriotic citizens *when* to be Chinese.

It would be easy to conclude this section by highlighting, once again, how National Humiliation Days have been a successful part of state-driven propaganda campaigns in the past and present. Indeed, I could underline how both the ROC and the PRC used various methods to enforce a solemn patriotic commemoration of National Humiliation Day, and thus keep demonstrations that valued sarcasm, satire, entertainment, and commerce at bay: in addition to schools and shops, bars, dancehalls, brothels, and amusement parks were closed on May 9th.

But this would only be telling part of the story. National Humiliation Day was, after all, originally declared and celebrated as an act of resistance by a nonstate actor – the National Teachers' Association – and was enthusiastically adapted as a popular holiday by many other nonstate groups. While most assume that the state is the actor producing identity for a passive audience, this shows how the state is also the audience that needs to respond to nonstate actors.

Moreover, this holiday was not only a criticism of Japan, but a self-criticism of China itself. In 1915, there was much political debate about on which day the humiliation should be commemorated: May 7th when Japan made the Twenty-one Demands, or May 9th when the Chinese president accepted them. Should patriots criticize the Chinese self or the Japanese other? In the Republican era, this debate was never settled, showing the tension between criticism and self-criticism entailed in National Humiliation activities.[32]

And debate over the proper time to commemorate national humiliation is not over. New national humiliation days actually keep being declared in unofficial and semiofficial spaces to address new security crises. In 1919, May 4th originally was named a *second* national humiliation day, as was September 18th in 1931, and November 4th in 1946.³³ Even after National Defense Education Day was declared in 2001 to stand for – and supplant – popularly commemorated national humiliation days, calls for a more specific and more official National Humiliation Day continue. In 2007, an NPC delegate proposed a law

> to observe September 18 nationwide "simultaneously" as National Humiliation Day because . . . an outstanding nation is one that will always keep its history firmly in mind. . . . Remembering this humiliating part of history will help Chinese people feel the need to safeguard peace and work hard for the rejuvenation of the nation.³⁴

Although this attempt to create a new National Humiliation Day as part of the reform of China's Golden Week holidays was unsuccessful, it is evidence of a gnawing desire among Chinese citizens that can be seen on Internet bulletin boards and in the blogosphere.³⁵ Although the party-state deliberately engineered National Defense Education Day as a nonhistorical holiday to address traditional and nontraditional security threats in the abstract, the vagaries of the calendar are outside its control. Since it commonly falls on or near September 18th, this ambiguous national holiday provokes popular historical memory to unambiguously recall defeat at the hands of a specific enemy, at a specific time and place.

In addition to refocusing the historically inflamed ire of Chinese citizens on Japan's past atrocities, new national humiliation days have been mooted for NATO's May 7th bombing of the Chinese embassy in Belgrade in 1999 and for the April 1st reconnaissance plane collision in 2001.³⁶ While the Century of National Humiliation focuses primarily on European and then Japanese aggression, these recent humiliations expand the focus to target the United States. New enemies generate new humiliations, which in turn not only lead to a quest for military strength to deal with foreign threats, but to a new construction of national identity to rally the masses at home. This unruly proliferation of national humiliation days shows how traditional and nontraditional securities are joined in the service of nation unity.

Comparing the texts from the early 1990s and the mid-2000s shows that even though there was a grand celebration of the final cleansing of the national humiliation with the return of Hong Kong in 1997, the narrative of national humiliation never ends. National humiliation discourse creates a desire for *xuechi* – which can be rendered broadly as "cleansing humiliation" or sharply as "revenge" – that is difficult if not impossible to satisfy. Hence, proclaiming National Humiliation Day continues to be a political act that incessantly constructs identity and security long after the Century of National Humiliation ended in 1949.

How: Ritual Performances on National Humiliation Day

In *Festivals and the French Revolution*, Ozouf asks: "[C]an a festival that is ideally conceived as a festival of Enlightenment represent doom and gloom? . . . [A]nd anyway, how does one celebrate one's misfortunes?"[37] To Ozouf, these are rhetorical questions; of course there is no proper way to celebrate one's misfortunes. Even more, there is no proper way to celebrate a nation's misfortunes. But the Chinese experience provides a concrete answer to Ozouf's rhetorical question. Chinese essayists address the same problem of unhappy holidays, but come up with different solutions. As we saw earlier, Chen Yunjie does not think that celebrating National Day is enough; Chinese citizens need to commemorate National Humiliation Day to produce and guard their nation. As Ah Yuan writes in the popular newsweekly *Outlook [Liaowang]*, "on special days we promote the commemorative activities of national humiliation education and national crisis education so people can have a more peaceful and better life today."[38]

After the grand inauguration of the provisional president in 1912, the Republic of China quickly descended into a period of disunity and violence. Hence National Days from the 1910s through the 1930s became problematic. Playing on the full meaning in Chinese of National Day as "National Celebration Festival – *Guoqing jie*," in 1926 a newspaper columnist asked "What is there to celebrate? . . . Are we celebrating imperialist oppression and warlords, or the soldiers, bandits and destruction, or the chaos of our communication and education systems, or perhaps freedom and equality?"[39]

Hence, in 1915 insecurity was added to security, and commemoration to celebration: Chinese people added "May 9th National Humiliation Commemoration Day" to complement "October 10th National Celebration Day" on their list of national holidays. Not surprisingly, the practices in May were similar to those in October. Indeed, much thought and preparation went into framing this national humiliation event as a solemn occasion of national unity: "What is worth discussing is that any official commemoration day for any nation must have a solemn and grand meaning. When the commemoration day comes, people must know its meaning with all their heart, and must hold a grand ceremony."[40] Like on National Day, there were parades, conferences, speeches, flags, songs, poems, and editorials. Merchants flew National Humiliation flags and banners. Patriotic youths wore National Humiliation armbands, pasted up wall posters, and performed street theatre to mobilize the masses.[41] Much like mass protests on May 4th, these activities typically were woven together for a full day of commemoration.[42] Firstly, schools, shops, factories, and entertainment venues were pressured by nonstate actors to close for the day. Indeed, some businesses took out advertisements on the front page of newspapers to proclaim that they were patriotically closing on May 9th.[43] This economic patriotism occurred not just in China, but among overseas Chinese in Southeast Asia too; in the 1920s and 1930s, Chinese-language newspapers in Bangkok closed on May 9th to observe the holiday.[44]

Patriotic performances often started with a parade through the city that culminated in a meeting either at a public park or in an auditorium. The agenda from a Shanghai meeting to commemorate a decade of national humiliation in 1925 is typical: (1) opening ceremony; (2) chairman gives report; (3) salute national flag; (4) section heads report situation of the past year; (5) sing National Humiliation Anthem; (6) speeches from the floor; (7) more mourning, including speeches and theatrical performances; (8) take photograph of delegates; (9) close meeting.[45] Across town, a student meeting had a similar agenda, but ended on a more entertaining note. After the speeches, salutes, and anthems, the last item instructed the children "to enjoy entertainment" including opera performances, stand-up comedy, traditional Chinese music, dancing, drama, storytelling, Western music, a speech on women's rights, and finally to end the proceedings, a magic show.[46] Another Shanghai school included a "National Humiliation Commemorative Gymnastics" routine that equated physical strength and national strength.[47] (See Figure 1.2.) In New York on May 10, 1938, the various diverse overseas Chinese associations joined together as nationals for a parade that protested against Japanese aggression in China; many "Americans" joined in the demonstration, while others "spontaneously cheered [the parade] along its downtown route."[48] National humiliation commemoration, thus, was itself a popular performance that expressed the tension between centralized solemnity and localized entertainment.

Even so, an enormous amount of earnestness is displayed in these celebrations; this can be seen in newspapers' editorial commentary. In 1922, for example, an unsigned article prescriptively instructs citizens in "Things You Should Do on National Humiliation Day." In addition to stopping work, attending meetings, and flying the flag at half-mast, it tells readers how to *feel*: "On National Humiliation Day you should shut yourself up in sadness, and draw a lesson from bitter experience." The objective is to formulate policies for a better future of national unity and stability, as underlined in the last prescription: "National Humiliation Day should make a glorious Republic of China which will last forever in the Orient."[49]

Such earnest activity also provoked satirical comment about the fleeting nature of Chinese patriotism. "An Analysis of Five Minutes of Enthusiasm" brutally satirizes the National Humiliation Day meetings:[50]

1st minute: Fly into rage. Be resentful. Gnash one's teeth. Be extremely antagonistic.

2nd minute: Have meetings and form associations. Unite to resist. Sacrifice our money. Love our country and resolve to do something.

3rd minute: Send a circular telegram and ask questions. Have a meeting to discuss it. Strategize to take a break. Pretend politeness and agreement.

4th minute: Speak up to avenge our national humiliation. Be incapable of action. One person alone cannot save the nation. Have no alternative.

5th minute: Scheme for personal gain. Forget about hatred and national humiliation. Surrender to the foreigners.

Sadly, much of the fun and satire increasingly indicative of National Humiliation Day performances in the 1920s was lost after the Nationalists took over Shanghai in 1927. The Nationalist Party turned independent political associations into corporate groups linked to the party, and limited participation in the commemorative activities to the leaders of these chosen groups. Outwardly, the meeting agendas were much the same, except a few items were added to celebrate the Nationalist Party and its ideology: the party flag was saluted, the party anthem sung, and party slogans shouted.[51]

In 1929, the government proclaimed that unauthorized parades would not be tolerated, and declared that "Each person should not go beyond the limits of today's national humiliation commemoration" because "May 9th National Humiliation Commemoration Day is being used by reactionaries and communists to mislead the public and create chaos."[52] For the fifteenth anniversary of National Humiliation Day in 1930, the government declared that there would be no closure of factories, shops, or schools. The official commemoration meeting was held in Shanghai's Fenglai Theatre for the leaders of corporate groups; likewise participation was limited for the twentieth anniversary in 1935 when the meeting was held at the Municipal Party Headquarters in Nanjing.[53] The Nationalist Party also churned out commemorative booklets to guide the activities and direct the meaning of National Humiliation Day.

After national humiliation discourse was revived in 1990, numerous days of national humiliation have been celebrated. No single nationwide humiliation holiday existed before 2001, so people marked national humiliation on a host of different commemoration days. The dates are quite similar to the Nationalist Party's calendar of twenty-six official national humiliation holidays. Indeed, there is an officially sanctioned textbook called *100 National Humiliation Days*.[54] However, in general, the temporal organization of humiliation holidays is quite different in the twenty-first century. Rather than following a twelve-month annual calendar, the PRC's commemoration activities follow a ten-year calendar: key National Humiliation Days are celebrated according to their 50th, 60th, 70th, 75th, 100th, and 150th anniversaries.

Thus, as a reaction to the Tiananmen movement, national humiliation activities started in 1990 as a commemoration of ninety years since the Boxer Uprising and 150 years since the Opium War. Likewise, the textbook *The Indignation of National Humiliation* was published to mark the 150th anniversary of the beginning of the Opium War.[55] The sixtieth anniversary of the September 18th Japanese conquest of Manchuria was commemorated in 1991. In 1995, National Humiliation articles centered on the fiftieth anniversary of the World War II victory, and the hundredth anniversary of defeat in the Sino-Japanese War. In 1997, the return of Hong Kong was celebrated with fanfare, while the seventieth anniversary of Japan's 1937 invasion of China proper was marked, along with the seventieth anniversary of the Nanjing massacre. In 1999, there was a muted celebration of the return of Macao, and the national humiliation cleansed by that event. And then it started again, with the hundredth anniversary commemoration of the Boxer Uprising in 2000, the seventieth anniversary of the September 18th Manchurian Incident in 2001, the sixtieth anniversary of the World War II victory in 2005, the seventy-fifth anniversary of the September 18th Mukden Incident in 2006, the seventieth anniversary of the Rape of Nanjing in 2007, and so on. Humiliation holidays thus are characteristically celebrated according to the decade-long calendar.

Yet, this does not mean that the activities are the same for the fiftieth and sixtieth anniversaries of the defeat of Japan in 1945. The decade-long calendar provides the template for commemorative activities whose intensity varies according to the contingencies of China's domestic and international politics. For example, in early 2005, Beijing planned a muted commemoration of the end of World War II that placed the anti-Japanese war in the context of a global war against fascism. Yet, the anti-Japanese riots that rocked urban China in April 2005 forced authorities to scale up the activities and focus them on Japan as part of the patriotic education campaign.[56]

The PRC marks these national humiliation days with many of the same activities that we saw in the Republican period. Indeed, they carried the same logic, because people participated in state-organized activities primarily as members of party-sponsored corporate groups: associations of students, workers, soldiers, party members, women, patriotic religious groups, national minority groups, and so on. But the PRC with its strong state power is able to organize and control these political performances much more effectively than the Nationalists.

A report on the activities planned for the handover of Hong Kong in 1997 – one of the few national humiliation days where humiliation was cleansed – gives an idea of the party-state's comprehensive approach. A Beijing school district organized activities for 120,000 primary and secondary school students that included chanting patriotic slogans (including "cleanse national humiliation," "peace through strength," and "understand historical facts"), explaining the history of Sino-British relations, singing songs (including "Our Great China"), and following a special countdown calendar of 200 days to the handover. Special textbooks were produced, including, *China's Hong Kong* and *Stories of the National Flag*. These special activities took place according to countdown calendars of 200, 100, 50, 30 days and so on. While the party-state prominently reversed chronological time with its electronic calendar on Tiananmen Square that counted down years, months, days, and seconds to the final return of Hong Kong, individual students were able to rip off a page a day (each with a special message) from another hundred-day countdown calendar. The Moral Education Committee declared the campaign a success: a test of high school students showed that 70 percent had an understanding of the fundamental concepts of national humiliation and the return of Hong Kong.[57] As we saw in Chapter 2, this success is not an anomaly; the patriotic education campaign has been the CCP's most successful mass movement.[58]

Most national humiliation day meetings took place to commemorate a specific day. For example, the trade journal *Contemporary Auditing* reported on a day trip of the Jingyu County Auditors Association to commemorate September 18th with a program called "Never forget national humiliation, rejuvenate China." At the patriotic site, "They cherished the memory of fallen heroes, visited the commemoration hall, reviewed history, and listened to personal experiences recounted by heroic veterans who fought the enemy under the leadership of the CCP."[59] The auditors, the article tells us, vowed to audit with these patriotic lessons in mind.

Like editorial opinion essays in newspapers in the early twentieth century, editorials in trade journals since 1990 have been a common way of marking national humiliation holidays. An editorial in *China Construction Materials* closely links the welfare of its industry with a cleansing of national humiliation: "Backwardness leads to being beaten. Only by being strong and powerful can we have national dignity. For our country to be great and strong, our construction materials industry must be great and strong."[60] The All China Women's Federation likewise organized a meeting in 1995 to commemorate the end of World War II (but on July 7th, the day that Japan invaded China proper in 1937). Old cadres from the women's federation testified to the brutality of the Japanese invasion, especially toward women. As the article title tells us, "National Humiliation Cannot Be Forgotten, the Anti-Japanese Spirit Endures."[61]

Like in the 1920s, national humiliation days are commemorated with more traditional performances: films, storytelling, speeches, slogans, and songs. As we saw in Chapter 2, the feature film *The Opium War* was a key sovereignty performance. It premiered to great fanfare in Beijing on June 9th (the national humiliation day when the unequal treaty in question was signed with Britain).[62] Poems by both professional and amateur writers were a particularly popular way to commemorate the return of Hong Kong: for example, a poem entitled "Never Forget National Humiliation, Rejuvenate China" was published in *Jiangsu Statistics*.[63] This and other such poems were quite formulaic; but focusing on the content would miss the point of this performance of China's national aesthetic. It is significant because it mobilized hundreds of people to express their pessoptimist patriotism in dozens of publications from across China's social spectrum. Poetry actually has a long history of performing China's pessoptimist national aesthetic: as the "Preface" to *Ode to National Humiliation* (1947) tells us, "National humiliation poems have been written since the end of the Opium War."[64] The recent fashion for proposing September 18th as China's official National Humiliation Day positively promoted new activities: flying flags at half-mast, simultaneously sounding air-raid sirens, and observing three minutes of silence. It also proposed a set of new restrictions reminiscent of the Republican era: while newly weds marched proudly in the 1999 National Day parade, National Humiliation Day weddings are discouraged, as are other "celebrations or entertainment activities" in both the public and the private sector.[65]

Because the PRC has been more successful at policing these activities, opportunities for popular resistance have been limited. Rather than direct criticisms of National Defense Education Day, resistance has largely taken the form of "unease." Ambivalence to a passionate commemoration of National Humiliation Day emerged in 2005 when China's traditional

Mid-Autumn Festival fell on September 18th. As an essayist in *Outlook* magazine wrote, this calendrical coincidence provoked "mixed feelings" that are both positive and negative: "This timing is an accidental coincidence, but in terms of feelings this pairing of the happiness of the traditional family reunion holiday with the sadness of National Humiliation Day makes some people feel uneasy."[66] In a similar spirit, a newspaper reported that many couples were postponing their weddings in spite of the convenience of the Mid-Autumn Festival falling on a weekend. As one bride surmised, "This year's September 18th is actually a fine day, but it makes me uneasy to have my wedding celebration on the 'Day of National Humiliation.'"[67] The *Outlook* essayist resolves this conundrum pessoptimistically by suggesting that people engage in both happy celebration and solemn commemoration: "plan the normal things to celebrate the Mid-Autumn Festival, and also do special activities of National Humiliation education and National Crisis education. We should be able to view both with equanimity."

While Chinese media commentators increasingly take September 18th as National Humiliation Day in order to "to arouse citizens' patriotic spirit," in a September 18, 2007 *Huanqiu ribao* [*Global Daily*] article Yuan Xiaoming stated that this was problematic for China's new role as a responsible great power.[68] While he can appreciate how many see September 18th as an "eternal national humiliation" that demands revenge, Yuan feels that "this way of understanding it makes it hard to get away from the 'hatred' that comes with 'September 18th.' Although hatred can become a motivating force, it can also work against us ... and serve as an excuse for a new breed of militarist power" in Japan.

Yuan thus suggests that Chinese people need to understand September 18th in a different way that moves beyond this "honor and shame" dynamic to frame political memory as an issue of "right and wrong." To do this, he compares the September 18th attack with Japan's attack on Pearl Harbor in 1941. While Chinese writers typically see Pearl Harbor Day (December 7th) as America's National Humiliation Day, Yuan tells us that Americans understand the attack on Pearl Harbor and World War II in general in terms of "right and wrong" rather than in terms of "honor and shame." Reading Roosevelt's Declaration of War and the Pearl Harbor memorial Web site, Yuan argues that the US response was motivated more by justice than by revenge. By framing it as a "Just War" against fascism, he feels that Americans were able to produce a different set of outcomes than China's incessant memories of national humiliation. The war crimes tribunals in Germany and Japan, which punished wartime leaders as criminals,

Yuan tells us, enabled the eventual rehabilitation of these former enemy states into friendly allies. Yuan thus argues that China's goals as an emerging great power are best served by understanding "September 18th" more as a legal issue of "right and wrong," than as an enduring national humiliation.

Yuan Xiaoming thus is not only commenting on the usefulness of commemorating a national humiliation day; he questions the whole logic that Chinese people use to understand the Century of National Humiliation. Rather than search for a complete truth about September 18th, Yuan is satisfied with a relative understanding of these events that looks more to "justice" and less to "shame." Hence while some are proposing new national humiliation days to target the United States, Yuan uses an American example to push beyond the choices of being pro- or anti-Chinese (and pro- or anti-American) fostered by the party-state's pessoptimistic structure of feeling. Regardless of whether we agree with his characterization of American (or Chinese) understandings of war, it is fascinating to see an essay that encourages readers to positively think about different ways of being Chinese published in an official newspaper. This more aesthetic view of Chinese identity, where we have to work hard to interpret the meaning of historical events, again shows how space is opening up for more meaningful political debate in the PRC.

Conclusion: Consuming Nationalism

The celebration of national humiliation days over the past century shows the interplay between security and insecurity, domestic and foreign, and official and popular culture as they construct national identity. These performative techniques reveal a shared logic of national humiliation day. At its heyday in the 1920s the meaning is clear: national humiliation day activities and essays stress the need for national salvation from an impending national extinction [*mieguo*]. The term "national humiliation" emerged in popular movements in 1915 as a sign of China's new modern, national, and Republican government that was the outcome of its 1911 revolution. After China's entry into modern politics, Chinese intellectuals expected their nation to be treated with more respect as a "free and equal sovereign state." But the transition from empire to nation-state did not impress the European, American, or Japanese governments who maintained their unequal treaties. As an editorial on National Humiliation Day in 1927 put it: "After the 1911 revolution we thought that things had changed, and that the great powers would change their previous attitude, and not bully newborn China." So Chinese were surprised and dismayed "in 1915 when Japan wanted to invade China with the Twenty-one Demands that would exterminate it."[69]

Hence, National Humiliation Day marked a national tragedy much greater than simply Japan's Twenty-one Demands; it reminded Chinese citizens that "friendly countries" (the contemporary designation for Britain and America) would not defend China against Japan. National salvation was in their own hands; Chinese had to defend themselves not just against Japan, but against imperialism in general. Commemorating National Humiliation Day thus was one of the many sovereignty performances (including National Day) that sought to produce a strong Chinese nation. Indeed, the money donated to the National Humiliation Fund in 1915 was gathered to buy military arms to guard China's national security.

But in the early twenty-first century, there is no sovereignty crisis comparable to those in the early twentieth century when imperialists were busy dividing up China. Rather, with the Tiananmen crisis and the disintegration of communist parties in the Soviet bloc, the CCP was facing a nontraditional security threat: regime security, ideological security, and cultural security. Thus, after 1989, there was a shift from primarily producing nationalism, as in the 1920s, to concentrate on *containing* nationalism. To contain the nation, it is necessary to construct insecurities such as National Humiliation Day, which then limits the expression of identity to approved activities and feelings. National Humiliation Day emerged after 1989 as one way to positively distract students from criticizing China's domestic corruption, and thus refocus their critical energies on foreigners as the primary enemy. As the National Defense Education Day (2003) poster tells us, identity not only marks the border between us and them, but also contains "us" in China: "National Defense connects you, me and others in the national borders that peacefully hold together millions and millions of families [in China]." Yet, the state is never totally successful; nationalism and humiliation both keep crossing the official boundaries to go in unexpected directions to produce unorthodox identities.

This chapter's wide and varied examples of national humiliation day activities show how the Chinese nation performatively emerges through the interplay of state and popular culture. Rather than engaging in a conceptual battle to resist the restriction of community to the nation (and open it to other gender, class, or regional identities), it is important to note that National Humiliation's popular resistance activities still seek to produce the proper Chinese nation – albeit a different Chinese nation.

Yet, what kind of nation is emerging from public commemoration? If history is a security issue, then the conclusions of this chapter are not encouraging. There was great fanfare in 1997 with the return of Hong Kong, which as we were repeatedly told, cleansed humiliation once and for all. However, just a few days later, Japan was criticized in the commemoration of the seventieth anniversary of July 7th invasion of China, and again a few months later with the anniversary of the December 13th massacre in Nanjing. Although National Defense Education Day is directed at a general enemy, new humiliations increasingly target new enemies, such as the United States (which only played a secondary role in the imperialism of the Century of National Humiliation). Far from memory fading with the march of time, national humiliation days, textbooks, and other activities and media products continue to proliferate.

To achieve stability in East Asia, many scholars tell us that China, Japan, South Korea (and the United States) have to construct normal diplomatic relations by resolving the history question rationally and objectively.[70] This chapter uses the example of National Humiliation Day performances to show how Chinese texts are not reacting to a rational objective historical legacy, as much as constructing a particular history, in a particular context, as part of a particular *national* project. In the Republican era, the humiliation holidays buttressed a history that sought to produce the proper Chinese nation as a modern entity in distinction to (both Chinese and foreign) empire. Since 1989, national humiliation discourse has aimed to maintain and contain the Chinese nation by focusing on the external "other" as a hostile enemy. While the early-twentieth-century discourse used nontraditional modes of popular culture to address the dramatically traditional security crisis of foreign invasion, discourse in the early twenty-first century uses a traditional vocabulary of war and foreign relations to address the nontraditional security issue of the CCP's political legitimacy. Patriotic education here appeals to national time to differentiate Chinese citizens from the foreign other, which in turn recreates the Chinese nation while redirecting criticism from domestic corruption to imperialist aggression.

It is common among scholars and officials in both China and the West to see nationalism as a "problem" that needs to be addressed by the state, arguing that foreign affairs would improve if Japanese and Chinese leaders, for example, simply revised their negative views of each other.[71] But national humiliation discourse is not completely directed at external Others – it has always targeted both foreign invasion and domestic corruption. The self/Other relations generated by national humiliation discourse will not cease if the leadership decides to change course because there is leakage from national containment, especially as the discourse is increasingly produced in the media market rather than by the party-state. The meaning of national humiliation thus is not exhausted by state-directed propaganda that seeks to instrumentally construct public memory as a way to legitimate the nation. Increasingly, identity and public memory are negotiated in popular culture where nationalism is not imposed by elites so much as it resonates with people's feelings as it circulates in the market.

It is thus necessary to think about more than how the state produces nationalism; we also need to consider how people *consume* National Humiliation Day, and thus produce their own identity. Not surprisingly, the *Shenbao* provides clues to national humiliation consumption. In addition to news, essays, and editorials, this newspaper published advertisements that urged readers to commemorate national humiliation by purchasing "national products" in the form of patriotic cigarettes, straw hats, and face towels: "When you use the national humiliation towel every day to wash your face, think of how it is even better to wash away humiliation at the same time as you are washing your face."[72] (See Figure 3.3.) As historian Karl Gerth concludes, "With the [National Products] movement, consumption became a way for ordinary Chinese to practice nationalism and anti-imperialism everyday."[73]

Since 1990, national humiliation activities have spread from state-sponsored rituals to the market: commemorating national humiliation has become a brand, with icons from national patriotic education sites

Figure 3.3 Never forget national humiliation cigarettes (1925). *Shenbao*, May 9, 1926.

such as the ruins at Beijing's Garden of Perfect Brilliance imperial palace being reproduced on t-shirts, hats, bottled water, playing cards, and novelty calendars. (See Figures 1.3, 3.4, and 3.5.)[74] Indeed, each time I visit such national humiliation sites, I am able to purchase new and more interesting

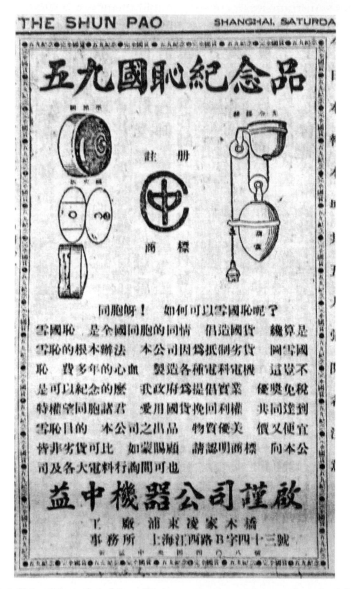

Figure 3.4 "May 9th national humiliation commemoration products" ad from a consortium of electrical goods producers. *Shenbao*, May 9, 1925.

patriotic commodities. This commercialization of commemoration certainly resists the state's objective of using solemn rites to produce national unity; but this resistance also reifies the nation as the central patriotic identity site for Chinese citizens.

But it would be a mistake to limit our understanding of consumption to financial transactions. Like in other countries, identity in China emerges through the circulation of images in a symbolic economy where production and consumption entail each other, and where state and nonstate actors are

Figure 3.5 Consuming nationalism with playing cards. Beijing baqixuan sheji gongzuoshi.

intertwined. Buying and playing poker with national humiliation cards, for example, is both a production and a consumption of national identity. By focusing on what people do (in popular culture and consumption), rather than what they think, this chapter has examined how Chinese consume nationalism through a commodification of humiliation. Identities thus shift from being constructs of the state to products that take shape through exchange and circulation in the market. Likewise, nationalism is best understood as a continual pessoptimistic performance that includes both National Day and National Humiliation Day.

The debate over the proper use of the Garden of Perfect Brilliance illustrates the tension between ideology and the market, and between official and popular culture in China's identity politics. While one group feels that it should be a solemn park that preserves the historical ruins in order to commemorate national humiliation for patriotic education, another group argues that it should be rebuilt to its former glory as a theme park that is entertaining for profit.[75] As one critic of renovation concludes, "Overwhelmed by commercialism, the Yuanming Yuan Ruins Park appears anything but solemn and melancholy."[76]

Rather than understanding the Garden of Perfect Brilliance in terms of either solemn commemoration or the entertainment market, I think that the park illustrates the creative tension between the state and the market, and between official and popular culture. It is a national humiliation theme park where people produce and consume both identity and security as patriotic edutainment that takes many forms. The party-state certainly uses it to stage commemorative events on National Humiliation Days: the first National Defense Education Day in 2001, the return of Hong Kong in 1997, and the 130th anniversary of the looting itself in 1990. The ruins park is also employed for the party-state's more positive internationalist events, including part of the Asian Games' opening ceremonies in 1990.

But the ruins park also takes on meaning through the popular activities of China's new middle class, which in the past decade has enjoyed increasing amounts of leisure time and disposable income. (See Figure 3.6.) The Garden of Perfect Brilliance thus is a vast site where young lovers, for example, can find some privacy to romantically ponder the apex of Chinese civilization and the nadir of European barbarism. Like at its height in the Qing dynasty, the park once again is a pleasure garden with multiple, often sentimental, meanings.[77] The palace ruins from the Second Opium War (1860) thus have become a "souvenir" both in the sense of a solemn remembrance and a hedonistic leisure commodity. In this way, China's

Figure 3.6 Families enjoying a national humiliation icon. Courtesy of William A. Callahan.

pessoptimistic identity/security dynamic is the product of both state policy and popular resistance, involving both domestic initiatives and interactions with foreign bodies. More importantly, it shows how people are moving beyond the "leadership of the communist party" to consume patriotism in new and often unpredictable ways.

Chapter 4

Where Is China?: The Cartography of National Humiliation

While we assume that we can easily locate China on the map, Figures 4.1 and 4.2 give a sense of the complexities of China's engagement with the world, and the range of possible answers for the question "Where is China?" The map in Figure 4.1 shows China as a confident world power that has global influence. It charts the Ming dynasty voyages of Admiral Zheng He from China to (what we now call) Southeast Asia and South Asia, eventually reaching Africa's East coast. What is noteworthy about this particular map from 1418, which was discovered by a Chinese collector in 2001, is that it also charts Zheng's voyages to the East, suggesting that the admiral "discovered" America before Columbus.[1] And as we know, "discovering America" is part of the symbolic politics of being a great power.[2]

If the map in Figure 4.1 asserts a confident outward-looking China, then the map in Figure 4.2 represents China's fears of national disintegration. This map, which was published on the cover of the best-selling hypernationalistic book *China's Road under the Shadow of Globalization* (1999), presents China as the victim of an international conspiracy to divide up the PRC into a clutch of independent states including Tibet, Manchuria, Inner Mongolia, East Turkestan, and Taiwan.[3] The authors tell us that this is a popular map in the West and have the "original" English-language version on the back cover, with a Chinese translation on the front cover. This map is thus taken as evidence of Western plans to keep the PRC from achieving its natural status as a great power on the world stage.

Although both maps assert their authenticity as evidence of either Chinese discovery or Western conspiracy, it turns out that neither map is

Figure 4.1 Map of Zheng He's American voyage (1418). Courtesy of Liu Gang.

authentic in the sense of representing what it purports to represent. Because it is full of anachronisms and has an unclear provenance, there are serious doubts about the authenticity of the world discovery map – most people now see it as a hoax.[4] Although the authors of *China's Road* say that it is a popular map in the West, no one has been able to track down its source.[5]

Yet a search for "authenticity" misses the point of such maps: they are not reflecting reality so much as asserting a normative image that resonates with China's national aesthetic. The two maps are aspirational, first in the positive sense of presenting China as a united and a great power with global influence, and second in the negative sense of what China doesn't want to be: "carved up like a melon" to use a popular Chinese phrase from the early twentieth century. Indeed, this is not strange; even many official Chinese maps are actually imaginative and aspirational, inscribing territories that are not under state control – but could and should be part of China's sovereign territory: PRC maps record Taiwan as a province of China, and until recently Republic of China (ROC) maps included Outer Mongolia as well. This illustrates how national maps are not simply scientific reflections

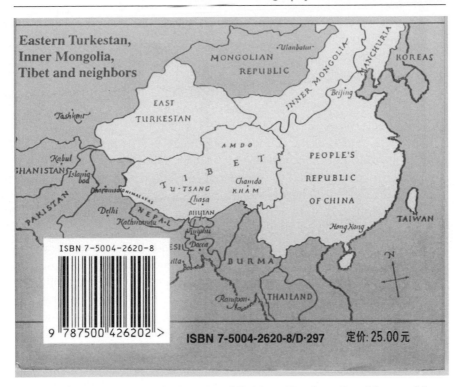

Figure 4.2 Back cover of *China's Road* (1999). Wang Xiaodong, Fang Ning, and Song Qiang, *Quanqiuhua yinxiang xiade Zhongguo zhi lu.*

of the territory of the "real world"; maps are technologies of power used for political projects. Chinese atlases from the early twentieth century, for example, characteristically state that the new Republic (founded in 1912) needed national maps to know just what it was ruling.[6] The title of a recent academic article shows how the enduring goal of Chinese cartography is in line with China's national aesthetic: "A Century of Anticipating the Unification of the Motherland."[7]

Here, I follow those who treat maps and cartography as political practices that seek to produce what historian Thongchai Winichakul calls the national "geobody," which is "not merely space or territory. It is a component of the life of a nation. It is a source of pride, loyalty, love, . . . hatred, reason, [and] unreason."[8] As mass-produced visual artefacts, maps are more than scientific representations of "reality"; they constitute a structure of feeling that can mobilize the masses. In this way, maps not only tell us about the geopolitics of international borders; when they inscribe space as a geobody, maps also tell us about the pessoptimistic politics of national identity.

93

Thinking of territory in terms of the geobody is especially useful for China; when the national body politic emerged in the early twentieth century, China was known as the "Sick Man of East Asia," whose life needed to be saved [jiuguo]. As we see, re-membering territories that have been dismembered [fenge] is a key way of imagining – and then managing – China's geobody in a way that combines symbolic politics and geopolitics, and integrates soft power with hard power.

Hence the borders of the Chinese geobody are neither obvious nor fixed; they are contingent on historical events and are framed by cartographic conventions. China's borders are the product of debate and struggle as the country has gone through major transitions, first from an empire to a nation-state in the early twentieth century, and now from an isolated revisionist state to an engaged superpower in the early twenty-first century. Hence the struggle over the proper size and shape of China is not only with foreign countries along frontier zones, but also within China in debates among different groups, each of whom draw different "national maps" to support their preferred geobodies. While it is popular to analyze European and American images of China to criticize Western imperialism, this chapter is more concerned with the identity politics of Chinese images of its own region, which as we see, grow out of the collision of imperial Chinese cartography and modern scientific maps.

Thus rather than just trace the geopolitics of how the shape of China has changed in its encounter with modernity, to understand the extent of Chinese territory, we need to explore the conceptual issues of mapping. To locate China's geobody, we need to engage in comparative cartography – but rather than compare East and West, we need to consider China's uneasy shift from premodern unbounded understandings of space and territory to bounded understandings of space and territory in the early twentieth century. Simply put, I question the common argument that there has been a shift from the late imperial Chinese concept of unbounded domain [jiangyu] to a modern understanding of bounded sovereign territory [zhu-quan lingtu].[9] The maps show how imperial domain and sovereign territory both still work – often in creative tension – to inscribe the PRC's twenty-first century geobody on the Chinese imagination.

This creative tension is manifest in a set of "Maps of China's National Humiliation," which, I argue, form a link between imperial China's unbounded cartography and its modern maps of sovereign territory. These national humiliation maps help us understand the emergence of China's geobody because they are produced for mass education to chart how China "lost territories" to imperialist aggressors starting with the Opium War in 1840. Yet, these national maps do more than publicly register China's aspirational claims to various neighboring territories. I argue that these normative national maps actually tell us more about China's pessoptimistic identity politics than about the geopolitics of Asian security.

To understand how China's geobody emerges at the confluence of un-bounded imperial domain and bounded sovereign territory, it is helpful to see how Thailand used three strategies to claim many of its vassals as sover-eign national territory.[10] The first strategy for claiming imperial possessions as national territory is to deny the difference between imperial domain's hierar-chical unbounded space and sovereign territory's homogeneous bounded space. The second strategy is to establish the stories of China's sovereign territoriality within the context of modern international politics – particular-ly colonialism – as opposed to China's own history of imperial conquest. The third strategy is to read territoriality exclusively from Beijing's point of view, and thus suppress any rival perspectives – from Lhasa, Kashgar, or Taibei – that might dispute the scope of China's expansive geobody. As we see, Chinese cartography employs these three strategies to transform the Qing Dynasty's imperial domain into the PRC's national sovereign territory.

This chapter has two general aims: (1) to demonstrate how China's current national maps have emerged through the creative tension of un-bounded imperial domain and bounded sovereign territory, and (2) to show how the cartography of national humiliation constructs China's geo-body. The goal thus is not to determine China's correct boundaries in legal discourse or geopolitical space. Rather, like with our examination of patri-otic education and national humiliation days in Chapters 2 and 3, we examine what Chinese maps of China can tell us about their hopes and fears, not only in the past or present, but also for the future. The analysis, therefore, is not limited to the standard questions of political geography and border disputes; by asking the question "Where is China?" it examines how China's image of itself interacts with its image of the world.

Comparative Cartography (1): Imperial Domain and Sovereign Territory

Normative maps certainly are not exclusive to China. Mappa mundi in late medieval Europe also represented normative space: not how the world was, but how it should be. The map "Europe as a Virgin" (1592), for example, presents a literal geobody of Europe with the Iberian peninsula as the Queen's head and Denmark and Italy as her arms, with a medallion over her heart in Bohemia where the map was produced.[11] Starting in the sixteenth century, Europe used more scientific maps both to conquer the world and to create the world map to divide up the globe into sovereign territories divided by clear boundaries. Thus, Walter D. Mignolo argues that the symbolic politics of drawing maps to claim imperial space and sovereignty was a key part of conquering the world because this new cartography "coloniz[ed] the imagination" of both the conquered and the conquerors.[12]

To understand the interplay of imperial domain and sovereign territory on twentieth-century Chinese maps, we need to consider late imperial Chinese cartography. The untitled map (1743) in Figure 4.3 presents a good example of one of the key genres of imperial Chinese cartography; it reflects the style of a "Huayi tu" – a Map of Civilization and Barbarism.[13] If we look closely at this large and complex map, we can see that the borders are not between territories so much as between peoples and cultures: civilization and barbarians. Cartography, then, is like other sites of Chinese identity politics where the structure of feeling is informed by the "civilization/barbarism distinction" [*Huayi zhi bian*].[14]

This genre of imperial map presents China at the center of the world, and often as the world itself. On such maps, foreign countries – even Vietnam and India, let alone Portugal, England, and America – appear as small and insignificant islands off China's coast.

It is difficult to read late imperial maps if you don't know the conventions of Chinese cartography – which suggests that reading modern mathematical maps is not natural, either, but depends on unspoken conventions.[15] Simply put, the main convention of imperial Chinese maps is hierarchy. Such maps represent not a homogeneous space of equal sovereignty and legitimacy, but a hierarchy of concentric circles with diminishing sovereignty as one travels from the imperial capital out to the periphery of provinces, vassal states, and finally the barbarian wilderness. The result of this style of cartography is that imperial maps of China's domain are very detailed at the center, but very vague at the margins. Rather than the single-line boundaries that define the sovereign territories of the Westphalian international system, imperial Chinese cartography often mapped an ambiguous and unbounded domain of empty or overlapping frontiers.

While normative maps are a curiosity in Euro-American cartography, they have enduring value in China: the first truly modern map of China based on scientific surveys was published for public consumption in 1934.[16] Hence, any clear division between late imperial aesthetic maps and modern scientific maps is misleading; China presents a case where normative mappamundi of imperial domains inform and overlap with scientific cartographs

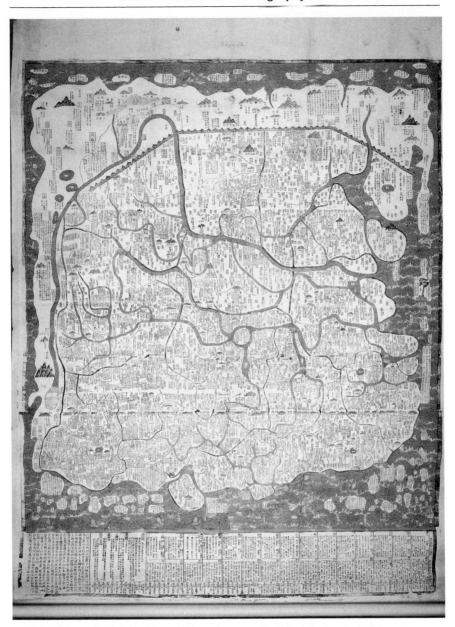

Figure 4.3 Untitled (1743): Map of civilization and barbarism. Courtesy of the British Library Board, Shelfmark: 15406.a.28.

of sovereign territory. Chinese cartography, thus, inscribes a coalescence of the two distinct worlds of cosmography and geography; China's twentieth-century maps exemplify the simultaneous appeal to two quite different readings of space: the ambiguous frontiers of the imperial domain and the clear national boundaries of the international system.[17]

To chart the emergence of China's geobody, I analyze a set of "Maps of Chinese National Humiliation" that were first published in China between the founding of the ROC in 1912 and Japan's all-out invasion of China in 1937, and then reappeared after the Tiananmen movement (1989) as part of the PRC's patriotic education campaign. These national humiliation maps are important for three reasons. First, they graphically show the tension between the two ways of mapping China outlined earlier; they thus provide a colorful link between the cartographies of imperial domain and sovereign territory.

Second, they are very deliberately published as part of patriotic education campaigns for public edification. In the Republican period, these large wall maps of national humiliation were an important part of the emergence of nationalist geography education in China; they were published by government bodies, geographical societies, and commercial presses for classroom use and public consumption alongside mainstream national maps. National humiliation maps published at the turn of the twenty-first century are likewise very public artefacts that are part of the PRC's multimedia patriotic education campaign.

Third, national humiliation maps not only make expansive and aspirational claims to huge tracts of land as China's national territory, but they also address the enduring Chinese anxiety of falling apart seen in Figure 4.2. Indeed, many have noted that an obsession with unity is not simply a modern concern that arose in reaction to China's Century of National Humiliation. While Euro-American philosophy asserts a solid objective reality that needs to be deconstructed, "in the Chinese case, in contrast, it is of a dispersed reality, in the face of which a reconstructive need has often struggled."[18] Similar national humiliation maps from the turn of the twenty-first century suggest that this search for "Great Unity" [da yitong] is not only part of China's enduring national aesthetic – it continues to be one of the main theoretical frameworks for historical geography in the PRC.[19]

To see how these three strategies of the cartography of national humiliation crafted China's geobody, we need to look at how the interplay of positive and negative images actually constructed the map of China that is familiar today.

Defining China's Borders (1): Outside/In

To understand how the geobody emerged through an interplay of imperial domain and sovereign territory, it is helpful to see how on Chinese maps the outside defines the inside, and the inside defines the outside. The first official map of the Republic of China, which was published in the Republic's founding *Almanac* (1912), graphically shows the ambiguity of China's borders (see Figure 4.4). This *Almanac* is interesting precisely because it does not simply list dates and places. As we saw in Chapter 3, the *Almanac* actively asserts a new time for a new China by instituting a new calendar, complete with tables to convert dates from the old imperial Lunar calendar to the new Republican Julian calendar. Likewise, the *Almanac*'s "Map of the Republic of China" carves out a new space for this nascent nation-state; as with the new calendar, the new map was "issued for enforcement."[20]

Still, this map of China and its Asian neighbors does not assert clear boundaries between the ROC and other sovereign states; it is actually hard to pick "China" out from the rest of the continent. The map is thus like the first constitutions of the Republic, which state that "The sovereign territory of the Republic of China continues to be the same as the domain of the former Empire."[21] However, this simply begs the question of defining the domain of the Qing Dynasty – which as we saw earlier, relied on a different way of mapping the world. While maps of the late Qing Empire are characteristically dotted with textual annotations,[22] the Republican map is largely blank. On this 1912 national map, physical and economic geographies are more important than political geography: the lines marking rivers and railroads are more prominent than those defining international boundaries. The first official map of China thus shows that in the early twentieth century it was not clear how the Qing imperial domain would map onto the sovereign territory of the new Republic: if we look closely we can see that this map is already claiming much of Central, East, and Southeast Asia as lost territory for the Republic. While the Qing Dynasty's late imperial maps marked various places as vassals, the *Almanac*'s map of the Republic marks Korea, Vietnam, and other territories as "originally our vassal, now a vassal of Japan/France/Britain." Like on the untitled map of civilization and barbarism (1743), China *is* Asia. China's first national map thus reproduces the logic of imperial cartography to frame neighboring territories as part of China's domain.

The "Map of Chinese National Humiliation" (1916, Figure 4.5) and the "Map of China's National Humiliation" (1930, Figure 4.6) graphically

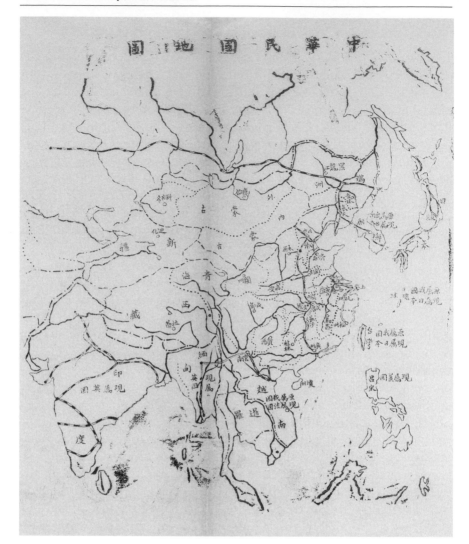

Figure 4.4 First map of the Republic of China (1912). *Zhonghua minguo ditu*, courtesy of the British Library Board, shelfmark: 15298.a.66.

demonstrate both the anxiety of China unraveling, and the importance of asserting a new unity through the Republic.[23] But these maps link imperial domain and sovereign territory in an interesting and unexpected way. Rather than focusing on China's geopolitical torso and showing how various territories have been ripped off, it does the opposite to stress how the outside defines the inside. In ways similar to the *Almanac* map (1912), China is portrayed as empty, blank, and white, while "lost territories" are

Figure 4.5 Map of Chinese national humiliation (1916). *Zhonghua guochi ditu*, courtesy of Cornell University Library.

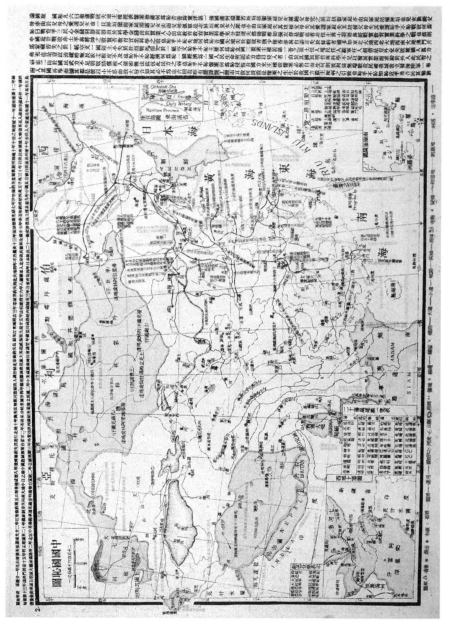

Figure 4.6 Map of China's national humiliation (1930). Bai Meichu, *Zuixin Zhonghua minguo gaizao quantu*.

inscribed in living color: on the 1916 map, Central Asia, the Russian Far East, Korea, Taiwan, Southeast Asia, Bhutan, and Afghanistan are shaded bright red; on the 1930 version, Central Asia, Mongolia, Russian Far East, Sakhalin Island, Taiwan, northern Burma, and Tibet are colored yellow, while Korea, Southeast Asia, the Sulu Islands, Bhutan, Nepal, and Afghanistan are colored pink.[24] These maps thus highlight China's boundaries in an odd way. Identity and territoriality are negative: the maps tell you what you don't want to be, rather than what you want to be.

Importantly, these maps of national humiliation each chart a different set of lost territories. Instead of using mathematical surveys to clarify China's territorial boundaries, they appeal to the contingencies of historical geography. Rather than China's borders settling down as the ROC adjusted to being a nation-state amongst other nation-states in its first few decades, its geobody was actually very unstable. As the differences in the 1916 and 1930 maps show, there was no obvious agreement about just which territories were "lost." Other maps confirm that the territorial claims of China's national humiliation maps actually were *expanding* in the 1920s and 1930s.[25]

In a technical sense, these maps invert the hierarchical logic of China's imperial maps of civilization and barbarism. The imagination shifts here from the center to the periphery: the outside defines the inside, and bleeding wounds define the geobody. The trauma of national humiliation generates a national community by setting its normative and aspirational boundaries. These semiofficial maps are important because they were produced for popular consumption and mass education. As the cartographer of the "Map of China's National Humiliation" (1930) explains, the aim is "to make beautiful maps with simple explanations... that are fun for the youth... and help common people to be patriotic."[26] According to a recent commentary, such maps were quite effective politically, if not scientifically: they successfully "spread patriotic thought which aroused the Chinese people to save our country."[27]

Defining China's Borders (2): Inside/Out

Another set of modern Republican maps reproduces the logic of imperial maps in a more direct and obvious inside/out way. The "Map of China's National Humiliation" (1927, Figure 4.7) reasserts the imperial cartography of hierarchical concentric circles on a modern map.[28] It is important to note that the outer ring, which claims an extraordinarily expansive imperial domain as China's sovereign national territory, is labeled the "old *national* boundary" – not the old boundary of the Qing Empire. Compared with the maps in Figures 4.5 and 4.6, this "Map of China's National Humiliation" claims an even larger domain as Chinese national territory. As on other "inside/out" national humiliation maps,[29] a graphic display of lost territories is complemented by a textual list of lost territories in an inset box. The 1927 map lists fifteen lost "homeland territories," fifteen lost "vassals," four "territorial concessions," and another fourteen lost and disputed "maritime territories."

Some of these "lost territories" now seem obviously "Chinese": Hong Kong, Macao, and Taiwan were ceded in treaties to the British, Portuguese, and Japanese empires. But other lost territories are not so obviously Chinese possessions: the map claims most of the countries in what we now call Southeast Asia and Central Eurasia, as well as Korea and the Russian Far

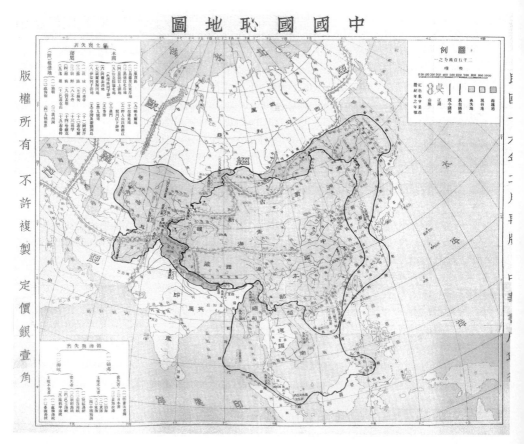

Figure 4.7 Map of China's national humiliation (1927). Chinese University of Hong Kong.

East in Northeast Asia, and the Himalayan states of South Asia. Moreover, all the national humiliation maps dot China's geobody with notes (often in red ink) that mark treaty ports, massacres, and other wounds to the geobody from the Century of National Humiliation.[30] The *Geography of China's National Humiliation* (1930) textbook makes the political purpose of such illustrations and annotations clear; it states that since China has lost more than half its territory, it is necessary to "compile a geographical record of the rise and fall of our country in order to craft a government policy to save it."[31]

This set of national humiliation maps of lost territories thus seeks to combine the expansive cosmology of late imperial maps with the scientific geography of maps of China's sovereign territory. Through the logic of outside/in and inside/out, China's early-twentieth-century cartography asserted the proper shape of "the real China" as a combination of late imperial and modern notions of space.

Defining China's Borders (3): Post-Tiananmen Maps

With the eruption of World War II in Asia in 1937, the normative cartography of national humiliation was displaced by the massive national crisis of the Japanese invasion of China proper, which eventually led to the Communist revolution in 1949. Although maps of lost territories continued to be published in history and geography textbooks, the PRC's new national and historical maps generally followed a different path to highlight the more affirmative ideological politics of class struggle and revolutionary victory. This is what makes the reemergence of national humiliation maps in the PRC after a fifty-year hiatus remarkable: they became popular again in China's modern history textbooks in the 1990s as part of the Central Propaganda Department's wider policy of patriotic education and national humiliation education. As I argued earlier, national humiliation discourse reemerged after the June 4th massacre as part of the Chinese Communist Party's (CCP) multimedia campaign that aimed to refocus the Chinese youths' critical ire on foreign enemies rather than on the internal corruption of the party-state.

The best example of recent national humiliation maps is the book *Maps of the Century of National Humiliation of Modern China* (1997), which contains eighty-six pages of maps, pictures, charts, illustrations, and explanations.[32] It shares many themes with similar maps from the early twentieth century. The way China's territories were lost to Russia, for example, is recorded on the "Map of Czarist Russia's Occupation of China's Sovereign Territory" much as it is on the "Map of Chinese National Humiliation"

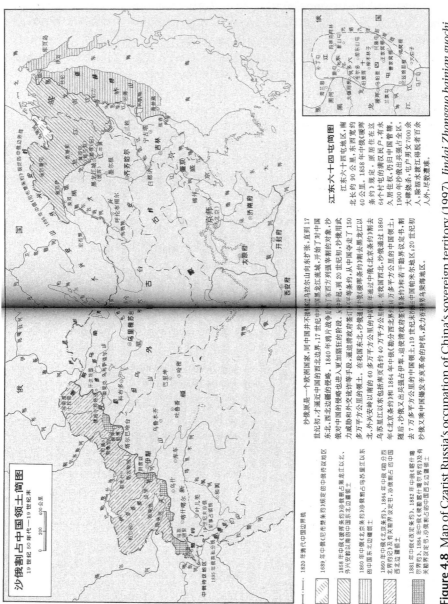

Figure 4.8 Map of Czarist Russia's occupation of China's sovereign territory (1997). *Jindai Zhongguo bainian guochi ditu*, 25–6.

(1916) – down to the details of the different styles and colors of shading to mark territories that were lost at different times (see Figures 4.5 and 4.8).[33]

But the 1997 atlas of national humiliation raises the stakes because it argues its case much more forcefully and in much greater detail than earlier wall maps. While national humiliation maps from the early twentieth century were published by geographic societies, provincial governments, and commercial presses, the 1997 atlas of national humiliation was edited by the Cartographic Department of China's official People's Press and was distributed as a mass market publication through the Central Propaganda Department's network of New China Bookstores. Moreover, the book launch of this official publication was a major media event timed to mark the return to Chinese sovereignty of a key lost territory: Hong Kong. Interestingly, the tone of *Maps of the Century of National Humiliation* does not follow the official slogans to "celebrate the return of Hong Kong to the bosom of the motherland." Rather, the cartographic agony of early twentieth century is republished as a new anxiety about China's geobody in 1997, in ways that echo the cinematic anxiety of *The Opium War* (1997) over China's modernization strategy that we saw in Chapter 2.

This concern is manifest in the map of "Imperialism's Division of China into Spheres of Power in the Late Nineteenth Century" (see Figure 4.9), which revives the turn of the twentieth-century theme "carving up China like a melon and gobbling it up" for the turn of the twenty-first century.[34] This resonates both with the map of the unraveling of China on the cover of *China's Road* (1999) (see Figure 4.2) and with a famous 1898 Chinese cartoon of European, American, and Japanese empires gobbling up China's territory (which is duly reproduced in the 1997 atlas).[35] To drive home the continuing importance of the cartography of national humiliation in the twenty-first century, *Maps of the Century of National Humiliation* was republished in 2005, on paper of higher quality and with a sturdier binding, to mark the sixtieth anniversary of China's victory over Japan in World War II.

Like maps from the 1910s to the 1930s, post-1989 Maps of National Humiliation also combine the cartographies of imperial domain and sovereign territory to naturalize the borders of the PRC. Indeed, to claim unbounded frontiers as sovereign national territory, these national humiliation maps employ the three strategies outlined earlier. The maps very directly deploy the first strategy of denying the difference between imperial domain's hierarchical unbounded space and sovereign territory's homogeneous bounded space to craft China's modern geobody as a clearly defined national sovereign territory.

Following the second strategy of placing territorial changes in the context of the modern international politics of foreign imperialism, both early

107

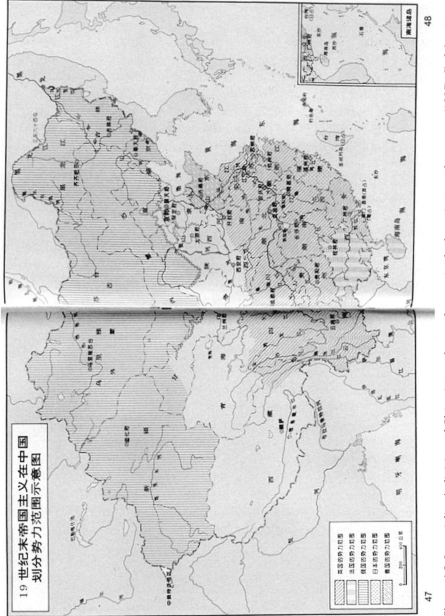

Figure 4.9 Imperialism's division of China into spheres of power in the late nineteenth century (1997). *Jindai Zhongguo bainian guochi ditu*, 47–8.

and recent maps frame the struggle as between China and the imperialist powers from Europe, America, and Japan that stole China's territories. This "Western imperialist" framework suppresses an alternative story: China, Russia, the West, and Japan were rival expansionists, fighting over the same territorial prey – the vassal states, semi-states, and frontier zones on the periphery of the Qing imperial domain such as Mongolia, Korea, Vietnam, and Siberia.[36] Indeed, spaces marked as "lost territories" on twentieth-century maps were conventionally marked as "gained territories" on the Qing Dynasty's eighteenth-century maps.[37]

While the *Geography of China's National Humiliation* (1930) lamented the halving of Chinese territory, as a conquest empire, the Qing Dynasty actually doubled the size of China. But since "talk of 'Chinese imperialism' is heresy ... official discourse refers to Qing expansionism as 'national unification.'" Because Beijing insists that China only experienced imperialism as a victim, this grand territorial expansion is analyzed as "borderland studies" rather than "colonial studies."[38]

Generally, these national humiliation maps employ the Westphalian international system's grid to reduce, classify, or exclude the voices of quasi-states, and allow only the story of the "Great Unity" of the emerging Chinese nation-state to be heard. This, then, is a prime example of the third strategy: read territoriality exclusively from Beijing's point of view, thus suppressing any rival perspectives that would produce alternative geobodies.

The result of these cartographic strategies is paradoxical: rather than evidence of a loss of national territories along Siberian, Central Eurasian, Northeast Asian, and South Asian frontiers, these national humiliation maps show how China has asserted national sovereignty over an ambiguous imperial domain, transforming the periphery into an integrated sovereign territory that includes some, although not all, of the former Qing realm. National humiliation maps and impassioned discussions of "lost territories" therefore have actually *helped* China to strengthen its claim to frontier zones in Xinjiang, Tibet, Manchuria – and Taiwan. Both dismembering and re-membering thus are key strategies in the production of China's national geobody.

Comparative Cartography (2): National Maps and National Humiliation Maps

While these maps of national humiliation are certainly interesting and raise serious questions about the proper size and shape of China, it is easy to dismiss them as the exception to the rule of China's standard practice of national sovereignty. Yet, an examination of a wider selection of China's official and popular maps from the early twentieth century and the turn of the twenty-first century shows that these national humiliation maps are an integral part of the emergence of mainstream cartography in China.[39] The same geographical societies and commercial presses that published national humiliation maps often simultaneously published "national maps" containing the same images and information. The "Map of China's National Humiliation" in Figure 4.6 is actually the second map in the *Atlas of the Republic of the China* (1930) – the first map is labeled simply the "Republic of China." Moreover, most "normal" and official maps of the ROC contain important references to China's national humiliation: they characteristically mark lost territories and list unequal treaties, treaty ports, and territorial concessions. The "Latest Detailed Complete Map of the Republic of China" (1923) is literally framed by the cartography of national humiliation's now familiar inset maps, annotations, and charts. Its inset maps, for example, show the details of particular lost territories, while the main map labels surrounding countries like Korea and Annam [Vietnam] as countries that used to be "our vassals," and now are Japan or France's vassals.[40] As with the *Geography of China's National Humiliation* (1930), an impassioned statement is written along the bottom margin of "Latest Detailed Complete Map," declaring that Chinese people can "cleanse their national humiliation" only by studying this map which shows how their country's sacred territory was lost to Europeans and Japanese through a series of unequal treaties.

The "Patriotic Map: National Humiliations and National Assets in One View" (1929) shows how the cartography of national humiliation informs mainstream national maps in China in a different way.[41] This map shows how recording and publicizing China's territorial humiliations has always been closely tied to expressions of patriotism, national pride, and thus to campaigns for national salvation. Alongside annotations celebrating the strength of China's industry and infrastructure (Chinese-owned factories, mines, orchards, etc.), there are red-dotted notes marking the wounds of treaty ports and lost territories. Together, these cartographic strategies produce China's national geobody by linking imperial domain with sovereign territory.

The pessoptimistic pattern of cartography at the turn of the twenty-first century is similar. Like those of the 1920s and 1930s, recent national humiliation maps are not only very similar to the standard maps found in the *Atlas of Modern Chinese History* (1984); the editors of *Maps of the Century of National Humiliation* (1997) credit this and other modern Chinese history atlases as their main sources.[42] Although it doesn't use the phrase "national humiliation," the monumental and comprehensive *History of China's Modern Borders* (2007) not only employs the same national aesthetic to combine the cartographies of imperial domain and sovereign territory in the service of asserting China's "Great Unity," but it also utilizes the now familiar maps of China's ancient borders and Czarist Russia's subsequent theft of Chinese territory.[43] Recent national humiliation maps also overlap considerably with a patriotic education atlas produced by the CCP's Central Propaganda Department: the *Atlas of One Hundred Patriotic Education Sites* (1999).[44] These and other Chinese maps thus show how the cartography of national humiliation is an integral part of official, scholarly, and popular imaginings of China's geobody.

These national humiliation maps are more than historical curiosities. They show how scientific cartography has paradoxically reenchanted China, producing a modern geobody that is at the same time a sacred national space. The maps vigorously promote China's pessoptimist structure of feeling through appeals to civilization and victimization.

Border Diplomacy

These national maps and national humiliation maps have shown how, starting with the Opium War in 1840 and continuing through the Republican revolution against the Qing Dynasty in 1911, the Communist revolution in 1949, and economic reforms in 1978, China has experienced dramatic changes not only politically, but also spatially. Modernity introduced not only contingent concepts to China, but also contingent borderlands. Indeed, both the imperial era and the Cold War were characterized by border wars for China; from 1949 to the 1970s, the PRC engaged in a series of border wars with almost every neighboring country, most famously with India (1962), Russia (1969), and Vietnam (1979). After the PRC fired missiles in the Taiwan straits confrontation (1995–6), many were again concerned about Chinese irredentism.[45]

Maps are a key part of such border disputes: after the Sino-Indian War (1962), Delhi complained about "Chinese aggression in maps," and in the 1990s, Beijing's Southeast Asian neighbors worried about "cartographic aggression" after China published official maps that include a "historic claim line" that digs deeply into the South China Sea in ways reminiscent of national humiliation maps.[46]

However, political scientists Allen Carlson and M. Taylor Fravel have separately argued that a close analysis of border disputes shows that the

PRC often prefers to negotiate solutions with its neighbors – even if this means giving up more than half of the disputed territory.[47] Carlson explains that the PRC shifted from military coercion to a policy of normalizing borders through diplomacy and international law as the economic reform policy took hold in the 1980s. This was a part of Beijing's broader understanding that acting as a responsible member of international society would contribute to the peaceful international environment that is crucial for the success of China's domestic economic reform project. Fravel argues that the positive policy of negotiating boundaries began much earlier – in the early 1960s – and has less to do with economic reform policy than with China's national security problem of stabilizing ethnic politics along its frontiers. China compromised in border disputes when it faced internal threats to regime security from transnational ethnic groups that straddled international borders. The PRC thus often made territorial concessions to its neighbors in Central Eurasia in exchange for cooperation in stopping cross-border ethnic movements, which Beijing saw as "separatist movements." Whether because of economic reform policy or national security concerns, China has settled seventeen of its twenty-three border disputes, and is dealing with the remaining disputes largely in a noncoercive spirit.[48]

Yet Carlson notes that alongside this cooperative diplomatic strategy, there is a significant undercurrent among China's national security and foreign policy experts of "memories of the contraction of Chinese territory during the 'century of humiliation.'"[49] The PRC's boundary disputes since 1949 thus are an imperial legacy that continues to be informed by much broader "historically grounded understandings of the 'legitimate' scope of China's territorial sovereignty."[50] Although the PRC has negotiated most of its disputed boundaries, yearnings to recover a vast collection of "lost territories" continue to emerge in official, semiofficial, and popular discourse.

Because it is located at the crossroads of various empires, Manchuria exemplifies the pessoptimistic complexity of colliding geobodies.[51] Indeed, the only regional Map of National Humiliation represents Manchuria as a lost territory after Japan's 1931 invasion.[52] Manchuria's uneasy status thus provokes various forms of resistance both inside and outside China. So, for example, soon after China and Russia signed an agreement in 2004 to settle the disputed sovereignty of islands at the confluence of the Amur and Ussuri rivers, Beijing was harshly criticized on the *China Daily*'s online forum for the treasonous act of ceding Chinese territory. This critique, which was traced to the Web site of the China Cartographic Press, posted several very detailed satellite photographs of the islands and the controversial boundary settlement. Not surprisingly, the Chinese government quickly removed these Web pages.[53]

Other critiques of the Sino–Russian border continue to percolate among China's netizens, including items on the PRC's premier search engine Baidu, which rename the Russian Far East as "Outer Manchuria." This Web site marks Outer Manchuria as an area of lost territory on a national humiliation-style map, and the text explains that it has been China's sovereign territory "since ancient times," and was lost when it "was invaded and occupied by Czarist Russia."[54] Moreover, Maps of China's National Humiliation from the early twentieth century are continually rediscovered and posted in chat rooms to provoke patriotic discussion of lost territories among China's youth: one participant declares that we "must recapture the homeland," while others argue over the status of Mongolia and Korea.[55] On the Russian side of the border, there are palpable fears that China's "Yellow Horde" plans to employ "demographic pressures" to reclaim the Russian Far East from the dwindling ethnic-Russian population.[56] The cartography of national humiliation thus continues to animate Chinese (and Russian) popular understandings of China's proper geobody and provokes scattered protests on the Web. While we can't rely on Wikipedia-like sites for "objective truth," they do show how activist groups are producing, distributing, and consuming alternative understandings of China's geobody.

The "Koguryo controversy," by comparison, is a prime example of how the cartography of national humiliation is framing more official, academic, and diplomatic understandings of the geobody. Like with Russia, China has cartographic disputes with South Korea over Manchurian territories. While China's imperial and national humiliation maps commonly mark Korea as a vassal state, South Korean elites look to ancient history to claim what we now call Manchuria as Korean territory. These two discourses, which had largely bypassed each other for decades, collided when both North Korea and the PRC applied to the United Nations Education, Scientific, and Cultural Organization (UNESCO) to recognize tombs from the ancient Koguryo Kingdom (37 BC to AD 668) as world heritage sites. Popular opinion was inflamed on July 1, 2004 when UNESCO simultaneously recognized tombs in *both* North Korea and China as Koguryo world heritage sites. This led to a serious diplomatic dispute: on August 5, Seoul sent a senior diplomat to Beijing to protest China's "ongoing distortion of the history of Koguryo," and later that month Beijing sent a vice foreign minister to Seoul to iron out a five-point reconciliation plan.[57] Several years later, the controversy continues to smolder with newspaper articles and scholarly works regularly reigniting it.[58]

113

On the Chinese side, the UNESCO application was part of the "Northeast Asia Project" launched in 2002 by the same group that published the standard-setting *History of China's Modern Borders* (2007): the Center for the Study of Borderland History and Geography, which is part of the official Chinese Academy of Social Sciences think tank. The project's research on the Koguryo Kingdom, whose territory straddles the current PRC–North Korean border, concluded that this Korean dynasty was a vassal state in China's empire. Imperial history is thus reframed as "borderland history," while Koreans are refigured from an independent nation to one of China's many "ethnic minorities." The Chinese media refers to this kingdom as "China's Koguryo" (analogous to references to "China's Tibet"), and China's Foreign Ministry removed Koguryo from its Web page on Korean history.[59]

On the Korean side, Koguryo is central to national identity: the name "Korea" comes from this ethnic Korean kingdom. Koguryo thus is a foundational site of Korea's ancient history, not only for cultural reasons: this dynasty is particularly famous for resisting imperial China. Although the world heritage site is in North Korea, the controversy became a matter of national humiliation for South Koreans. Patriotic citizens were enjoined to once again resist the threat of Chinese aggression: as an editorialist in Seoul writes, "[T]his Chinese attempt to include Kokuryo as part of the history of China should be criticized for what it really is: an example of China-centered great-power chauvinism."[60] South Korea's National Assembly "called on China to cease its efforts to distort history," and the prime minister was pressured to set up the Foundation for the Study of Kokuryo as a direct response to China's Northeast Asia Project.[61] While Chinese scholars look to imperial and national humiliation maps that list Korea as a vassal, Korea's scholar-activists not only look to ancient maps to argue their case, but many have now drawn their own expansive maps of the Koguryo Kingdom and posted them on the Web (see Figure 4.10).[62]

Northeast Asia's early history thus is the focus of heated debates over the nontraditional security issues of national identity. But these historical issues also frame the very traditional security issue of the proper international border between Korea and China. Indeed, strategists on both sides agree that the Koguryo controversy is less about correctly recording "historical facts" than about the strategic intentions of the PRC and Korea in the twenty-first century. While some South Koreans worry about Beijing's plans to dominate Northeast Asia, many strategists in Beijing see the Northeast Asia Project as "preempting" any territorial claims that a reunified Korea would make on the Manchurian territories, where the PRC's nearly 2 million ethnic Koreans live.[63]

Figure 4.10 Map of the Koguryo Kingdom. http://www.kokuryo.com.

Thus, although the Northeast Asia Project and the Foundation for the Study of Kokuryo are on opposite sides of the Koguryo controversy, China and South Korea are both employing the strategies of the cartography of national humiliation. And Korea is not alone in using China's cartographic strategies to claim territory. While scholar-activists in South Korea argue that much of Manchuria is actually Korean, Thailand likewise has a history of seeking to claim its former vassals in Laos, Cambodia, Assam, Burma, and Yunnan as integral parts of a sovereign pan-Thai geobody.[64] Hence, South Korea and Thailand use a similar dual cartographic logic in their own narratives of "lost territories" to inspire normative and aspirational geobodies that encroach on China's own national map.

115

While China's diplomats are busy negotiating solutions to international border disputes, alternative voices continue to emerge both in China and abroad. This is evidence of the effectiveness of maps for patriotic education in China and other countries: all these nativists continue to crave the return of what they see as "lost territories." In a way, the cartography of national humiliation has been too persuasive; popular voices are now ahead of the party-state in promoting this view of China's lost territories. The symbolic politics of this geobody thus actually exceeds Beijing's diplomatic strategy that seeks to map China as a responsible part of the world.

Alternative Geobodies

Resistance to China's expansive geobody also emerges on the domestic front in the frontier areas of Xinjiang, Hong Kong, and Taiwan. Artisans in northwest China, for example, have woven the PRC out of a carpet map to highlight Xinjiang as its own entity (see Figure 4.11).[65] The carpet plays with the tension between two conflicting geobodies. On the one hand, the carpet's meaning is very official because the design is based on a road map of the Xinjiang Uyghur Autonomous Region found in any Chinese atlas. On the other hand, the carpet subversively portrays Xinjiang as separate from China because the design obscures the difference between internal provincial boundaries and external international boundaries. This carpet thus uses the cartography of sovereign territory to assert the geobody of Xinjiang as East Turkestan; it does not contest the logic of borders so much as reframe them from internal boundaries to external ones.

Resistance in Hong Kong and Taiwan, however, calls into question the cartographic conventions that are taken for granted on this Xinjiang carpet map. Rather than arguing over the correct borders of sovereign territory, in *The Atlas: An Archeology of an Imaginary City* Hong Kong novelist Dung Kai Cheung discusses the return of Hong Kong as a conceptual issue. While *Maps of China's National Humiliation* (1997) stresses the geopolitical and legal aspects of how Britain's gunboat diplomacy and unequal treaties stole Chinese territory, *The Atlas* treats the territorial border as a site of aesthetic sovereignty performances. Thus Dung does not resist British or Chinese sovereignty in the expected way by asserting Hong Kong as an independent sovereign territory. Rather, he takes a conceptual – and frankly satirical – approach to understand Hong Kong's contingent historical and geographic position. *The Atlas* thus makes sense of Hong Kong's messy history at the intersection of two empires by deploying a set of eccentric cartographic concepts: counterplace, commonplace, misplace,

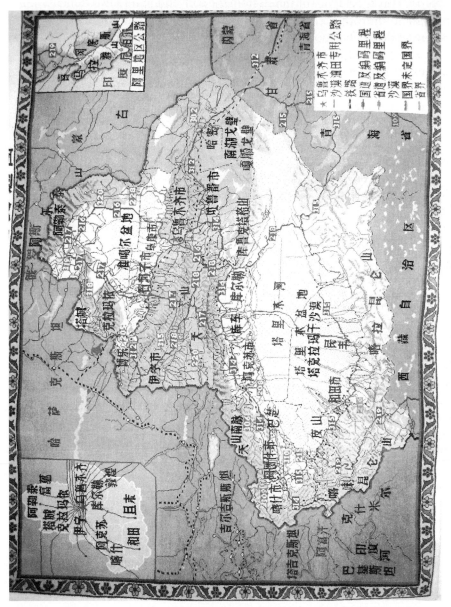

Figure 4.11 Untitled carpet map of Xinjiang (2005). Courtesy of Ablimit Baki.

displace, antiplace, nonplace, extraterritoriality, boundary, utopia, supertopia, subtopia, transtopia, multitopia, unitopia, and omnitopia. Dung's complex approach to cartography thus shifts from the conventions of a two-dimensional map to an overlapping and multiple space that undermines the hegemonic understanding of the modern notion of territorial sovereignty.[66] *The Atlas* therefore is quite good at capturing Hong Kong's transnational dynamic, which is difficult to represent on standard maps. Indeed, similar to Susan Sontag's *On Photography* which avoids using photos, one of Dung's tactics for resisting the discourse of territorial sovereignty is to refuse to display any maps at all.

While the carpet cartograph uses a standard map to resist the PRC, and Dung theorizes against maps to locate Hong Kong in transnational space, resistance in Taiwan employs both mathematical maps and critical cartography to contest Chinese hegemony. During the Cold War, maps of the Republic of China (whose government fled to Taiwan with the founding of the PRC in 1949) reflected the ROC's political aspirations to reconquer the mainland – and Mongolia too. Yet, with the rise of Taiwan's independence movement, which seeks to separate the island from Chinese sovereignty, new maps have appeared to sketch out a new autonomous geobody. In addition to simply drawing the island of Taiwan as an entity separate from the mainland, at times Taiwan's maps have resisted the conventions of modern Chinese cartography to assert their own perspective. Following the hegemonic cartographic practice of the Mercator projection, official maps in Asia put the north on top and the west on the left, thus generally valuing north over south and west over east.[67] On China's national maps, Taiwan is located in the worst symbolic quadrant: the Southeast.

In 2004, Taiwan's Secretary of Education unveiled a new "Series of Maps from Taiwan's Perspective" for use in the island's high schools, including the "Change the Perspective to View Taiwan" map (see Figure 4.12).[68] This fascinating map very deliberately challenges cartographic conventions to put Taiwan at the center of the map as an independent maritime nation rather than as a peripheral province of a continental power. As its notes tell high school students:

> Perhaps this map is confusing to people because it shifts from the normal situation where the North is up and the South is down to one where the Southeast is up and the Northwest is down. This map enables us to see our neighbors more clearly, from Japan on the left to the Philippines and Indonesia on the right. These East Asian countries are not only our neighbors; in terms of their geological environment they are Taiwan's brothers.

Figure 4.12 "Change the Perspective to View Taiwan" (2004). Council for Cultural Affairs, Taiwan.

Many proponents of Taiwan's reunification with China were outraged by what they saw as a "politicization" of Taiwan's map. But what is most interesting about the "Change the Perspective to View Taiwan" map is how this strange image highlights how we have to work very hard to interpret not only this map, but any map. The purpose of this map thus is not only to represent Taiwan; its notes instruct us that its goal is to "critically interrogate cartography's system of tools," which includes determining the map's "scope and position, the way it is projected, how its content is selected, the choice of map symbols, and so on."

While national humiliation maps fudge the contradictions between imperial domain and sovereign territory and thus obscure their own relations of production, the perspectival map of Taiwan is much more honest about how it uses conventions to create political meaning. While the national humiliation maps' annotations of lost territories (which we are told have been Chinese "since ancient times") tend to naturalize ambiguous space as national territory, the annotations on the "Change the Perspective to View Taiwan" map underline how it is created by and for a particular Taiwanese point of view; that is why it is so controversial – and so successful.

As in Xinjiang and Hong Kong, people in Taiwan creatively employ cartographic strategies to challenge China's simple conversion of imperial domain into national territory. They resist China's national aesthetics by shifting from asking "Where is China?" to "Where isn't China?" In this way, these three alternative geobodies resist the last cartographic strategy of drawing maps exclusively from Beijing's point of view.

These last two sections on border diplomacy and alternative geobodies underline the symbolic nature of the cartography of national humiliation. They show how the overlap is not only between imperial domain and sovereign territory; managing sovereign territory also is intertwined with managing ethnic(ized) populations both on the periphery and at the center.

The cartography of national humiliation can have a very material impact, however. Taiwan is still seen by many in the PRC as the final "lost territory" that Beijing needs to recover to complete China's fractured geobody and become a great power. According to this popular view, Taiwan was stolen first by Japan in the Century of National Humiliation, and then by the United States when it chose to defend the Republic of China during the Cold War. Official US policy supports a peaceful and noncoercive resolution of the Taiwan issue; but most Chinese see America as the main "obstacle" to China's natural national reunification. These map disputes thus concern much more than pedagogical issues; Taiwan is a huge security issue for the region because the United States would get pulled into a war if and when Taiwan and the PRC come to blows.

Conclusion

While we assume that we can easily locate "the real China" on a world map, these fascinating and perplexing maps show that the debate over where China begins and ends is ongoing, especially in discussions among Chinese intellectuals. These maps are a visual expression of China's pessoptimistic national aesthetic, which graphically shows how the transition from imperial Chinese cosmology to modern scientific geography has not been complete. Indeed, China's geobody actually emerges from the interplay of the otherwise contradictory cartographic conventions of imperial domain space and sovereign territory space. Yet, after over a century of crafting, China's geobody is still neither stable nor hegemonic; it faces cartographic resistance on many fronts.

Although the cartography of national humiliation isn't necessarily the dominant view, it is necessary to understand how it still animates official, scholarly, and popular understandings of national territoriality in China. After welcoming back Hong Kong (1997) and Macau (1999), it seems natural to many in China that Taiwan will soon be part of the motherland. As China gets stronger, people take for granted that their geobody will continue to "reunify" – and that anything that gets in China's way is a heinous "obstacle." Using Chinese-language materials that rarely emerge in Western analyses of China, the chapter has shown the rise of a strangely anxious popular countercurrent to Beijing's current positive images of the PRC as a "peacefully rising" power in a "harmonious world."

This is not to say that China has irredentist geopolitical ambitions to reclaim lost national territories in the twenty-first century. With the exception of Taiwan, the goal of national humiliation maps is no longer primarily to recover lost territory; it is to cleanse the stains of lost honor and pride. The desire is not so much for material territory as for symbolic recognition, acceptance, and respect. As the deputy director of the Olympics ceremonies declared, "I really hope that the people of the world can...get to know China, to understand China, to love China, and to desire China."[69] The challenges that China faces thus emerge more in identity politics than in geopolitics. Rather than emanate from some grand "Western conspiracy" (see Figure 4.2), these challenges arise in China's own backyard through its relations with Russia, South Korea, Thailand, Vietnam, the new Central

Asian states, and Taiwan. If anything, these maps suggest that rather than looking abroad for more territory, Beijing is most concerned with the challenges posed by ethnic groups like Koreans, Uyghurs, and Tibetans that occupy borderlands already inside China's sovereign territory.[70]

The Tibetan uprising and Chinese reactions to it in spring 2008 illustrate how maps and geobodies continue to animate popular movements. The patriotic Chinese video "Tibet WAS, IS, and ALWAYS WILL BE a part of China" that went viral on YouTube used imperial maps (that were quite anachronistic) to show Tibet as an integral part of China.[71] Tibetan activists and international scholars, on the other hand, produced their own maps of a greater Tibet that goes far beyond the boundaries of the Tibetan Autonomous Region (TAR). Figure 4.13 maps Tibetan territory by plotting where demonstrations took place in the TAR and the provinces of Qinghai, Gansu, Sichuan, and Yunnan, rather than according to current or traditional borders.[72] Thus, maps of Chinese and Tibetan geobodies take shape through the actions of activists both on the ground and on the Web.

A satirical twist was added to this battle of maps after Beijing cancelled the 2008 EU–China summit because French President Nicolas Sarkozy "hurt the feelings of the Chinese people" by planning to meet the Dalai Lama. A Chinese blogger responded by doing a keyword search of the *People's Daily* to see which countries had also "hurt the feelings of the Chinese people," which he then charted on a world map[73] (see Figure 4.14). This fascinating map of hurt feelings inverts the logic of cartography of national humiliation to map the "humiliators" rather than the humiliations.

Such popular maps show a shift in how and where maps are made, and how geobodies are produced and consumed. Until recently, map-making was a capital-intensive activity that required the institutional backing of the state or an elite geographic society. But in the digital age, anyone with a computer and internet access can make a map and craft a geobody. The patriotic Chinese video was created in a few days, and the Tibetan protest map was continually updated as the unrest spread in March and April 2008. Certainly, states still try to control map production: Vice President Dick Cheney famously blurred his official residence on Google Maps, and the PRC passed a law in 2007 forbidding unauthorized foreigners from mapping any part of China. But with new software from Google, Microsoft, and Yahoo, people can easily create customized maps both for utilitarian tasks and to express their dreams and nightmares. The director of the Center for Citizen Media thus explains, "The possibilities for doing amazing kinds of things, to tell stories or to help tell stories with maps, are just endless."[74] While MapQuest tells us how to get from here to there,

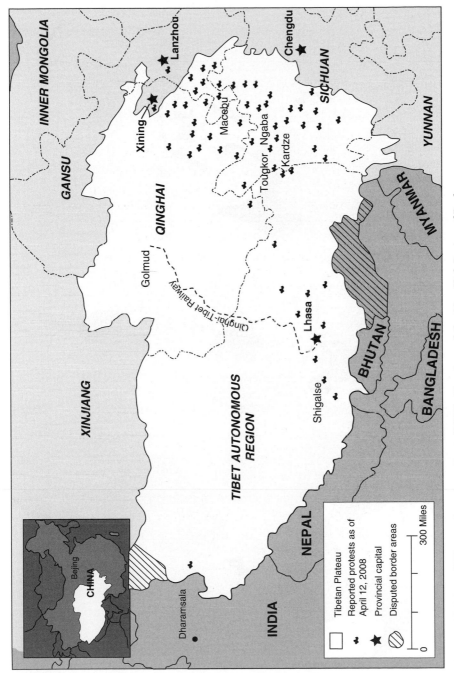

Figure 4.13 Map of Tibetan demonstrations (2008). Courtesy of the *New York Review of Books*.

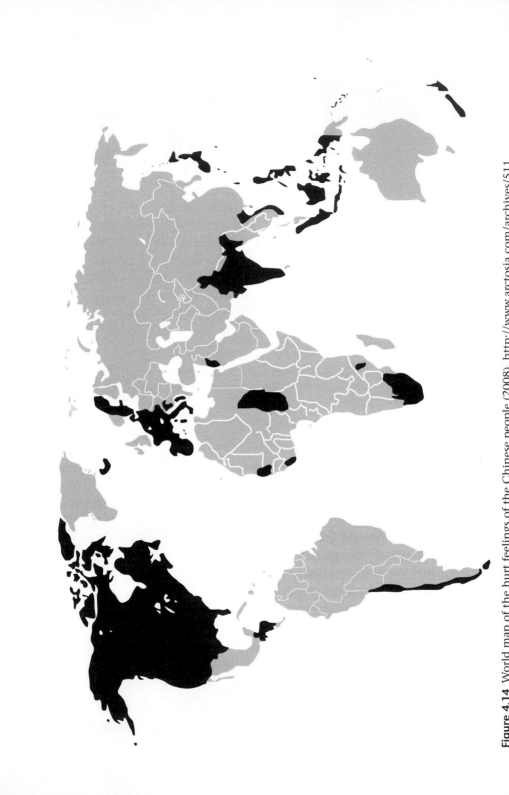

Figure 4.14 World map of the hurt feelings of the Chinese people (2008). http://www.arctosia.com/archives/511.

these maps of China show how cartography is an active part of the pessop-timist dynamic of identity politics. People are producing and consuming nationalism when they make, distribute, read, and recirculate such maps.

The cartography of national humiliation is uniquely prominent in China; but the symbolic struggles of its national geobody resonate beyond its borders. On the one hand, activists in other countries are also crafting aspirational geobodies to reclaim lost territories: Ireland, Israel, Mexico, and so on. On the other, some transnational groups are imagining normative geobodies as a way to get onto the current geopolitical map: Kurds, Basques, and so on. These alternative geobodies don't just imagine new territorial boundaries; they also manage the hopes and fears of peoples. While many are declaring a grand shift from the hard power of geopolitics to the soft power of identity politics, the cartography of national humiliation shows show hard and soft power are intertwined in a creative tension that pro-motes the management of territorial borders as it regulates the flow of hopes and fears.

Hence, national humiliation maps (like all maps) don't just tell us where we are, but also how to feel. In this way, national maps are part of the broader discourse of national security, which generally tell us less about the geopolitics of defending territorial boundaries than about the symbolic politics of "tell[ing] us who we must be."[75] And where we must be.

Chapter 5

Who Is China? (1): Foreign Brothers and Domestic Strangers

Using ethnicity to answer the question "Who is China?" seems obvious. Most countries in the world look to ethnic identity to define their national identity. But it runs into problems in China. While most outsiders assume that China is ethnically homogeneous, the People's Republic of China (PRC) defines itself as a "multinational nation-state." Here the Chinese word *minzu* is employed both for the plurality of China's fifty-six ethnic nationalisms and the singularity of its unified nation-state. *Minzu* as "nation" thus refers to diametrically opposed concepts in China: patriotic nationalism that is encouraged by the state, and ethnic nationalism that is seen as a threat. These contradictions are messy because the two conflicting ideas of nationalism typically refer to specific ethnic groups: while Han Chinese (including overseas Chinese) are taken as a bottomless reservoir of patriotic nationalism, the PRC's ethnic minorities (especially Uyghurs and Tibetans) often are seen as terrorist threats to China's national unity.

The Tibetan uprising in spring 2008 graphically demonstrated the explosive nature of the tensions between Tibetans and Han first in Lhasa, and then throughout the Tibetan plateau.[1] There were four days of peaceful demonstrations before the violent confrontation in Lhasa on 14 March, and then weeks of peaceful protests after this horrible event. But Chinese Central Television (CCTV) focused on the violence of 14 March, whipping up public opinion by playing looped video of barbaric Tibetans beating, burning, and killing Han Chinese; ordinary Chinese viewers thus demanded a strong response from the party-state to the crimes of these "rioters." As the uprising was spreading from Lhasa to the broader Tibetan plateau in March 2008, the party secretary of the Tibet Autonomous Region inflamed the interethnic frenzy even more by demonizing the Dalai Lama as a "wolf with a human face and the heart of a beast." The "one sided

propaganda of the official Chinese media had the effect of stirring up interethnic animosity and aggravating an already tense situation," according to
the few Chinese dissidents who criticized Beijing's violent crackdown.[2]

Some of the more sensational aspects of the Chinese reaction to the
Tibetan uprising actually did not take place in the PRC, but abroad. As
the Olympic Torch's "Journey of Harmony" passed through Europe, America, Australia, and East Asia, overseas Chinese groups increasingly targeted
Tibetans and their supporters in "pro-China" activities that ranged from
peaceful counter-demonstrations to Internet death threats to violent con-
frontations on the street. For trying to mediate between demonstrators who
supported Tibet and China, Grace Wang, a freshman at Duke University,
was denounced as a "race traitor" and physically threatened.

Yet overseas Chinese and ethnic minorities also are linked by the party-
state in more positive ways. In 1949, Mao Zedong included these two groups
as part of the "Political Consultative Conference of representatives of all the
democratic parties, people's organizations, democratic personages in all walks
of life, national minorities and overseas Chinese"; Mao repeated this inclusive
formulation of political identity with the foundation of the PRC on October
1, 1949.[3] This linkage of Chinese expatriates and national minorities continues to appear in official statements and history textbooks not only to
remember past victories, but also to recruit "all ethnicities" and "overseas
Chinese brothers and sisters" to "rejuvenate the Chinese race" in the twenty-
first century.[4] Yet, regardless of whether their interaction is positive or negative, neither national minorities nor expatriate Chinese are at the center of
Chinese politics. In grand declarations, they come at the end of a long list of
the PRC's various constituencies, and typically are followed by the catchall
phrase "and other patriotic elements."[5] Likewise, they are merely supporting
actors in the narrative of the Century of National Humiliation.

Both groups thus are outsiders looking in. What they share is not a
common political identity so much as the common role as "the Other" in
the imagination of mainland Han Chinese who, as we are repeatedly told,
dominate the PRC with over 90 percent of the population. Yet the integrity
of the Han race is not self-evident either. At the turn of the twentieth century
the father of Chinese nationalism, Liang Qichao, lamented the lack of a
single name for his race; after various tries he settled on "*Zhonghua minzu*" to
designate the Chinese nation. The Father of China, Sun Yatsen, similarly
worried that the Han were a "loose sheet of sand" who had little loyalty to
the Chinese nation. To forge China's various clan and regional identities
into a homogeneous "all-embracing idea of Han as the national group" Sun
decided to distinguish Han from both "external foreigners," namely the

Western and Japanese imperialists, and "internal foreigners" – Manchu, Tibetans, Mongols, and Hui.[6] At the same time that Sun was busy excluding non-Han groups as internal foreigners, he very actively recruited external support for his revolution from the expatriate Chinese community.

While previous chapters have examined how Chinese identity is constructed against external foreigners, this chapter will follow Sun Yatsen's curious approach to focus on the role of domestic strangers (i.e., national minorities) and foreign brothers (i.e., overseas Chinese) in China's pessoptimist national aesthetic. Certainly national minorities and overseas Chinese are important policy concerns in a positive way: both are the sources of things valued by the party-state. As we saw in Chapter 4, national minorities are key to China's territorial integrity; while they compose less than 10 percent of China's population their autonomous regions constitute 60 percent of the PRC, and "in many border counties of Xinjiang, Tibet, Inner Mongolia, and Yunnan, minorities exceed 90 percent of the population."[7] This frontier territory is crucial to Beijing for both political and economic reasons: it is a security issue because these ethnic groups straddle China's international border; it is an economic issue because their territory contains rich natural resources that are necessary for China's development strategy.[8]

While minority nationality policy often deals with ongoing security challenges, the PRC's ties with overseas Chinese play a more positive role in Chinese foreign policy by providing a diasporic bridge to foreign lands. Rather than being a source of natural resources, overseas Chinese communities are exploited by Beijing as a transnational resource of foreign investment, technical expertise, and managerial experience. Indeed, 80 percent of China's foreign direct investment has come from the Chinese diaspora in Southeast Asia. Expatriate Chinese are also a security issue because Beijing and Taibei compete for the lucrative loyalty of this transnational group.

However, this unlikely pair of domestic strangers and foreign brothers is important beyond China's economic and security strategies. The chapter will show how modern Chinese identity emerges in pessoptimistic tension with these "essential outsiders." Once again, the goal is not to discover the positive core Chinese civilization (i.e., "the real China"), but to examine how national identity is produced through a positive/negative structure of feeling that weaves together the majority with minorities, and the center with the margins. Certainly, non-Han groups and expatriate Chinese are very active in constructing their own identities in empowering ways to work both with and against the mainland Han majority; here, however, we will consider how domestic strangers and foreign brothers are employed in the PRC to answer the question "Who is China?"

The chapter thus examines the inclusive/exclusive logic of Beijing's nation-building strategies, but in a new way that explores how this positive/ negative, identity/security dynamic often reproduces the civilization/ barbarism distinction [*Huayi zhi bian*] discussed in previous chapters. National minorities are actually the original "barbarians," and the "Chineseness" of expatriates is often dismissed as derivative at best. In the PRC both "overseas Chinese work" and "nationalities work" – Beijing's official designations of these policy areas – increasingly look to China's imperial past for policy narratives. Chapter 2 showed how China sees itself as economically backward when compared to the West. But here China is both civilized and backward: mainland Han see themselves as civilized in relation with barbaric national minorities, and backward when compared with advanced expatriate Chinese capitalists. In this way, the dominant Han Chinese identity takes shape against foreign brothers and domestic strangers in ways that employ the civilization/ barbarism distinction. As we have seen, the civilization/barbarism distinction is much more than a cultural issue from the past. This dynamic continues to be popular in academic and policy journals to describe the formation of both the Chinese nation and the PRC's sovereign territory.[9]

This chapter concludes with an examination of how Jiang Rong's best-selling novel *Lang tuteng* [*Wolf Totem*] redeploys the civilization/barbarism distinction to use marginalized groups, once again, to construct the mainland Han majority.[10] The analysis will show how for domestic strangers and foreign brothers any appreciation of difference still needs to support the unity of One China, not just ethnically or territorially, but conceptually.

Barbarians, National Minorities, and the Construction of Chinese Identity

With the founding of the PRC in 1949, the government's policy toward frontier ethnic groups changed dramatically from the assimilation strategy of Republican China to a new policy that stressed equality and autonomy. Before the 1930s, the civilization/barbarism distinction was written into the orthography of Chinese characters, which defined some non-Han groups as dogs and insects. As part of its new policy, the PRC officially reformed the Chinese language to recognize the humanity of non-Han groups. Peoples who had previously been called "barbarians" were recast as "national minorities" [*shaoshu minzu*]. While imperial and Republican nationalities policies seemed to be formulated to "exclude and insult," the

PRC's policy aimed to enlist the various minority groups as loyal citizens of the Chinese nation.[11]

Yet China's problems over the past sixty years lead us to question this official narrative where Han Chinese heroically liberate national minorities. The Tibetan uprising of spring 2008 is only a recent example of ethnic unrest in China, which continues to simmer among other groups as well. While official policy stresses equality and autonomy, the Han majority still has an ambivalent attitude toward ethnic minorities that often works itself out in discriminatory practices. In "The Discriminatory Complex in Our Sub-consciousness," a prominent Chinese blogger explains why Han Chinese lacked sympathy for Tibetans in 2008. Because they resist assimilation into the Han majority, he argues, Tibetans are seen as backward barbarians: "those 'minorities' who dress in their traditional clothing are violent, cognitively not quite enlightened, and still at the primitive stage of development. Only pan-Han are 'civilized' people."[12] The Han Chinese graduate student who created one of the most popular anti-Western patriotic videos in 2008 confirmed this commonsense view: he "couldn't figure out why foreigners were so agitated about Tibet – an impoverished backwater, as he saw it, that China had tried for decades to civilize."[13]

Hence, rather than just highlight the progressive innovations of Beijing's national minorities' policy, it is important to recognize the policy *continuities* between the PRC, Republican China and imperial China. Indeed, Ma Rong, an influential ethnic policy theorist, argues that the PRC needs to rethink its current Soviet-influenced nationalities policy by reviving China's premodern strategy.[14] My argument is that the civilization/barbarism distinction continues to guide Han relations with other groups. The goal of civilizing the barbarians is not just to confirm the unity of the party-state, but to confirm the superiority of the Han race.

This is not to say that the civilization/barbarism distinction is simply reproduced as a constant throughout Chinese history. Certainly, China's current concept of civilization has been informed by Western, Japanese, and Soviet notions of nationalism. Drawing upon various sources, the concept of civilization thus has developed within China, changing from a simple binary opposition of civilization/barbarism in imperial China, to the "Republic of Five Races" in the early twentieth century, and finally to the fifty-six nationalities of the PRC. Although the number of official ethnic groups has expanded over the past century, the enduring need to define and classify minorities reaffirms the central role of the Han as the majority. China's civilizing project thus is an important part of its nationalizing project (and vice versa).

Civilization and barbarians in imperial China

To understand the role minorities play in China's national aesthetic, it is important to further develop our critical view of China's civilization/barbarism distinction. As we saw in Chapter 1, idealized versions of imperial Chinese civilization stress its openness and tolerance. Rather than seeking to conquer the violent barbarians who challenged it, we are often told how China's magnanimous civilization inclusively embraced difference. Rather than distinguishing people according to races and nations, Chinese leaders employed a cultural policy of civilizing various barbarian groups to include them in Confucianism's hierarchical world order. Imperial China's universal community of All-under-Heaven [*Tianxia*] was governed by a unified system of rituals that promoted the ideology of Great Unity [*da yitong*] for China's ethnic groups and territory.

While this idealized worldview is often employed to explain imperial China's foreign policy, it also informs what Beijing now calls "nationalities work."[15] Historical geographer Li Dalong discusses – at length – "the harmonization of ethnic relations in All-under-Heaven [*Tianxia*]," while Ma Rong explains that "the lessons Chinese may learn from their ancestors should benefit China in viewing and guiding ethnic relations at present time."[16] Historian Xiaoyuan Liu thus concludes that contemporary "devotees" to this view of ancient China see Great Unity as "the conceptual predecessor to today's *Zhonghua minzu* [Chinese nation]," which provides an "ambiguous yet enduring conception of Chinese ethnicism."[17]

However, China's universal system is not only about inclusion. It is also very exclusive, in ways that are similar to other imperial and colonial regimes. Like European empires, Chinese imperial ideology drew sharp distinctions between insiders and outsiders. To maintain its "Great Unity," China constantly needed to affirm itself as the center of civilization by distinguishing itself from "barbarians" on its periphery. Rather than embracing neighbors as equals, Lien-sheng Yang explains that the Sinocentric hierarchy is predicated on "China being internal, large, and high and barbarians being external, small and low."[18] Imperial philosophers, historians, and officials thus continually deployed this hierarchical inside/outside distinction to draw – and redraw – China's cultural, political, and territorial borders.

Alongside the classical passages that extol the inclusive tolerance of the Confucian world order is a parallel canon that radically divides civilization from barbarians. A passage from the *Book of Rites* (third century BC) provides the governing concept of the civilization/barbarism distinction: "the Chinese, the Rong, the Yi and the other peoples of the five quarters all have their own nature, which cannot be moved or altered."[19] The five quarters refers to the Sinocentric geography that we saw in Chapter 4 where civilization was at the center and the "outermost areas were reserved for barbarians, ferocious animals and evil spirits."[20] Barbarians, in this political cosmography, not only lack civilization, but lack humanity: "The Di and Rong are wolves."[21] This Confucian classic confirms that outsiders are not only barbaric, but essentially different: "If he is not of our race, he is sure to have a different mind."[22] In an oft-quoted phrase, Mencius declares that cultural influence can only go in one direction: "I have heard of the Chinese converting barbarians, but not of their being converted by barbarians."[23]

In his survey of China's philosophical and historical classics, Li Dalong underlines the enduring popularity of the civilization/barbarian distinction in imperial policy. It led to "long-term trends of discriminating against borderland minorities culture... which formed the foundation for dealing with frontier nationalities" over China's many dynasties.[24] While idealized views of the Chinese moral order stress how these were cultural rather than racial distinctions, the imperial regimes characteristically defined civilization as the people and practices of China's central plain [zhongyuan]. The general terms for civilization – Hua, Xia, and Huaxia – are generally glossed as "Han" in contemporary Chinese texts, while the names for barbarian – Yi, Man, Rong, and Di – are tied to China's current and past ethnic minorities.[25] Non-Han groups are not defined positively according to their own unique cultural practices, but negatively according to a "lack" of Han Chinese attributes. The civilization/barbarism distinction thus leads to a racial taxonomy whereby different ethnic groups are martialed into a set of binary distinctions that place the Han at the center as the dominant majority group, and others on the periphery as "national minorities" rather than independent nations or equal citizens.

Imperial China's frontier policy generally shifted between two distinct strategies: (1) construct and guard the border to conquer or contain barbarians, and (2) assimilate barbarians through education and intermarriage. The conquest and containment policy employed the strategy of "use barbarians to control barbarians," while the assimilation policy deployed the strategy of "use Civilization to transform the barbarian."[26] Many scholars differentiate between these approaches toward outsiders as "inclusive" and "exclusive,"[27] but I think that they are better understood as two aspects of the same hierarchical approach to dealing with difference. One conquers, the other converts; neither allows different peoples to survive on their own terms.

Forging nationalism in Republican China

At the turn of the twentieth century, a vigorous debate over politics and identity emerged in China, especially after the humiliating shock of China's defeat in the Sino-Japanese War (1894–5). As mentioned above, Liang Qichao lamented the lack of a single name for the Chinese race, and only settled on *Zhonghua minzu* after trying numerous other phrases. Even after the Chinese race acquired a proper name, the raucous debate continued in ways that reaffirm the civilization/barbarism distinction. Sun Yatsen's revolutionary slogan "Expel the Tartar Enemy and Restore China" is strikingly similar to "Expel the Northern Barbarians and Restore China," a popular Han slogan protesting Mongolian rule during the Yuan dynasty.[28]

While Sun's revolutionary goal was to expel Manchus from his imagined community, key reformers Liang Qichao and Kang Youwei were more inclusive with non-Han nationalities, whom they felt could help China in its impending "race war" with the West. Liang thus coined the phrase "Republic of Five Races" – Han, Manchu, Tibetan, Mongolian, and Hui – to unite the Yellow race in *Zhonghua minzu*. However, the civilization/barbarian logic still applies; Liang's goal was to assimilate the "small and weak" non-Han groups to produce an even stronger Han race.[29]

The Republic of China, which was founded in 1912, developed this notion of Chinese nationalism. According to its provisional constitution it was the "Republic of Five Races," complete with an official Five-Color Flag to represent these groups (see Figure 5.1). However, Sun Yatsen did not have a change of heart; rather he changed his strategy to include internal foreigners in the Chinese nation out of a concern that China's borderlands were being annexed by external foreigners. Rather than dividing Han from other ethnicities, Sun Yatsen's new slogan appealed to a more expansive view of the Chinese identity: "All-under-heaven is shared by everyone" [*Tianxia wei gong*].

Yet, non-Han groups were not included as equals. Sun Yatsen was still uncomfortable with a multinational China; in 1919 he even blamed the Five-Color Flag for encouraging separatism: "This ill-omened flag has been the cause of all the Republic's misfortunes."[30] Sun's notion of the Chinese nation gelled in his influential lectures on the *Three People's Principles* (1924), which stressed that the Chinese nation was actually the "single, pure race" of Han Chinese.[31] Since Mongolians, Manchurians, Tibetans, and Hui were small and insignificant "alien races," Sun concluded that radical assimilation was the only way to construct a strong Chinese nation. In another version of the "Three People's Principles" (1921), Sun argued

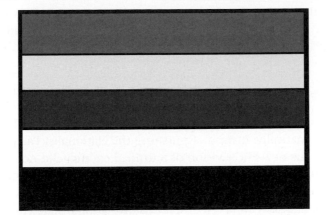

Figure 5.1 The Republic's five-color flag.

that "to constitute a single nation . . . we must facilitate the dying out of all names of individual peoples inhabiting China, such as Manchus, Tibetans, etc."[32] Anthropologist Dru Gladney thus concludes that "Sun Yat-sen's nationalism – either as a means of excluding barbarians, or assimilating them – thus set our commonsense view of a homogeneous Han as well as that of ethnic groups as national minorities."[33]

When Chiang Kai-shek came to power a few years later, he vigorously pursued an assimilation policy that entailed cultural suppression. In his influential book, *China's Destiny* (1943), Chiang even denied the difference of non-Han groups, whom he declared were actually "branches of the same race." Since their differences were merely "religious and geographical," they thus could be assimilated by the dominant Han Chinese.[34] In fact, Chiang and his contemporaries showed little interest in Manchurians, Mongolians, Tibetans, and Hui as fellow citizens; they were primarily interested in reclaiming the borderlands as "national territory."

National Humiliation history textbooks in the 1920s and 1930s thus understand these issues as a "territorial crisis" rather than as a "nationalities question." Cao and Huang's *Short History of National Humiliation* (1932) has chapters on "The Tibet Problem," "The Outer Mongolia Problem," and "The Manchuria Problem."[35] Like with the national humiliation maps we examined in Chapter 4, the struggle here is framed as between China and foreign imperialism, rather than between, for example, Mongolians and Han.[36] Han Chinese at this point had very little interest in their neighboring nationalities; the vast frontier lands were seen as either empty or as populated by savages with strange customs. The one national humiliation history textbook that talks about Tibetan culture and society actually needs to confirm that "people live there," before describing the odd rituals of Lamaism.[37]

Nationalities work in the PRC

With the founding of the PRC in 1949, China's view of its ethnic periphery changed dramatically. Instead of pursuing the Nationalist Party's assimilation policy, the new PRC's vision of a unified country did not appeal to a homogeneous Chinese identity. Rather than all ethnicities being branches of the overarching Han race, China's constitution declares that "The People's Republic of China is a unitary multi-national state created jointly by the people of all its nationalities."[38] This view of China as a "pluralist-unitary structure" [*duoyuan ti*], where all ethnicities are equal, is widely accepted among scholars and officials in the PRC. China's plural unity is not simply seen as a modern accomplishment of the Chinese Communist Party (CCP). Various documents, including Beijing's "National Minorities Policy and its Practice in China" white paper (2000), appeal to both ancient and modern history to argue that China has been "a united multi-ethnic country since ancient times."[39] The top social scientist in China, Fei Xiaotong, argued in an influential essay that "the Chinese people became a conscious national entity only during the past century, as a result of China's confrontation with the Western powers, but their formation into a single nation has been the result of a historical process of millennia."[40]

Yet as we will see, the PRC's new nationalities policy is still part of China's Han-centric national aesthetic; it combines Marxism–Leninism with imperial China's "Great Unity" ideology in a way that revives the civilization/barbarian distinction. Like with previous Chinese regimes, national unity is the guiding theme in Beijing's "nationalities work." To understand how minority groups create and maintain unity in the PRC, Taiwanese political scientist Chih-yu Shih explains that it is necessary to examine how the issues of autonomy, ethnicity, and poverty together "lock the local communities within the policy agenda of the state."[41]

AUTONOMY

The PRC's understanding of non-Han groups grows out of the CCP's pre-liberation contacts with borderland groups. While the Nationalist Party government had little contact with most non-Han groups on its periphery, Chiang Kai-shek's anticommunist military campaigns pushed the CCP to engage with "fierce barbaric tribesmen" during the Long March (1934–5).[42] To survive this arduous trek through the borderlands, the CCP made deals with non-Han groups including the Shan, Miao, Yi, Tibetans, Mongols, and Hui. Once safe at its new headquarters in Yan'an, the CCP further appeased the Hui and Mongols by recognizing them as separate nationalities, which included setting up China's first autonomous regions.[43] At this point, autonomy included the right for minority groups to secede from China, which was enshrined in the Constitution of the Jiangsi Soviet Republic in 1931. But with the founding of the PRC in 1949, the meaning of autonomy changed from the right to self-determination into a duty to preserve the territorial integrity of China.[44] China's "National Minorities Policy" white paper (2000) underlines how autonomy still needs to enhance China's unity: "The practice of regional autonomy should be beneficial to the unification of the country, social stability and the unity of all ethnic groups."[45]

A national humiliation-style reading of China's revolutionary history guides this shift from the possibility of national self-determination to the necessity of national unity. Rather than Tibetans or Mongolians expressing their national consciousness, Fei tells us that their independence movements were the result of the evil schemes of internal and external foreigners: "Working in collusion with the traitors of the various nationalities, the imperialists tried to split the country and fostered secessionist movements."[46] To support his argument, Fei quotes a poem by Mao Zedong:

> Long was the night and dawn came slow
>> to the Crimson Land
> For a century demons and monsters danced
>> in a sinister band,
> And the union of five hundred million people
>> was not at hand.

The "National Minorities Policy" white paper thus argues that in modern times all nationalities shared the "common destiny" to unite and struggle against foreign "imperialist invasion, oppression and humiliation"[47] – as opposed to struggling against Han domination. Thus, while autonomy is understood in China as the positive solution for a "unified multi-national country," self-determination is seen in terms of the negative problem of "splittism." Ma Rong, for example, cites the Soviet and Yugoslavian examples to explain how self-determination is a "political weapon" employed by internal and external enemies to split the nation-state; such poor ethnic relations thus lead to "disintegration and violence," "foreign invasions," and other calamities where the "entire society is turned upside down."[48] While autonomy is presented by Ma and others as the basis of a successful multiethnic society, autonomous regions actually endure even greater political surveillance by the party-state than regular provinces.

ETHNICITY

Just as Beijing needed to survey China's sovereign territory to know the geographical extent of its rule (as we saw in Chapter 4), after 1949 the party-state needed to survey the country's ethnic groups to know just whom it was ruling. As Fei Xiaotong explains, "how could a People's Congress allocate its seats to deputies from different nationalities without knowing what nationalities there were? And how could the nation effect regional autonomy for the nationalities without a clear idea of their geographical distribution?"[49]

In order to transform China's unmanageable assortment of "barbaric tribes" into a standardized set of "national minorities," China engaged in one of the largest ethnographic research projects that the world has ever seen. The "distinguishing nationalities" [minzu shibie] project started in the early 1950s, and continues to this day. Beijing first sent out a call for non-Han groups to register for recognition from the party-state. However, after over 400 groups responded, Beijing decided that it needed to scientifically determine which groups to include and which to exclude. After years of ethnographic fieldwork that employed Stalin's nationality criteria (common territory, language, economic life, and identity based on cultural heritage), the State Council determined that forty-one national minority groups would be recognized in the PRC's first census in 1953. By the 1964 census there were fifty-three official nationalities, and since the 1979 there have been fifty-six nationalities (including the Han).[50] Other groups are still being considered, and 734,438 people were listed as "unidentified" in the 2000 census.[51]

The "distinguishing nationalities" project included national minorities in interesting ways. To survey non-Han areas, the party-state recruited ethnic cadres, who were trained in newly created national minority institutes before returning to their home region first to conduct fieldwork, and later to enforce government policy.[52] These minority cadres were trained not only in social science methods, but also in scientific socialist ideology. Thus rather than assimilating unruly tribes according to the Confucian world order as in imperial China, the party-state now seeks to convert these national minorities to China's particular form of Leninist-nationalism.

The "distinguishing nationalities" project thus is the current form of China's enduring practice of "distinguishing between Civilization and barbarism," while the training of ethnic cadres and their subsequent nationalities work is the latest example of "using Civilization to transform barbarians." Xiaoyuan Liu thus argues that the party-state's nationalities policy is a continuation of China's previous strategies for addressing difference on its frontier.[53]

However, in a way, nationalities work is backfiring. While many communists expected national minority identities to fade away as ethnic groups were assimilated into the socialist state, these officially assigned ethnic labels "have taken on a life of their own." China's national minority policies tend to harden ethnic identities even as they work to domesticate them. Indeed, Gladney reports that instead of assimilating the Hui's future leaders into the party-state's "Han vision of the state," nationalities institutes actually foster broader and closer ties within the Hui national minority group.[54]

Rather than assimilating to the Han-centric view of Chinese nationalism, there has actually been a significant growth in the population of national minorities. While many people expected Manchus to disappear as a distinct group as they were absorbed into the Han race, Manchus actually had the highest population increase (128 percent) of any nationality in the 1980s.[55] These figures cannot be explained simply by higher birth rates. Actually, what they show is how people formerly categorized as one nationality are now demanding recognition as another nationality, both as individuals and as groups demanding autonomous status.[56] While Fei Xiaotong tells us that "The Hans as a nation grew by attracting non-Hans and assimilating them,"[57] this population movement shows the weakness of China's assimilation argument. Rather than national minorities converting to Han, Han are also converting to national minorities.

POVERTY

The "distinguishing nationalities" project did not just recognize and register non-Han groups; it also ranked national minorities on a hierarchical scale. While it used Stalin's nationality criteria to differentiate various groups, it employed Leninist categories to rank each official nationality into a hierarchy of political–economic stages: primitive, slave, feudal, capitalist, and socialist. Once recognized, each nationality was assigned a place on the timeline of China's political–economic development. While the Han were seen as operating in the feudal and capitalist stages, other nationalities generally were placed at earlier stages of development, and

139

thus "denigrated as less civilized than Han."[58] Once again, Han civilization is designated as the standard and model, while national minorities are classified as poor and backward; this is what the Chinese blogger cited above meant when he described unassimilated nationalities as barbarians who are "still at the primitive stage of development."

The ranking of national minorities as "less than Han" is pervasive in official and academic understandings of the "National Minority Problem." While Han are presented as farmers who are tied to the land in an orderly civilization, nomadic minorities who rely on animal husbandry are seen as an unstable barbaric threat.[59] As Elena Barabantseva argues, this stereotype locates non-Han groups along China's Western frontiers which are seen as poor, backward, and barbaric. Han, on the other hand, are located in the East which is wealthy, modern, and civilized.[60] Han areas have the human resources necessary for modernization, while non-Han areas are "richly endowed with natural resources needed for industrial production." Non-Han groups need Han expertise to utilize these resources because, as Fei Xiaotong explains, "the national minorities are generally inferior to the Hans in the level of culture and technology indispensable for the development of modern industry."[61]

There are many counterexamples that contest this Han-centric view: ethnic Koreans, for example, live in the northeast and have the country's highest educational achievement. However, looking for contradictory facts would miss the point of national minority discourse: "The more backward, or 'primitive', the minorities were, the more advanced and civilized the so-called Han seemed, and the greater the need for a unified national identity."[62]

Beijing's nationalities work thus follows the civilization/barbarian distinction to modernize these backward groups. Jiang Zemin's "socialist spiritual civilization" campaign, which aimed to "raise the population quality" of the Chinese people, specifically targeted national minorities.[63] Hu Jintao's current Harmonious Society policy also seeks to balance the income and well-being of Han and non-Han groups, as it seeks to have a more equitable modernization of coastal and interior areas. The Great Western Development Project is specifically designed to develop the infrastructure of minority areas, and various "Aid the Poor" campaigns target impoverished ethnic groups. Yet Chih-yu Shih concludes that the party-state's poverty alleviation programs actually backfire because they characteristically "begin by condemning the cultural backwardness of indigenous communities," which "often confirms their inferior self-images."[64] On the other hand, the Han's unsympathetic response to Tibetan unrest confirms that national minorities are seen as backward populations that need to be modernized, civilized, and Sinicized – for their own good, whether they like it or not. According to the Chinese blogger who discusses the Han "Discriminatory Complex," minority groups that resist assimilation garner little respect because Han believe that "those who submit to me will survive and thrive, those who resist me will be destroyed."[65] Thus, as Shih argues, the issues of autonomy, ethnicity and poverty "all point in one big direction – the unity of the Chinese nation, which means that autonomy points to political unity, ethnicity to cultural–national unity, and poverty to economic unity."[66]

NEW POLICY CHALLENGES

China's nationalities work includes a pessoptimist mix of positive and negative policy strategies. On the negative side, when non-Han groups push for real autonomy or independence the party-state cracks down ruthlessly with extensive patriotic education campaigns, mass arrests, and even public executions. Recently this negative policy has exacerbated the situation as part of a vicious circle. Increased patriotic education has been one of Beijing's main policy reactions to the spring 2008 unrest in Tibet. Zhang Qingli, the hardline party secretary of Tibet who called the Dalai Lama a "wolf with a human face and the heart of a beast," declared after the riots that "propaganda and education are our party's greatest advantages. These are the most useful weapons with which to defend ourselves against the Dalai Lama group. So let the propaganda department work more actively to expose its plots."[67] Yet such compulsory patriotic education, which denounces the Dalai Lama as a terrorist and Tibetan culture as backward, was one of the factors that led to the demonstrations in the first place.[68] The party-state's solution, thus, risks further entrenching the problem.

On the positive side, the party-state provides significant rewards when non-Han communities cooperate. For most national minority groups, the main issue is not independence; rather, they try to use the party-state's ethnic categories to pursue more modest economic, cultural, and political objectives. While Han Chinese dominate politics by controlling communist party positions in autonomous regions, non-Han elites can have meaningful control over "the administration of resources, taxes, birth planning, education, legal jurisdiction, and religious expression" through their government positions.[69] Some Han thus are converting to non-Han because it has become valuable – culturally, politically, and economically – to be a part of a minority group. Still, the economic benefits of the party-state's large-scale development projects often benefit Han migrants much more than the resident non-Han groups, leading to further interethnic problems.[70] Like with Beijing's negative security strategies, these positive economic strategies risk exacerbating racial and ethnic tensions in China.

To address China's "nationalities work" problems, Ma Rong suggests some new policy directions.[71] Like Fei Xiaotong and others, Ma supports the party-state's objectives of stability and national unity. To avoid any misunderstandings encouraged by the use of the same term "nationality-*minzu*" for both the Chinese nation and national minorities, Ma suggests that Beijing employ "ethnicity-*zuqun*" as the official term for China's fifty-six nationalities. His purpose is to stress national unity, and thus end any "confusion" that national minorities have the right of self-determination.

However, Ma's policy suggestions go far beyond mere semantics. As we saw above, he is also concerned that China could splinter like the Soviet Union and Yugoslavia. Ma is actually one of those who assumed that ethnic identity would fade away in socialist China; he is alarmed that the power of non-Han groups not only endures in China, but is growing. Ma blames this splittist tendency on Beijing naïvely following the Soviet Union's nationality policy that "politicized" ethnicity by creating a collection of ethnically defined republics and autonomous regions. Hence while most would agree that China's nationalities work seeks to domesticate non-Han groups, Ma argues that they need to be "depoliticized" even more.

Here Ma departs from China's official policy that presents autonomous regions as the answer to the country's nationalities question. While Beijing largely follows Fei Xiaotong's "pluralist–unitary structure" for China's multinational nation-state, Ma proposes a new "political unity–cultural pluralism framework" that stresses the importance of national unity even more. Here ethnic groups would shed their special political and economic rights, and focus more on maintaining and developing their own cultural traditions. Ma thus hopes to "depoliticize" China's nationalities work by "culturalizing" China's ethnic minorities.

To argue his case Ma looks to two examples: imperial China's civilization/barbarism distinction and modern America's assimilation policy. Ma rehearses the now familiar narrative of the "more 'advanced' Han Chinese" civilizing the "relatively less advanced minority 'barbarians'" who are at a lower stage of development.[72] In this idealized view of All-under-Heaven [*Tianxia*], barbarians are acculturated and assimilated by Han Chinese. To apply this imperial policy to modern China, Ma looks to the American "melting pot." Using a very dated view of American society and an exaggerated view of the powers of the federal government, Ma argues that China also needs to "likewise" more actively assimilate its ethnic minorities. This entails a shift from a "politicization" of national minorities that sets up boundaries between ethnic groups – including the territorial boundaries of autonomous regions – to a "culturalization" that blurs social boundaries into a national identity shared by all Chinese citizens. As part of his policy prescription Ma argues that Beijing should scale back its affirmative action-style benefits for non-Han groups because this support now is seen by the Han majority as reverse-discrimination. Ma concludes that with time the "tension among ethnic groups will fade and finally vanish, because there will be no need to encourage minorities to fight for their rights and benefits. When that stage has been reached, the concept of ethnic identity will lose its political meaning, retaining its linkages only with cultural heritage."[73]

Certainly, Han China's encounter with non-Han indigenous groups is not unique; "civilizing the barbarians" was a common way of justifying European imperial expansion. Most modernizing nations, including the United States, Canada, and Australia, have waged brutal wars against indigenous groups. Therefore, as we criticize such policies and ideologies in the West, we should also note that similar things are still going on in China. Ma's policy advice is particularly noteworthy because it goes against a critical view of racial politics to revive imperial modes of governance for a rather right-wing nationalities policy.[74]

Understanding Ma's culturalization strategy is important because it resonates with popular views beyond the state and the academy; it reflects the common Han view of non-Han groups as "singing and dancing minorities," who perform their cultures as exotic entertainment not only for tourists but at national events. Indeed, at times it seems that the exotic costumes are more important than the ethnicity of people wearing them: at the opening ceremony of the Beijing Olympics, the children wearing costumes from China's fifty-six ethnic groups were all Han Chinese. This Han practice of dressing up as non-Han is quite common at other official events, and is not seen as problematic. It thus underlines how non-Han groups are an important part of Han identity politics.

Overseas Chinese and Modern Civilization

Chinese expatriates are one of the world's great diasporas. Before the debate about the rise of China emerged in the late 1990s, many people were talking about "Greater China" to describe the network of overseas Chinese business that was the main investor in China's dramatic economic rise. As one expatriate Chinese tycoon boasts, "We are the dealmakers, the ones that will provide investment and financing advice to a country in the throes of economic transformation."[75] Rather than simply being an investment opportunity, expatriate activities in China are changing the motherland in dramatic ways that some see as civilizing and others as barbaric.

The status of overseas Chinese thus has been unclear. No one is ever quite sure where their loyalty lies: to the motherland, to their host country, or to their clan. When abroad, ethnic Chinese rarely fit into the host country's national identity. When in China they call national identity into question because while they might "look" like their mainland compatriots, they often act differently. In this way, their marginal position as outsiders is quite similar to that of national minorities.

This problem is not new; overseas Chinese identity has been radically unstable for the past 150 years. Beyond the current hyphenations of "Sino-Thai" or "Chinese-American," the diaspora was called "domestic overseas Chinese" in imperial China, "foreign Orientals" in the Dutch East Indies, and "artificial Chinese" in Siam. Even the new generation of migrants that has left China since economic reform started in 1978 is often considered "pseudo-Chinese." Naming is no clearer in Chinese: the three dominant ways of categorizing this mobile group – *huaqiao, huayi, haiwai huaren* – overlap in confusing ways. *Haiwai huaren*, the standard term now used in mainland China, is a translation of "overseas Chinese," which in turn is a translation of *huaqiao*.

The problems faced by Wang Gungwu, the doyen of overseas Chinese studies, in even naming this population are indicative: again and again, he laments the difficulty of defining "Chineseness" and naming the overseas Chinese.[76] Although Chinese nationalism and the diaspora seem to be essential and separate identities, each actually take on meaning in relation to the other. Just as non-Han minorities are crucial in constructing the Han majority, "Chineseness" and "overseas Chinese" have been linked historically and conceptually, since they both became issues at the turn of the twentieth century.

While both non-Han groups and overseas Chinese are seen as lacking the virtues of traditional Chinese civilization, the Chinese diaspora is also seen as a key source of the modern civilization of global capitalism. The Han majority characteristically positions itself as modern in relation to backward national minorities, but here the mainland itself becomes "backward" in relation to the modernity of overseas Chinese. Diasporic Chinese, thus, are valued outsiders because they translate and Sinicize the modern civilization of science, technology, and business management for the benefit of the motherland. Nevertheless, the relationship is still uneasy. While expatriate Chinese cultivate the modern civilization of science and capitalism, there are lingering doubts in the PRC about their fundamental Chineseness, and thus their fundamental loyalty. After all, global capitalism is still seen by many in China as barbaric.

Expatriate identity

Although Chinese have been traveling abroad for millennia, the creation of a single term to name this group is quite recent, taking form at the same time that nationalism gained currency in China. Before 1893, there was a legal ban on unofficial overseas travel. The state saw these unofficial travelers as "vagabonds, fugitives, or outlaws" who risked beheading if and when they returned to China.[77]

Beginning in the nineteenth century, Chinese migrated in large numbers as a result of the economic and political dislocation that started with the "invasion of foreign countries' capitalism" after the Opium War.[78] The emergence of overseas Chinese identity, thus, is part of the gelling of the concept of national humiliation in China: "it was not until after several decisive defeats by the European powers in the second half of the nineteenth century that a name for these Chinese, their misfortunes and their achievements was found."[79] As Wang argues, the first term for overseas Chinese as a unified group – huaqiao – was crafted by the Qing regime "to encourage sojourners to identify with China and Chinese civilization."[80] Although huaqiao was a new word, it had an ancient pedigree that framed the overseas Chinese as an "elegant and respectable" group.[81] Thus, in the late nineteenth century, overseas Chinese were transformed from a disparate collection of outlaws who hailed from different regions into a single group of honored mandarins. The Qing dynasty's new imperial nationalism thus looked beyond China's shores for loyal citizen-subjects. Evidence of this transformation can been seen in the Sino-Thai exhibit of the Roi-Et National Museum in rural Thailand: it has a grand portrait in imperial dress of a local prosperous overseas Chinese who returned to China to take up an official post.[82] (See Figure 5.2.)

This is not simply a history lesson, for the dynamic of nationalism and diaspora is again producing Chinese identity in familiar ways. For the past twenty years, PRC policy has been not only to recruit overseas Chinese as patriotic investors and technocrats, but to reeducate the diaspora in their proper "national" history. Alongside the rise of Chinese nationalism in the PRC, overseas Chinese identity reemerged in the late 1980s because of two factors that accompanied Deng's economic reforms. The open door policy

Figure 5.2 Roi-Et businessman becomes an imperial official. Courtesy of Somchai Phatharathananund.

invited the older generation of wealthy Chinese expatriates to return and invest in their homeland as part of the economic network of "Greater China." It also allowed a host of "new migrants" to leave China to pursue postgraduate education in science and technology in the West.

Since the late twentieth century, these new and old populations of overseas Chinese are again being recruited into the narrative of national humiliation as patriotic "sons of the Yellow Emperor" who form "a part of China's history that is splattered with blood and tears."[83] Thus the party-state has gone beyond luring overseas Chinese investment into the PRC; overseas Chinese work also aims to socialize the diaspora by reeducating it according to both the glory of Chinese civilization and tragedy of China's modern history.

While focusing on shared civilization to bind together Han Chinese at home and abroad, mainland understandings of the overseas Chinese experience also look to the history of national humiliation. Similar to the patriotic education textbooks examined in Chapter 2, mainland texts list the reasons for the diaspora as stemming from both foreign invasion and domestic corruption: "among the foreign reasons we must stress the frenzied plunder of China's cheap labor by the foreign invaders, among the domestic reasons we must stress the basic corruption and ineptitude of the Qing state, which was powerless to protect our people from the foreign invaders' human trafficking."[84] Books like *The Coolie Trade: The Criminal Activities of the Abduction and Pillage of Overseas Chinese Laborers* are published by Beijing's Overseas Chinese Press as part of a "Never Forget National Humiliation History" book series.[85] The plight of overseas Chinese in the late nineteenth and early twentieth centuries also merits a chapter in many of the recent general histories of national humiliation.

Rather than focusing on the rags-to-riches stories of poor Chinese who succeeded abroad, these history books chronicle how they were exploited by heartless foreign capitalists. Chinese workers were traded like African slaves, Chen Shiwei's *Never Forget National Humiliation* tells us. Poor people were drugged by Chinese traitors, who then sold them on to evil Westerners, who transported them in "floating prisons" that resembled pig pens.[86] Once Chinese laborers arrived in the new land – Southeast Asia, Australia, or the Americas – they were treated "worse than slaves," according to Liang Zhanjun's *Record of the National Humiliation of Modern China*. Stripped naked and sold at human markets, overseas Chinese worked long hours in farms, mines, and factories to "build a heaven for Westerners" – before being banned from the United States altogether with the Chinese Exclusion Law of 1882.[87] Zhou and Zhang's *Record of National*

Humiliation reasons that the mistreatment of overseas Chinese "created deep hatred and pain for imperialist powers in the good hearts of the Sons of the Yellow Emperor. The Chinese nation's great humiliation and deep hatred can never be forgotten!"[88]

Before they left China, most of these people identified themselves in terms of their clan, village, or province. However, anti-Chinese discrimination in foreign lands forged together this disparate group into some of China's most ardent nationalists. The title of a poem from a student in the United States says it all: "I am Chinese" (1925):[89]

> I am Chinese, I am Chinese,
> I am the divine blood of the Yellow Emperor,
> I come from the highest place in the world,
> Pamir is my ancestral plain,
> My race is like the Yellow River,
> We flow down the Kunlun mountain slope,
> We flow across the Asian continent,
> From us have flowed many exquisite customs.
> Mighty nation! Mighty nation!

The national shame, therefore, is not just about the loss of China's geobody (as we saw in Chapter 4), but about the loss of many Chinese bodies. Chinese identity thus expands through national humiliation from being defined according to citizenship and territoriality to a wider transnational view of the Chinese race as "Sons of the Yellow Emperor," who are spread throughout the globe. Ethnic theorist Chen Liankai thus explains how the loyalty of Chinese expatriates confirms the unity of the Chinese race: "Even up until today, the Chinese race, particularly the overseas Chinese, are proud to call themselves Sons of the Yellow Emperor. They all take the Yellow Emperor as evidence of the early rise and unity of the Chinese race, and take this as their connection with the shared national feeling of the Chinese race."[90] Ren and Zhao also see the diaspora as part of China's comprehensive national power: "China is not just the most populous country in the world; it also has the most populous diaspora."[91] According to these sources, the thirty million diasporic Chinese constitute the third largest economy in the world.

As the popular verses of the "Song of Revolution" (1903) show, diasporic Chinese communities feel an anxiety about their overseas wealth, and the risk of diluting their authentic Chinese identity posed by living abroad. This song thus calls on overseas Chinese merchants to reclaim their identity by financing China's nationalist revolution:

> Let me call again to the *huaqiao* overseas,
> Compatriots to the distant ends of the earth! . . .
> What use is the accumulation of silver cash?
> Why not use it to eject the Manchus? . . .
> It is hard to be happy all one's life,
> You need but little conscience to feel shame.
> What then is the most shameful matter?
> To forget one's ancestors deserves the greatest hate!
> If not that, then to register as a foreign national
> Forgetting that you come from Chinese stock.[92]

This ditty, which was widely distributed between 1903 and the republican revolution in 1911, shows how economy and identity are closely linked: overseas Chinese merchants are enjoined to finance the revolution – or risk losing their Chineseness. Yet the song shows how this expatriate "Chineseness" takes particular forms: rather than looking to a multinational nation-state as discussed above, it replays Sun Yatsen's early form of exclusive nationalism. It seeks to construct the Han race as a direct descendent in the Yellow Emperor's bloodline by ejecting the Manchus. Moreover, the "Father of China" is not only known for gathering financial and political support from abroad during this period; he grew up overseas in Hawaii.

China's national humiliation histories thus labor to record the nationalist feelings and revolutionary activities of overseas Chinese patriots. Indeed, in the early twentieth century, some of the first Chinese nationalist activities emerged not in China, but abroad where they were organized by overseas Chinese merchants and students. As Chapter 3 showed, in the early twentieth century overseas Chinese associations, merchants, and newspapers participated in patriotic boycotts of Japanese goods, and marked May 9th as China's national humiliation day.

The purpose of founding a strong nation was not only to reunify China, but to protect diasporic Chinese who otherwise "deeply know the shame and pain of a weak country." Hence, according to mainland sources, overseas Chinese understand that "their own destiny is wrapped up in the destiny of the motherland."[93] Persecution of Chinese overseas during the century of national humiliation was not just physical or financial, but a question of "respect" – or the lack of it: "If Chinese people were bullied locally, that was because China received no respect internationally."[94] While expatriates were humiliated by anti-China demonstrations in spring 2008, the status of overseas Chinese in the United States would improve, according to Chinese-American leaders, "due to the respect China gained from the Olympics."[95] Overseas Chinese experience thus not only becomes a chapter in the history of national humiliation textbooks as a problem to be solved, but as a "reflection of the development of modern Chinese history" itself.[96] Expatriates and patriots are thus woven together in the party-state's version of China's national identity.

Overseas Chinese work

The PRC and Taiwan still struggle for the loyalty of overseas Chinese as part of their transnational national reunification strategies: Ren and Zhao's book title says it all – *Overseas Chinese and Nationalist Party–Communist Party Relations*. Taibei and Beijing both have Overseas Chinese Affairs Offices (OCAO) to coordinate such "overseas Chinese work." Thus one of the common activities of both regimes has been to "re-Sinicize" overseas Chinese populations by supporting education and cultural activities. By 2008, for example, the Chinese state had opened over 150 Confucian Institutes around the world to teach national language and culture, like Germany's Goethe Institute. While the task of the Goethe Institute is to spread German language and culture to foreigners, the Confucian Institute targets Chinese expatriates as well. The Confucian Institute at the University of Manchester, for example, works closely with the Education Section of the city's Chinese consulate to teach language and culture to the region's large ethnic Chinese community. The Confucius Institute in Bangkok is even more ambitious; it now trains ethnic Chinese businessmen, and even officials from Thailand's Royal Court.[97]

Confucius Institutes are only the latest example of Beijing's official policies to cultivate the loyalty of ethnic Chinese around the world. Throughout the twentieth century, various Chinese governments have sought to recruit overseas Chinese to their cause. After the revolution in 1949, the PRC called upon expatriates to "return to serve the country," and thus help to build "New China." After the financial and technical expertise of expatriates was exploited in the 1950s, during the Cultural Revolution overseas Chinese became a political target – along with anyone else who had foreign ties. Overseas Chinese thus were famous during this era mostly for fomenting socialist revolution in Southeast Asia.

As Elena Barabantseva's research on Beijing's overseas Chinese work shows, official policy has shifted in the past three decades from international revolution to domestic modernization, and from old migrants to new migrants.[98] In 1977, Beijing began rebuilding ties with expatriate Chinese. When Beijing's OCAO was reconstituted after the Cultural Revolution, it focused on reestablishing ties with the "old migrants" who had left China before 1949. When the CCP revived its mass organization for overseas Chinese – the All-China Federation of Returned Overseas Chinese – its first slogan was "building bridges out of overseas Chinese connections."[99] Because the *qiao* in *huaqiao* is similar to the word for "bridge," Chinese expatriates have been seen on the mainland as a bridge between China and the world. But rather than using this bridge to promote world revolution, these new expatriate bridges seek to develop the economic and political strength of the motherland.

With Deng Xiaoping's Open Door policy, Beijing again looked to the older generation of wealthy Chinese expatriates as a financial resource to fund China's economic development. Although it is common to credit the investment of western multinational corporations for China's massive economic growth, the bulk of China's foreign investment came from overseas Chinese in Southeast Asia. In the 1990s, China's policy toward overseas Chinese expanded from the old migrants in Southeast Asia to address "new migrants" who had left the PRC through Deng's Open Door. Since China relaxed its travel laws in 1985, over 1 million students have gone to graduate school in North America, Europe, and Australia primarily to study science and technology. After graduating, many of these new migrants chose to stay in the West – indeed many of the engineers in Silicon Valley were born in China.

Rather than seeing this as a "brain drain," Beijing has crafted new policies to cultivate the loyalty of these new expatriates. While the old migrants' investment in factories has been crucial in developing China's exports of consumer goods, the skills of new migrants are crucial for developing China's new knowledge economy. Patriotic overseas Chinese were enjoined to "return to serve the country" after the 1949 revolution; new migrants now are encouraged to "serve the Chinese nation" by cultivating transnational networks. In 1993, this new approach was summarized with a twelve-character policy slogan: "support study overseas, promote return home, maintain freedom of movement." As Richard P. Suttmeier's research on transnational networks of ethnic Chinese scientists shows, new migrant professors in the United States have developed close ties with their counterparts in China, which include joint research projects and recruiting elite Chinese graduate students for American universities.[100]

The PRC's overseas Chinese work with new migrants is both positive and negative: while promoting transnational ethnic Chinese networks among professionals, it also discourages young Chinese from going abroad for primary and secondary education. Only "ripe" Chinese who "were born in New China, and grew up under the Red Flag"[101] are encouraged to study abroad, primarily as graduate students. New migrants who have been so-cialized by the party-state's patriotic education are trusted as more sympa-thetic to the economic, political, and culture policies of the PRC. The "socialization gap" between graduate students in their thirties and under-graduates in their late teens was seen in the controversy at Duke University in April 2008: the freshman Grace Wang was chastised by much older graduate students for mediating between Tibetan and Chinese protestors.

Beijing does not just rely on properly "ripened" new migrants. Over the past two decades, it has formed close ties with the "three pillars" of overseas communities: overseas Chinese organizations, Chinese schools, and Chi-nese-language media.[102] The Education Sections of China's consulates maintain close relations with Chinese student organizations abroad. The OCAO has likewise focused on national and regional expatriate Chinese associations. In 2002, for example, the OCAO implemented a three-year plan to "Develop the Motherland and Assist Overseas Chinese."[103] The goal is to increase the quantity and quality of interactions between old and new migrant communities, and deepen links between overseas communities and China. With Beijing's support, overseas Chinese organizations have become much more institutionalized and centralized in Europe, Australia, and the Americas.

Beijing has instituted similar policies to foster and guide Chinese-language schools and media as a way to influence the identity of ethnic Chinese people of all ages. As part of its struggle for the loyalty of overseas Chinese, it presents the PRC as the source of traditional Chinese culture: "Chinese cultural roots are in China, not in Taiwan."[104] Official national humiliation texts also are increasingly copublished in Hong Kong in tradi-tional Chinese characters for overseas distribution that is directed squarely at expatriate audiences. For example, in the preface to a slick national humiliation text, the Director of the Chinese Revolutionary History Muse-um in Beijing explains that the book "will help overseas Chinese, especially our young friends overseas, to understand this period of the motherland's history."[105] Confucius Institutes run special classes for ethnic Chinese chil-dren, and the party-state organizes summer camps in China for these kids to rediscover their Chinese roots. By cultivating the three pillars of expatri-ate communities, Barabantseva concludes that "the PRC presents itself as a hub giving impetus to the globalization and intensification of Chinese networks and associations."[106] Anne-Marie Brady's study of the CCP's pro-paganda system also concludes that a "key task of foreign propaganda work" is to gain influence over such overseas Chinese groups in order to "turn them into propaganda bases for China."[107]

The world saw the result of these policies in spring 2008 when Chinese at home and abroad reacted to international criticism of Beijing's crackdown on Tibet. Rather than wondering why Tibetans would question Beijing's rule, the overseas Chinese groups followed Beijing's lead to criticize foreigners for sympathizing with Tibet. While the popular demonstrations and official statements from overseas groups in support of Beijing appeared to be spontaneous, they actually can better be explained as the fruits of the PRC's overseas Chinese work.

The Olympic Torch Relay in London, Paris, San Francisco, Canberra, and Seoul provoked pro-Tibet demonstrations, and then pro-China counter-demonstrations by overseas Chinese. As the Torch Relay progressed, the demonstrations grew on both sides, with the pro-Chinese side becoming increasingly more organized and more aggressive – with the help of the Chinese government. In Australia, the Chinese embassy helped organize pro-China demonstrations, for example, by bussing in thousands of Chinese students from other cities. The Chinese students were able to overwhelm pro-Tibet groups in Canberra by shear force of numbers, at times surrounding people holding Free Tibet signs with even larger Chinese flags.[108] In Bangkok, the Chinese Embassy again provided transportation and gave students patriotic shirts to wear.[109] The worst violence erupted in Seoul where mobs of Chinese expatriates and students hurled rocks, water bottles, and pipes at South Korean protestors and police: "Near [Olympic] park, Chinese students surrounded and beat a small group of protesters."[110] Anti-Tibet and anti-Western protests by overseas Chinese students continued after the Torch Relay, spreading to many North American and European university campuses where pro-Tibet supporters were harassed on the Web, in the classroom, and on the street.

Overseas Chinese organizations and media also cooperated with Beijing's transnational anti-Tibet campaign. The Council of Chinese-American Associations held a seminar in New York to "eloquently prove" China's sovereignty over Tibet.[111] Other overseas Chinese organizations and media in South Korea, the United States, Mexico, Egypt, the Czech Republic, Cote d'Ivoire, Australia, and Bulgaria likewise reproduced Beijing's patriotic narrative of these new national humiliations.[112] Steven Wong, the acting chairman of the United Federation of Chinese Association (United States), said that claims of Tibetan independence "arouse[d] indignation among all Chinese people including the overseas Chinese." The chairman of the China–Bulgaria chamber of commerce declared that "Chinese businessmen in Bulgaria are firmly committed to our home country's reunification and territorial integrity, supports all efforts made by the Chinese government to attain the goal, and hope that the riots will not affect the upcoming Beijing Olympics." The vice president of the Australian Chinese Community Association said that "overseas Chinese have the obligation and duty to tell the truth about the riots to the people of the countries where they reside so that they would not be influenced by distorted reports defaming China." New Zealand's Chinese-language weekly *Home Voice* reported that "the Lhasa riots were masterminded and incited by the Dalai clique," while the Chinese-language *World News* of the Philippines condemned any plan to boycott the Olympics. Xinhua reported that "*Singtao Daily's* European edition also covered the truth of the Lhasa riots, quoting China's Xinhua news agency."

Diasporic Chinese, therefore, are not simply a resource for China's economic modernization. The dynamic of diasporic persecution and continuing national humiliation is used as a symbolic resource for producing Chinese national identity. Curiously, these financial and symbolic resources, which are transnational and deterritorialized in the diaspora, are used to consolidate the identity of the Chinese nation in particular ways. The more obvious the national difference abroad, the greater the need for a strong Chinese state to protect the diaspora both diplomatically and militarily.

It is common to conclude that diasporic Chinese nationalism ended in the 1950s, with the end of migration from the PRC and the rise of postcolonial nationalism in Southeast Asia. However, nationalism continues to grow both at home and abroad. Over the last century, a series of atrocities provoked national outrage among new and old migrants: at the turn of the twentieth century by anti-Chinese immigration policies in North America and Australasia, in the mid-twentieth century by the Anti-Japanese War and the Rape of Nanjing, and at the turn of the twenty-first century by the rape and murder of ethnic Chinese in Indonesia (1999). In 2008, the new atrocities of Han Chinese being attacked in Lhasa and Paris added to this sense of crisis-induced national identity. In other words, although we often assume that nationalism is defined by positive norms, there is nothing like a humiliating atrocity to unite a diverse and dispersed population into a community.

In addition to gathering around glorious Chinese civilization, diasporic Chinese communities increasingly identify with the national humiliation of such atrocities. As Ian Buruma concludes, "It is, it appears, not enough for Chinese-Americans to be seen as the heirs of a great civilization; they want to be recognized as heirs of their very own Holocaust."[113] Hence, overseas Chinese not only network for economic gain, but for social and political projects, to produce a transnational form of nationalism. Still, this transnational nationalism gains power from very primordial sources; it is based on Han China's essential bloodline from the Yellow Emperor. Expatriate nationalism certainly has been growing among Chinese overseas; but as the clashes in spring 2008 show, it can come at the expense of international sympathy and support for Beijing. According to the BBC World Service poll of global attitudes, China's positive ratings fell in countries that hosted the Olympic torch run.[114]

Conclusion

Overseas Chinese communities and national minority groups are an odd place to look for answers to the question "Who is China?" However, these essential outsiders show how the party-state works both at the local level and in transnational space to recruit domestic strangers and foreign brothers into its national aesthetic. Although nationalities work and overseas Chinese work both insist that this unlikely pair has been part of China since antiquity, national minorities and Chinese expatriates are both very modern actors. They emerged as political groups in China just as Chinese nationalism itself was taking shape in the early twentieth century. The Chinese state certainly created these pessoptimistic categories as a way to recruit (and exclude) outsiders in the Chinese nation. Nevertheless, as this chapter has shown, outsiders also define the inside. The role of assimilation in nationalities' work and overseas Chinese' work is telling: for Chinese expatriates assimilation to non-Han cultures is seen as the problem, while for national minorities assimilation to the Han majority is seen as the solution. In this way, nationalities' work and overseas Chinese' work each reinvoke and reinterpret China's enduring civilization/barbarian distinction to construct the Han as the majority race of the Chinese nation. This pessoptimist understanding of national minorities and overseas Chinese is part of the PRC's very modern national aesthetic, whose dynamic structure of feeling once again integrates the positive factors of civilization with the negative factors of humiliating victimization.

While the civilization/barbarism distinction seems to provide a solid foundation for the unified primordial identity of "the real China," this structure of feeling is quite dynamic, taking on new forms all the time. The fantastic success of Jiang Rong's novel *Lang tuteng* [*Wolf Totem*], which is based on his experience living in the Mongolian grasslands during the Cultural Revolution, shows how flexible the boundaries of civilization can be.[115] *Wolf Totem* has sold over 25 million copies since it was published in 2004, making it China's no. 2 bestseller of all time after Mao Zedong's *Little Red Book*. The novel is popular abroad as well: its English translation won the inaugural Man Asian Literary Prize.[116]

Wolf Totem is an autobiographical story about a Han Chinese student who leaves his intellectual family in Beijing to go to the grasslands of Inner Mongolia at the height of the Cultural Revolution. Chen Zhen, the main character, lives and works with nomadic Mongolians. As a shepherd, Chen becomes fascinated with wolves and the role they play in the local economy and culture of the grasslands. He is drawn to the wolves' strength, cunning, and ferocity, and adopts a wolf pup to "scientifically" study how they "think." However, in the end Chen has to kill the wolf pup because it can't be tamed to live among humans.

Wolf Totem is praised for its environmentalist sensibility: the Han student criticizes how his people are invading the Mongolian grasslands economically, if not militarily. Chen watches as Han settlers ruin the grassland ecosystem when they try to turn it into farmland. The novel ends with a plea to Han Chinese to preserve the grasslands and its ecological balance of nomadic Mongolians, sheep, and wolves. This environmental message was popular among foreign readers; the Man Asian Literary Prize judges praised *Wolf Totem* for giving a "passionate argument about the complex interrelationship between nomads and settlers, animals and human beings, nature and culture."

However, *Wolf Totem's* environmental message is wrapped up in a broader political message about China's national rejuvenation and international politics. Indeed, Jiang Rong is a pseudonym for Lu Jiamin, a political scientist who spent time in jail for participating in the Tiananmen Square movement in 1989. His ideological program is outlined in detail in the novel's sixty-four page appendix "Rational Exploration: A Lecture and Dialogue on the Wolf Totem," which is not included the English translation.[117] Like Europeans and Americans, Chinese people generally fear wolves, seeing them as a serious problem that needs to be exterminated.[118] This fear is metaphorical as well as literal: in 2008 the CCP's worst epithet for the Dalai Lama was "wolf with a human face," and historian Yuan Weishi worries that educating China's youth with the "wolves' milk" of xenophobic history textbooks is turning rational citizens into the violent indignant youth.[119] *Wolf Totem*, on the other hand, lionizes the ferocity, strength, and violence of wolves, turning them from a problem into the solution to China's future development.

Following a theme popular in modern Chinese literature (discussed in Chapter 2), Jiang stresses how "reform in China is not just about the transformation of the economic and the political system, but about the transformation of national character."[120] Echoing a popular idiom from the early twentieth century that saw China as the "Sick Man of East Asia," Jiang tells us that the Chinese people have been weakened over the centuries by a Confucian culture that only teaches them how to be followers. Since "the root of the China syndrome is the sheep syndrome," Jiang argues that the nomads' wolf-nature is the best model for China's national character. Many Chinese authors now tell us how China needs to reclaim its civilization to assimilate national minorities and fight western barbarians. Hence, *Wolf Totem* is interesting because it reverses the civilization/barbarian distinction by directly criticizing Han Chinese and Confucianism, while praising the freedom and independence of nomadic ethnic groups.

To argue his case, Jiang rewrites Chinese history from the mythical Yellow Emperor up through the Qing dynasty. Going against the grain of official dynastic historiography, which he argues is warped by a reverence for Confucianism, Jiang reverses the standard argument of how civilization transformed barbarians and tamed conquest dynasties. He asserts that the Yellow Emperor came from grasslands in the Northwest, and that China's first Great Unity [*da yitong*] in the Qin dynasty did not come from Confucianism, but from wolf-nature's attack on Confucianism. Because Han are soft and weak, Jiang explains, outsiders prey on them – just as wolves prey on sheep on the grasslands. Jiang thus argues that throughout history fierce nomads from the Mongolian grasslands and the broader northwest have continually conquered and occupied China proper. This is not seen as a problem, but as an important contribution to the greatness of the Chinese race. It is not simply a metaphor of nomadic cultural influence; one of Jiang's main arguments is that the soft "sheep-nature" of the Chinese race has been strengthened, again and again, through transfusions of Mongolians' ferocious blood (through rape and/or inter-marriage).

Wolf Totem's revision of history also explains why the "Western race" was able to dominate China, and become the most advanced civilization in the world. Europeans are ferocious, Jiang explains, because they have wolves' blood from the same inner Asian sources: attacks from Huns, Turks, and Mongols. The Europeans' wolf-nature then was used to conquer Asia:

> The Westerners who fought their way back to the East were all descen-
> dents of nomads. . . . The later Teutons, Germans, and Anglo-Saxons grew
> increasingly powerful, and the blood of wolves ran in their veins. The
> Han, with their weak dispositions, are in desperate need of a transfusion

of that vigorous, unrestrained blood. Had there been no wolves, the history of the world would have been written much differently.[121]

Therefore, while nomads are dismissed as the most backward element in China's nationalities work, according to *Wolf Totem* China must now look to them since "the most advanced people today are descendents of nomadic races. . . . What is hard to learn are the militancy and aggressiveness, the courage and willingness to take risks that flow in nomadic veins."[122] Like with nomadic Mongolians, Jiang revalues the Western race from "barbarian enemies" to "civilized wolves" who should serve as the model for China's national character. His goal then is to transform Han Chinese from being "civilized sheep" first into "civilized wolves," and finally into "civilized humans" who have democracy and the rule of law. The main problem for Jiang is how to release and contain the power of what he calls the "thermonuclear reaction" of wolf nature – whose ferocity can not only save a nation, but also risks destroying a society.[123]

By reversing the civilization/barbarism distinction to value Mongolian nomads over Han civilization, Jiang certainly is offering a fresh perspective. Indeed, a few years before the novel was published, cultural theorist Wang Hui lamented that in the PRC there was "not a single Chinese postcolonial critique of Han centrism from the standpoint of peripheral culture."[124] Yet, although Jiang's narrative reverses the civilization/barbarism distinction, it still reproduces the same zero-sum structure of feeling that divides humanity into binary opposites: wolves and sheep, nomads and farmers, Chinese and Westerners. Such reversals don't question the idea of essential identity, and actually tend to reinforce its zero-sum logic of violent confrontation. Rather than looking to international society's rules and norms, Jiang sees international relations as a series of violent Darwinian race wars between wolf nations and sheep nations. In this struggle for the survival of the fittest nation, wolf-nature is worshipped for its strength, ferocity, and violence. This is an odd way to get to Jiang's goal of democracy and the rule of law, and provides a rather negative counterpart to *Wolf Totem's* generally positive calls for environmental protection.

Lastly, it is important to note how Jiang's ideological program shifts our attention from the particulars of the Mongolian grassland wolf to general prescriptions about wolf-nature as the key to success in today's ruthless social environment. *Wolf Totem's* popularity thus comes from more than its nostalgic description of an exotic past; businesses and the military use *Wolf Totem* to train managers and officers with strategies for success in today's dog-eat-dog world. The novel's epilogue ends with the disappearance of wolf-nature on China's Inner Mongolian frontier: Chen returns thirty years later to find that the wolves are gone, the grasslands have been turned into desert, and the Mongolian nomads have been overwhelmed by Han settlers. The wolf survives only as a ferocious metaphor for what Han Chinese need to succeed in the twenty-first century. Once again, the minority is sacrificed for the majority. Discussions of outsiders like national minorities (and Chinese expatriates) tell us more about the insiders, mainland Han Chinese. When answering the question "Who is China?," we thus have to appreciate how minorities are employed to construct the majority, and violent barbarians are deployed to shape enduring civilization.

Chapter 6

Who Is China? (2): Trauma, Community, and Gender in Sino-Japanese Relations

The Sino-Japanese relationship is a paradox. The two countries' healthy economic relationship, which is based on complementary trade, aid, and investment ties, forms one of the most important partnerships in the global political economy today. The statistics are quite impressive: Japan's investment in China reached $60.7 billion in 2007, making it the second largest source of foreign direct investment. Two-way trade between the two countries grew by 13.9 percent year-on-year to $236 billion in 2007, making China Japan's number one trading partner, and Japan China's third. Japan is also China's biggest exporter and its third-largest export market.[1] This close economic relationship shows how the fortunes of China and Japan are tightly intertwined.

Yet, their political relations are cool. They went into a deep freeze while Junichiro Koizumi was Prime Minister of Japan (2001–6). This was largely due to China's outrage at Koizumi's numerous visits to the Yasukuni Shrine, which honors Japan's war-dead, including fourteen "Class A" war criminals. Since Koizumi resigned in 2006, Beijing has tried to rebuild relations with Toyko through a series of high-profile summits. Yet, the frigid metaphor persists even when describing successful bilateral meetings: Japanese Prime Minister Shinzo Abe's to China in 2006 was seen as "ice-breaking" and Chinese Premier Wen Jiabao's visit to Japan in 2007 as "ice-thawing." Even as they are improving, Sino-Japanese relations are still unstable; a Yasukuni Shrine visit would throw them back in a deep freeze.

This Sino-Japanese friction emerges not only in state-to-state diplomatic relations, but also in popular Chinese movements. Protests erupted in 2003 when Japanese businessmen hired hundreds of Chinese prostitutes for an "orgy" in Guangdong on one of China's national humiliation days: September 18th. In 2004, Chinese soccer fans rioted after Japan beat China in the Asia Cup finals, which were held in Beijing. To protest Japan's quest for a permanent seat on the United Nations Security Council, China's "history activists" collected over 22 million signatures in spring 2005 on an online petition. A flurry of anti-Japanese riots protesting new editions of Japan's history textbooks then rocked urban China's streets in April 2005, with mobs attacking Japanese embassies, restaurants, and businesses. These various protests – both on the street and on the Web – were not sparked by a military clash, a diplomatic dispute, or an economic crisis. Rather, they erupted because of the two countries' "history war." Chinese people were insulted, over and over again, by what they saw as Japan's failure to properly atone for its imperial crimes.

Like with Chinese nationalism, debate over the "history issue" generally concerns whether these protests are the result of the party-state instrumentally manipulating history for diplomatic gain, or whether they come from the Chinese people's genuine feelings, which constrain Beijing's foreign policy options.[2] But I think that this debate is misplaced since state policy and popular movements are intimately intertwined. The party-state certainly has laid the foundation for these protests through patriotic education that targets Japanese as "devils," who humiliated the Chinese people, first in the Century of National Humiliation, and now when they refuse to remember history correctly. But this state policy would not be successful if it did not strike a chord with popular Chinese memory, and broader structures of feeling that use Japanese barbarism to construct Chinese civilization. Once again, popular identity and state security are tightly interwoven.

While the earlier chapters have focused on Europe as the main enemy in the Century of National Humiliation, it is necessary to recognize that most of the atrocities in the long twentieth century are Japanese. Indeed, national humiliation discourse itself first emerged to explain China's shocking defeat in the First Sino-Japanese War (1894–5): In a memorial to the throne, Kang Youwei described this loss as China's "greatest humiliation in more than two hundred years since the advent of the Qing dynasty, and aroused the indignation of all the officials and people of the country."[3] This defeat was shocking because it reversed power relations; before the First Sino-Japanese War, Chinese saw Japan as a student of Chinese civilization. Now, many Chinese people see Japan as a barbaric "country of ingratitude" because it has turned on its teacher while still refusing to face up to its horrible crimes from the twentieth century.[4]

Figure 6.1 *Painful History of National Humiliation* cover (1919). Yi ming, *Guochi tongshi.*

While Chapter 4 examined the symbolic politics of the dismembering of the Chinese geobody, and Chapter 5 looked at overseas Chinese as lost bodies, Sino-Japanese diplomatic relations are frayed by memories of the literal mutilation of Chinese bodies during the Century of National Humiliation (see Figure 6.1). This politics of bodily mutilation is most graphically expressed in the horrible memories of the Nanjing massacre, which have been seared onto public consciousness in the People's Republic of China (PRC). While World War II started in 1939 in Europe, and 1941 in the Pacific, in East Asia it began in July 1937 with Japan's all-out invasion of China. After conquering Beijing and Shanghai, the imperial Japanese army set its sights on China's then capital city: Nanjing. Iris Chang's best seller, *The Rape of Nanking: The Forgotten Holocaust of World War II*, which describes the horrors of the city's conquest and occupation, brought this tragic tale to an international audience for the first time since the war.[5] "Nanjing massacre" refers to the horrific series of atrocities committed by the imperial Japanese army as it invaded and occupied the Chinese capital. For the six weeks between December 13, 1937 and late January 1938, Japanese soldiers killed hundreds of thousands of civilians and POWs, and raped over 20,000 women. The city-scape itself was mutilated: homes and shops were looted, and one-third of the buildings were set ablaze.

While Westerners had largely forgotten about "China's holocaust" before Chang's book appeared in 1997, Chinese people started talking about this atrocity in the early 1980s, initially in reaction to a new edition of a history textbook in Japan that whitewashed Japan's wartime atrocities. Chinese (and South Korean) anger continues to be aroused by right-wing Japanese politicians who periodically deny these war crimes.[6] In China, the party-state worked to turn a scattered collection of specific memories of the Nanjing massacre into lasting national institutions: to mark anniversaries of the massacre a memorial hall and museum were built, feature films distributed, and dozens of commemorative photo albums and hundreds of illustrated articles published. Paintings, sculptures, and novels about the Nanjing massacre also have appeared in the last decade, while more feature films, television series, and documentaries appeared to mark the seventieth anniversary in 2007.

The main purpose of these media products is to document the truth about the Nanjing massacre, often through the "undeniable evidence" of iconic photographs of mutilated Chinese bodies, especially beheaded men and raped women. Starting in the 1990s, these haunting images spread out into cyberspace, uploaded onto the military Web sites of official security studies think tanks in China, as well as patriotic Web sites maintained by transnational Chinese groups. When posted on the Web, these free-floating images are separated from any context that would help us to understand their meaning – except as a provocation for the raw hatred of foreigners as devils. On the military Web site, these graphic pictures have only short captions like, "Never forget national humiliation: Chinese women raped by

Japanese devils" and "Never forget national humiliation: Slaughtering our compatriots."[7]

A few years ago, I got the sense of how the troubles between China and Japan are more social than geopolitical – the Sino-Japanese rivalry works itself out into the deeply felt personal enmity that many individual Chinese feel for Japan. When a dinner conversation with Chinese colleagues steered toward the issue of international friendships, a Chinese specialist on US affairs told the group that although he didn't like the US government (particularly the Bush administration), he felt a certain empathy and fondness for the American people. Another person agreed, but pointed out how things were different with Japan; *everyone* hates Japan: Asians, Americans, Europeans, everyone. After a moment, I pointed out that Thais have a fondness for Japan and the Japanese – one of their most popular novels is about a wartime affair between a Thai woman and a Japanese officer. My Chinese friends were perplexed at this unthinkable possibility: the "rape" of Nanjing defines the relationship between China and Japan. After a pregnant pause, the discussion moved on to happy memories of vacations in Thailand.

This conversation was not an isolated incident. Friendship between individual Chinese and Japanese certainly exists; but it would be a mistake to characterize the relations of the two countries as friendly. In 2003–4, when a few prominent journalists and scholars suggested that China pursue a "normal" relationship with Japan that did not simply dwell on "the history question," they were publicly denounced as traitors to the Han race – and even received death threats. In 2000, Jiang Wen's film *Devils on the Doorstep*, which is about a Japanese prisoner of war (POW) in China who is befriended by Chinese villagers, won the Cannes Grand Prix. But it was censored in China because, as the Film Censorship Committee explained, "the Chinese civilians don't hate the Japanese" enough; rather, they are as "close as brothers" with him.[8] Discussion of China's relations with Japan therefore is defined by a combination of official censorship and vigilante harassment, showing how state policy and popular movements work together to produce China's national identity. "People who hate Japan" thus is one way to answer the question "who is China." Indeed, China's national anthem "Ode to the Volunteers" is an anti-Japanese military song.

A critical examination of the magazine articles, textbooks, photo albums, films, novels, museums, and memorials commemorating the Nanjing massacre is important because this event is key to understanding the Sino-Japanese relationship in the twenty-first century, as well as modern Chinese identity politics more generally: *China Youth Daily*'s public opinion poll in the mid-1990s reported that 83.9 percent of young Chinese associated Japan above all with the Nanjing massacre,[9] and the "General Preface" to the twenty-eight-volume *Nanjing Massacre: Historical Materials* book series (2005–6) explains the meaning of this mammoth scholarly endeavor in terms of Sino-Japanese diplomatic relations.[10]

Certainly, the Nanjing massacre plays a pivotal role in the politics of Japanese historiography and national identity. It is the key event that divides the revisionist historians who deny it from the progressive historians and journalists who apologize for it.[11] Most discussions of the "history issue" thus outline the problems with Japan's history textbooks, semiofficial denials, and halfhearted apologies.[12] However, the problems of Japanese textbooks should be put into perspective: the history textbook that generated massive protests in China and South Korea in 2001 and 2005 was adopted by less than 1 percent of school districts.[13] Hence in a way, the "history problem" is more a media event than a pedagogical issue.

While it is necessary to recognize the horror of Japanese atrocities in World War II, and criticize those who deny them, this chapter has a different goal: to recognize the pivotal role that the Nanjing massacre plays in Chinese identity and security. Indeed, even though Japan has had a "Peace Constitution" for over fifty years, the image of a barbaric and militarized Japan continues to be circulated in Chinese texts as a way of building China's national identity against Japan in the twenty-first century. The party-state and popular movements together produce China's relation with Japan by setting limits on how to understand the "other," differentiating what is commonsense from what is unthinkable.

Although China's patriotic education texts have many positive images of Chinese civilization, nationalism here is more *negative*; it is produced more from China's "resistance" (to Japan, the West, and foreigners) than through any positive core values of Chinese culture. In this way, the unity of China's body politic is produced through the mutilation of specific Chinese bodies. The chapter thus explores the question "Who is China?" through a process of describing, cataloguing, and displaying such atrocities, where Chinese nationalism is defined against a standard of (Japanese) barbarism, rather than with a standard of (Chinese) civilization. Most texts thus appeal to the photographs and statistics as "evidence," not only to document Japanese guilt, but also to nail down "nationalism" as the dominant theme in the Chinese imaginary. But as we see later, the visual narrative uses gendered images of beheaded men and raped women to promote a specific sort of militant masculine nationalism in China. But this is not the only message of the Nanjing massacre; a critical reading of these visual texts can help us question the hegemonic theme of "nationalist resistance" in ways that allow "resistance to nationalism" to emerge in different spaces.

The visual is increasingly powerful, shifting more and more from the goal of reflecting reality to be a mode of "targeting" enemies.[14] Thus, I have to be careful here about how I display the images for analysis. Beverly Allen encountered similar problems in writing about rape warfare in Bosnia: "It is extremely difficult to write about such things. Every phrase risks misinterpretation; every analytic moment risks being incomplete."[15] Thus I have tried to get the right tone – respectful, but still critical – because any analysis of the visual politics of the Nanjing massacre risks offending women and men, Chinese and non-Chinese people.

Nationalist Resistance

The aim of this section is to put the free-floating images of the Nanjing massacre back into a historical and political context. But as we see later, this does not mean that the images have a stable relationship with a singular Chinese history. Like in other countries, national history in China is constructed through a deliberate editing of what to include in and exclude from the official story. Indeed, rather than "authoring" *The Rape of Nanjing* pictorial, Shi Young and James Yin see their work as "compiling and editing this book" of pictures.[16] History writing likewise involves more than conveying the "undeniable facts" of "the real China"; historians must actively employ the historical narrative in order to tell a story of a particular kind: a national history, a regional history, or a class history, for example. The politics of this constructive process become even more opaque in commemorative photo albums because photographs, which seem to reflect reality, take on an even more important "evidence function" in knowledge production.

Chapter 2 examined how patriotic education policy and the national humiliation curriculum grew out of the Chinese Communist Party (CCP)'s propaganda system's response to the Tiananmen movement of 1989. But this was not the first time that official history was rewritten in the PRC. Geremie R. Barmé argues that politics is always in command for Chinese historiography: "every policy shift in recent Chinese history has involved the rehabilitation, reevaluation, and revision of history and historical figures."[17]

Nanjing massacre texts, images, and memorials are interesting because they emerge just as Chinese historiography was undergoing seismic shifts in the early 1980s: what was "true" one month could be "false" the next – with little

167

or no explanation offered for the reversal.[18] Under Mao, history was written in terms of Marxist class struggle. The main enemy was Nationalist China on Taiwan. Hence, the Chinese civil war (1946–50) received much more attention than World War II (1937–45). Since Chiang Kai-shek and his Nationalist Party were the main enemies, Chinese historiography also treated wartime Japan along class lines, differentiating between Japan's heinous leaders and the exploited Japanese masses. According to this story, a small clique of Japanese militarists brought death and destruction not only to China, but also to the vast majority of Japanese people as well. At this time, China was wooing Japan to gain official diplomatic recognition, so the party-state restricted historical research and public education on potentially "embarrassing" topics like Japan's wartime atrocities.

China's official historiography changed in the early 1980s as an ideological reaction to the social problems generated by economic reform. As Chinese society became more complex, there were fears that rapid and uneven economic development was ripping the country apart. Thus, the Chinese leadership decided to shift from the guiding historiography of class struggle to a more nationalist historiography that would better unite China. This strategy revalued Taiwan and the Nationalist party from archenemies into compatriots to be wooed for eventual reunification. In terms of national history, this meant that World War II rose to new prominence, both to acknowledge Nationalist victories and, more importantly, to capitalize on the strong negative commonality of a shared enemy: Japan. Once Japan recognized the PRC as the one-and-only China in 1972, Beijing no longer needed to woo Tokyo so actively – or restrict research on Japanese atrocities.

Thus a Chinese nationalist historiography emerged that pursues two opposite, but ultimately complementary, images of China: China as a "victim state, persecuted by the international community," and China as a "victorious great power, ready to take its rightful place on the world stage."[19] These pessoptimist national narratives are often gendered, with China as a victim represented as feminine, and heroic China represented as masculine. Like in gender politics more generally, feminine victim and masculine hero are not exclusive opposites; each is necessary to constitute the other in the production of Chinese identity. This productive tension between China as a victim and China as a victorious great power can be seen in the Nanjing massacre's role in three historical narratives: the Century of National Humiliation, the War of Resistance against Japan, and the city of Nanjing. Each of these historiographies has produced its own set of texts, albums, and memorials.[20] Each has its own narrative logic and set of lessons – yet all three stories work hard, not only to provide evidence of imperial

Japan's war crimes, but also to continue to produce China's national identity by warning readers to "beware of resurgent Japanese militarism."

Nanjing Massacre in the Century of National Humiliation

National humiliation textbooks pursue the "China as victim" narrative. The Nanjing massacre constitutes one event among the many described in textbooks such as *National Humiliation: Chinese People Should Never Forget*.[21] The book follows the general narrative of the Century of National Humiliation; its "Preface" declares that Chinese civilization is the best in world history, but also reminds us that China's modern history is one of defeat and humiliation. China's youth must study their country's national humiliation because, as the preface paraphrases Confucius, only if the nation has a sense of shame, can it be courageous.[22]

Dozens of atrocities and 427 pages later, Che's edited volume contains a four-page description of the Nanjing massacre by Zuo Yi'na.[23] Although one would expect middle-school students to be shell-shocked after reading hundreds of pages about China's bloody modern history of invasions, occupations, and massacres, Zuo does not pull any punches in describing the Nanjing massacre. Because they are mass-market textbooks, national humiliation histories generally don't include pictures – but the book's descriptions are still quite graphic. Following the guiding historiography, Zuo begins by summarizing how in December 1937, the invading Japanese army's bloody massacre in Nanjing "turned the ancient capital of six civilized dynasties into hell."[24] After a tactical analysis of Japan's invasion and occupation of Nanjing, which lists the relevant military statistics of the invading Japanese and retreating Nationalist armies, Zuo graphically describes the Japanese occupation as "a bloody massacre that shocked the country and the whole world. . . . when [Japanese soldiers] saw a man they would kill him; when they saw a woman they would rape her, and then kill her after the rape; when they saw a house, they would burn it, when they saw a bank or a store, they would loot it."[25] In order to document the facts of the atrocity, Zuo then describes in gruesome detail the slaughters, rapes, arsons, and lootings. The purpose of this is to stress the *barbaric* nature of the Japanese army's excesses: "In the great massacre, the Japanese army didn't just use modern weapons, but also used various primitive barbaric ways of killing, like decapitation, hacking skulls, stabbing bellies, digging into hearts, drowning, burning and quartering people, skinning people alive, and bayoneting vaginas and anuses."[26]

The sexual violence against women is likewise documented in detail in this middle-school textbook: "like beasts" Japanese troops raped over 20,000 women and girls. After raping Chinese women, the text tells us that the Japanese soldiers then murdered them as a standard procedure to eliminate witnesses. But the brutality continued after death with the soldiers mutilating the still-warm bodies: "they dug out breasts, and bayoneted heads and bellies until intestines spilled out. Some [victims] suffered the ill-fate of having their bodies ripped open and unceremoniously burnt."[27]

The last paragraph of the four-page section sums up the universal lessons of the Nanjing massacre: "It was something seldom seen in human history. This record of atrocity in the history of modern warfare is the most barbaric and shameful page in the history of human civilization."[28] The trauma of the Japanese atrocities set the barbaric standard that is used to define "nationalist resistance," and thus Chinese identity. To be Chinese patriots, the book instructs us, it is necessary to visualize the mutilation of specific Chinese bodies and the Chinese body politic. Chinese identity in the twenty-first century thus is produced against the threat of foreign invasion through popular education texts that vividly – indeed, almost visually – describe imperial Japan's wartime atrocities.

Nanjing Massacre in the War of Resistance

When the Nanjing massacre is narrated in the context of World War II, the horrible event shifts from the guiding narrative of China as a victim to China as a victorious great power. Indeed, the most common way of naming World War II in Chinese is the "War of Resistance Against Japan" [*KangRi zhanzheng*] (the War of Resistance [*kangzhan*] for short). Moreover, the director of the national War of Resistance Museum in Beijing insists that the war is not a "national humiliation."[29] Rather than focus on humiliations, these museums, teaching materials, and commemorative albums frame the meaning of the Nanjing massacre in the larger context of China's *victory* in World War II. The foreword to a special book of illustrated flashcards for children put together in 2005 by China's Central [Communist] Party School explains:

> Sixty years ago, the Chinese people won a great victory in the War of Resistance against Japan. With the War of Resistance, the Chinese nation washed away the century of humiliation with blood, thus realizing the turning point of the national destiny in a great war of national liberation. In this war of national survival, the Sons of the Yellow

Emperor were no longer divided by party, faction, ethnic group or age. We united together … to defeat the Japanese fascists. In this war, the CCP united the people under one banner to resist Japan.[30]

This victorious narrative links mainland China with Taiwan through the shared enemy of imperial Japan; here, the Nanjing massacre plays the role of the horrible war crime that finally shocked the Chinese people into overcoming their various differences. In this way, the "Nanjing massacre" comes into the story to "feminize" all civilians as passive victims – disarmed men who are victims of brutal beheading and women who are victims of rape, murder, and mutilation – who need to be rescued and protected by the heroically masculine military. You can't help but feel that these pictorials are telling the same story as Jiang Rong's *Wolf Totem*, which we examined in Chapter 5: the world is divided up into wolves and sheep, and it is better to be a heroically masculine wolf than a passively feminine sheep.

While the Nanjing massacre only occupies a few pages in popular histories of the War of Resistance, these pages are quite grotesque, again displaying iconic images of beheaded men and raped women. As the caption to one photo tells us: "After raping this old woman, Japanese troops force her to disrobe."[31] Such pictures, as well as paintings inspired by the massacre, are displayed in the War of Resistance Museum's "Hall of the Japanese Army's Atrocities" in Beijing.[32] Children's magazines likewise have special commemorative articles that report their elders' war stories, not as heroic soldiers, but as common people who were abused and murdered by Japanese troops.[33] Thus, in most magazine articles, war histories, and museum exhibits, the Nanjing massacre is the only time that civilians take on a significant role in the war. But civilians take on a very specific role in these media products: while the grand narrative of World War II is built around heroic military resistance by both the Communists and the Nationalists, civilians in the Nanjing massacre chapter of the story are portrayed as passive victims who are in need of rescue, in ways similar to the narrative of the Century of National Humiliation.

While descriptions of the Nanjing massacre are short, they are necessary for the narrative of China's eventual victory, as well as for broader understanding of China's national identity. The Nanjing massacre takes on particular symbolic weight because of its pivotal placement in Chinese history and historiography. In terms of physical and spiritual trauma, the Nanjing massacre is both the worst atrocity for China in World War II, and the worst atrocity in the Century of National Humiliation as a whole. The physical trauma of these rapes and murders takes on symbolic significance: the Nanjing massacre represents the lowest point in modern Chinese history. Indeed, the sample sentence for "*zhenjing*-shock" in a prominent Chinese–English dictionary is "The Nanjing Massacre shocked the country and the whole world." Within the war itself, the Nanjing massacre is framed as a turning point whose barbaric atrocities "aroused the spirit of the Chinese race."

Yet, the Nanjing massacre and the War of Resistance victory tell us about more than China's struggle against Japan. The War of Resistance is often described as the "turning point" in modern history, where China went from being a humiliated victim to a self-confident great power:

> China always faced failure and humiliation in its struggles against large imperialist powers since 1840; a century before the War of Resistance Against Japan, China had little ability to bear international responsibilities.... The War of Resistance Against Japan was a turning point in modern Chinese history. It ended the divided situation in which China found itself since the Opium War of 1840. It aroused the Chinese people, filled them with a common hatred against the enemy, and enhanced their traditional national spirit as never before.[34]

The Nanjing massacre and the War of Resistance thus explain both the legitimacy of CCP leadership and the necessity of China's rise to world prominence.[35] As the Central Party School's flashcard history explains, through its wartime sacrifices China became a great power and "won the respect of all the nations of the world, raising China's international status to an unprecedented height."[36] The director of the War of Resistance Museum stated in 2005 that "today Chinese around the world are still receiving the benefits of the victory in the War of Resistance," when China went "in one step from being a bullied and backward country to having a permanent seat on the UN Security Council."[37] To understand the rise of China to world prominence as a great power, he tells us that it is necessary to remember the mutilation of the victims of the Nanjing massacre. The humiliation and mutilation of defeat is recognized in order to pave the way to final victory. The horrible photographs underline how even the generally positive narrative of China becoming a confident great power still depends on a patriarchal nationalist narrative where all civilians are "feminized" as helpless victims who can only be saved by masculine military heroes.

Nanjing Massacre: Six Weeks of Living Hell

The third historical narrative of the Nanjing massacre is much like the first two: it presents the imperial Japanese army as a barbaric force whose atrocities united the Chinese nation in order to first win the war, and ultimately to wash away the shame of the Century of National Humiliation. But as we see later, the third narrative of the Nanjing massacre is slightly different from the first two: as it reaffirms the dominant message of "nationalist resistance" it also opens up avenues for "resistance to nationalism." While the first two narratives frame the Nanjing massacre in terms of long-term national history stories – the *Century* of National Humiliation and the *eight year* War of Resistance – this narrative focuses on a very short period of time: the first six weeks of Japan's conquest and occupation of the Chinese capital. Nanjing as a "hell on earth" is documented by commemorative picture albums published in mainland China, Hong Kong, the United States, and on the Web: *Photographic Evidence of the Nanjing Massacre* (1995), *The Nanjing Massacre* (1995), "WWW Memorial Hall of the Victims in the Nanjing Massacre" (1995), *The Rape of Nanking: An Undeniable History in Photographs* (1996, 1997), the *Picture Collection of the Nanjing Massacre and the International Rescue* (2002), *The Nanjing Massacre* (2005), *Historical Materials of the Nanjing Massacre*, vol. 28: *Historical Images* (2006), *Collected Images of the Exhibitions of the Memorial Hall of the Victims of the Nanjing Massacre by the Invading Japanese Army* (2008), and "The Memorial Hall for Compatriots Killed in the Nanjing Massacre by Japanese Invaders" Web site (2007–9).[38] These albums tell the now horribly familiar tale of how China's "ancient capital of six dynasties" suffered the "fascist invasion of Japanese barbarians," who engaged in an orgy of "slaughter, rape, arson, and looting" in the first six weeks of the occupation of Nanjing.[39]

There is very little text in these publications – brutal pictures are worth even more than a thousand words. Attention to how these "editors and compilers" constructed the visual narrative of these massacre albums thus is particularly important. The atrocities of machine-gunning, shooting, stabbing, bayoneting, decapitating, disemboweling, burying alive, raping, gang raping, and sexual mutilation of bodies that were graphically described in the middle-school textbook *National Humiliation: Chinese People Should Never Forget*, are even more grotesquely displayed with hundreds of photographs in these albums. Certainly, like in the other two narratives the story of the massacre is told in national terms: "Japanese" people killed "Chinese" people, and Japanese men raped Chinese women. But in another way, the photographic narrative strategy shared by these albums also stresses the impact of the massacre on specific people, rather than on abstract nations. Although many people sacrificed themselves to resist the Japanese invasion, that is not the focus of these photo albums. The siege of

Nanjing was not characterized by the heroic resistance that dominates Chinese narratives of World War II. Rather, the Nationalist Chinese army leadership was noteworthy for its cowardly retreat from Nanjing under cover of darkness the night before the city fell. Nanjing residents and refugees were abandoned by the Chinese leadership; testimony of people who survived the many mass slaughters shows how they had to sneak away from the killing fields after dark to survive as individuals, rather than as an example of nation salvation.

This narrative strategy has crucial implications for the organization of the commemorative picture albums that mourn the atrocities of the Nanjing massacre. Some of the albums try to recapture the heroic narrative by including short descriptions of resistance by Chinese or by recounting how a few Westerners protected thousands of Chinese refugees from Japanese troops in the Nanjing Safety Zone (more later).[40] However, the dominant photographic narrative in these albums highlights the violent chaos of the time: each album displays page after page of beheaded men and raped women. Dozens of Chinese men are shown being executed, accompanied by still more photos of decapitated heads lying alone, lined up in row, strewn in piles, or held as trophies by executioners. Along with the photos with captions like "Japanese soldier rapes woman" and "Japanese soldier humiliates woman," the text tells us how Japanese soldiers not only violated women's bodies, but violated civilized categories: they did not distinguish between old women and very young girls, day or night, indoors or outdoors. After these "perverse rapes and gang rapes, they killed the women and mutilated their bodies in a tragedy beyond comparison."[41] One album has a chapter of pictures that catalogues the imperial Japanese army's "Killing Methods"; the following chapter displays more gruesome photos over captions like "A woman who was gang raped then mutilated by bayonets."[42] These visual narratives thus focus tightly to display the details of the mutilation of Chinese bodies to represent the mutilation of both the Chinese spirit and the Chinese body politic.

The photo albums have a complementary relationship with the official Nanjing Massacre museum, the "Memorial to the Victims of the Nanjing Massacre by Japanese Invaders," which exhibits large blowups of the same images. Many of the books end with a tour of the memorial, including pictures of Chinese schoolchildren on field trips, as well as specially guided tours of Japan's guilt-ridden veterans, penitent peace activists, and apologizing leaders. While these visitors are impressed by the overwhelming evidence of Japanese war atrocities, here we shift from the photo albums' objective presentation of historical facts, to the war memorial's more deliberate artistic figuration of historical trauma.

The Nanjing massacre memorial was commissioned in 1983 just as China's official historiography shifted to target Japan. It was built on the site of an actual killing field, and opened in 1985 to commemorate the fortieth anniversary of the end of World War II. In 1993, a second phase of the memorial was commissioned just as Beijing's post-Tiananmen Square patriotic education campaign was gaining traction. It was dedicated on December 13, 1997, the sixtieth anniversary of the Nanjing massacre. The planning for the third phase of the memorial began in 2005 at the low point of Sino-Japanese relations, and it opened for the seventieth anniversary of the Nanjing massacre in December 2007. Like war memorials in other countries, the Nanjing memorial commemorates the dead for giving the ultimate sacrifice for the nation. It is the most popular history museum in China, with a viewership of over 11 million visitors.

Although the photo albums see their task of presenting the evidence of the massacre as self-evident, the memorial's award-winning architect, Qi Kang, was quite self-reflective about the architectural (including visual) problems he faced in properly representing the trauma in three dimensions. To express the "social and national feelings" of the Nanjing massacre, Qi chose to "embody the historical disaster in the entire design of the environment."[43] For the first phase of the memorial (1983–5), Qi used the central idea of "to live and to die" to "give expression to [the themes of] 'disaster,' 'indignant grief,' and 'depression.'"[44] He accomplished this by constructing an enclosed plaza paved with gray pebbles and sculptures of dead trees; the anguish of the Chinese people is represented by a sculpture of a woman crying out in pain. This "bleak, desolate, and wild" space is surrounded by walls of panel sculptures representing the Chinese victims of the massacre. These sculptures work to illustrate the themes of "catastrophe, slaughter, and mourning." While the photo albums have pictures of nameless individuals, the memorial further abstracts and nationalizes war memory by framing the barren plaza with panel sculptures of mutilated men and raped women, including a terrified naked woman cowering from an unseen Japanese soldier (see Figure 6.2), beheaded men, and various severed body parts floating along the fractured wall. A stairway from this scene of desolation leads up to a grass lawn that symbolizes life, and the Chinese peoples' resistance to Japanese aggression. It contains a panel sculpture of people making a religious sacrifice to those who died in the tragedy, and has the inscription "Never Forget National Humiliation." The official Nanjing massacre memorial remembers the specific and unique murders and rapes of hundreds of thousands of people in Nanjing through a collective representation of archetypal victims – rather than the unknown soldier, it presents the unknown victims.

175

Figure 6.2 Section of panel sculpture at Nanjing massacre memorial. Courtesy of William A. Callahan.

Ten years later in phase two, the themes of the Nanjing massacre memorial shifted from a contemplative mourning of the victims to a more active focus on China's unfinished historical business with Japan: here Qi's organizing themes are "pain" and "hatred."[45] A massive sculpture entitled "Disaster in Jinling [Nanjing]" dominates phase two. It includes a huge decapitated man's screaming head, the frantically outstretched arm of a buried-alive victim, and a city wall that has been mutilated by artillery fire. Qi's aim here is for the memorial sculpture to be "resonant with the wails and shrieks of the dead."[46] Once again, the horror of the Nanjing massacre is embodied in larger-than-life visual images of mutilation. In this way, Qi has returned to his initial problem of how to properly represent unfathomable and unendurable atrocities – a problem that he shares with commemorations of the Holocaust. Qi writes that phase two is not figurative but "is really a portrayal of the actual scene, and of that part of history written in blood and tears."[47] The feelings of "pain" and "hatred" provoked by memories of the Nanjing massacre gain in reality as they are circulated. Indeed, like in Sino-Japanese relations more generally, since the 1990s, the Chinese people's painful hatred of Japan is overwhelming the more contemplative grief seen in the Nanjing massacre memorial's first phase built in the mid-1980s.

A decade later, phase three more than tripled the amount of space occupied by the museum compound, including a five-fold increase in exhibition space. The museum curator worked with the Art Engineering Company of the Lu Xun Academy of Fine Arts to create a state-of-the-art experience of historical memory and national commemoration;[48] the exhibits expand upon the now sadly familiar themes of slaughter, rape, arson, and looting to give a detailed multimedia view of Japan's invasion and occupation of Nanjing.

But the museum's appeal to "historical facts" is framed in phase three by an appeal to emotions. Visitors are greeted at the entrance to the museum compound by a huge new statue of a bare-breasted woman holding a dead baby; a poem, "Family Ruined," is inscribed on its plinth:

> Never returns the son killed
> Never returns the husband burned alive
> Sorrow drowns the wife raped.
> Heavens ...

While waiting in line to get into the museum, people can ponder a set of bronze statues that represent ordinary Chinese who were sucked up into the storm of war. The caption for the statue of a half-naked woman is "Never will a holy soul bear the humiliation of the devils! Only to die!

Only to die! Only death can wash away the filth!" Another statue has a man warn his son: "Japanese devils are coming!" A mother carrying her baby yells: "Run! The devils are coming..."

At the other end of the park, the museum visit ends in "Peace Square." This appeal to world peace is encouraging; the square has a "Peace Tower" at the end of a long reflecting pool. On top of this obelisk is another mother and child sculpture, here signifying peace and hope. Yet alongside the reflecting pool, a bronze statue of a Chinese soldier trumpets victory on his bugle, with one foot triumphantly on a Japanese helmet. This statue is in front of a large bas-relief sculpture of battling soldiers and triumphant Chinese called the "Wall of Victory." Peace here is intimately tied to military strength.

Women thus frame the Massacre Memorial Hall first as humiliated victims and then as symbols of peace who can only be saved by warriors. Although he didn't design it, the third phase continues to develop Qi's themes of "pain" and "hatred." It evokes China's national aesthetic of hatred and revenge to target Japan not only as the enemy, but as the devil that needs to be violently resisted.

The memorial and the visual texts that focus on six weeks of hell in Nanjing reproduce the narrative of China as a victim of shocking persecution on a world scale. Like historical narratives of the Nanjing massacre that are framed by the War of Resistance and the Century of National Humiliation, the ultimate message of these visual media products is the *victory* of "nationalist resistance" to Japanese aggression that followed the atrocity. Hence, rather than moving from a Maoist victory narrative to a reformist victim narrative of China's modern nationalist history, the Nanjing massacre texts show how these two seemingly opposite historiographies productively coexist in complementary tension, each feeding-off and encouraging the other in order to produce China's pessoptimistic identity.

War Pornography and Patriarchal Nationalism

As the shocking textbook descriptions, photo albums, and memorial halls all graphically display, the Nanjing massacre is about more than China's uneasy relationship with Japan. In addition to asserting China as a world power, the written and visual texts promote a very gendered view of Chinese identity and history through the recurrent categories of "beheaded men" and "raped women." As the visual texts suggest, although Japan's mutilation of Chinese bodies was certainly very physical, it was also symbolic: the Japanese army sought to humiliate the Chinese nation in very gendered ways – there are no images of men being raped or women being beheaded – that reinforce the notion that rape is about a desire for power more than a desire for sex. As literary theorist Lydia Liu explains, the symbol of raped women also helped build Chinese identity according to a patriarchal nationalism:

> As a sign of symbolic exchange, the raped woman often serves as a powerful trope in anti-Japanese propaganda. Her victimization is used to represent – or more precisely, to eroticize – China's own plight. In such a signifying practice, the female body is ultimately displaced by nationalism, whose discourse denies the specificity of female experience by giving larger symbolic meanings to the signifier of rape: namely, China itself is being violated by the Japanese rapist.[49]

This gendered nationalism is not unique to the Nanjing massacre or to China.[50] Political scientist Cynthia Enloe, for example, argues that "becoming nationalist requires a man to resist the foreigner's use and abuse of his women." Thus "nationalism typically has sprung from masculinized memory, masculinized humiliation and masculinized hope."[51] Most wars in the twentieth century hence are understood as rapes: the media referred to the beginning of World War I as the "Rape of Belgium," the beginning of the Gulf War in 1991 was called the "Rape of Kuwait," and later in the 1990s, rape came to symbolize the Bosnian war. Women here are enlisted as national symbols not in positive ways – the Statue of Liberty, Britannia, or France's Marianne – but in negative ways as the violated national bodies that challenge national honor – and demand nationalist revenge. The purpose in these narratives is not to stop the rape of specific women and bring particular soldiers to criminal justice.

The use of rapes for nationalist mobilization was much the same in China. The first Nanjing massacre photo album, *A Faithful Record of the Atrocities of the Japanese Invaders*, was published by the political department of the military committee of China's ruling Nationalist party in July 1938.[52] Indeed, many of the horrible pictures in photo albums published since 1989 are reproduced from *A Faithful Record*; the introduction to *Historical Materials of the Nanjing Massacre*, vol. 28: *Historical Images*, for example, goes out of its way to credit this 1938 book as a central source, as does the Nanjing Massacre Memorial Hall's Web site.[53] The purpose of these albums is not merely to provide objective evidence of Japanese war crimes, but to reproduce the gendered discourse of female victims that stokes desire for masculine military revenge.

Yet a nuanced understanding of the symbolic politics of the Nanjing massacre can open up avenues of critical resistance. When we question the links between women, war, and patriarchal nationalism asserted by the memorial and the photo albums, then we can criticize the resulting militarized masculinity that fosters violence in both personal space (rapes and murders) and geopolitical space (war). Rather than just frame the problem as *Japanese* militarism, we thus can also criticize the *militarization* of Chinese society produced through such memories of "nationalist resistance." It is also necessary to explore how these photo albums risk becoming complicit not only in reproducing patriarchal nationalism and Sino-Japanese conflict, but also being complicit in encouraging a voyeuristic consumption of the rape photos as exotic erotica, especially as this war pornography spreads on the Internet.

Photo albums and Web sites work hard to excavate and display the horrible truth about the war. *Photographic Evidence*, for example, prides itself not only for being the first book of Nanjing massacre photographs published in the PRC, but also for "provid[ing] an objective view of the Nanjing massacre's historical background." In addition to helping future generations of Chinese to understand this tragic period of their history, Liu and Bo are proud of how their professional work has "raised the quality of historical research to a new level."[54] Still, the provenance of the Nanjing massacre photos is problematic. Japanese revisionists typically try to prove either that the photographs are not of Japanese troops, or that they were not taken in Nanjing in winter 1937–8.[55] That is not my argument. Rather than saying that the provenance of the pictures is unclear, I find that the *clarity* of the provenance is problematic: most of the photographs of raped Chinese women were shot as war souvenirs by the men who raped them.

But rather than seeing this war pornography as a problem, the editors of *Photographic Evidence* see rape pictures taken by Japanese troops as a particularly compelling source of evidence. The introduction to the album's "Brutally Raping Women" section concludes: "This chapter's photographs of the rape and humiliation of women all were seized from Japanese POWs." The album also has a special section for "Pictures of atrocities taken by Japanese troops."[56] Many of the captions also recognize the military rapist provenance of photos: "After raping these women [the Japanese soldiers] first forced them to take off their pants for a photo, and then one soldier extended his hand to spread her legs." "The camera caught this Japanese soldier in the act of rape." "A young woman was bound to a chair to be repeatedly raped by Japanese soldiers. One of these criminals took this photo, which became one of the undeniable pieces of evidence of Japanese atrocities."[57] Hence, the mainland Chinese albums tend to celebrate the objective value of the photos, rather than critically engage with the ethical problems of reproducing war pornography.

The Chinese-American editors of *The Rape of Nanjing* photo album likewise skate over the controversial issue of war pornography. Rather than just celebrating the scientific source-value of war pornography, they appeal to a "civil liberties" logic to argue that any other editing of their book would amount to political censorship:

> In the process of compiling and editing this book, we showed parts of it to people from different walks of life. Many turned their faces away from these photographs taken 60 years ago. Some suggested that we censor the pictures and leave out those that are especially graphic and disturbing. Our purpose, however, is to record history, not to censor it.[58]

More than the other authors, Iris Chang is concerned about compounding the atrocities with what she calls "the second rape" of Nanjing. But this second rape is not of individual women; it is of historical memory and the Chinese nation: Japan's denial and refusal to apologize, for Chang, is the second rape. When Peter Hays Gries asked Chang "if she worried about committing a 'third rape' by reprinting graphic pictures of naked Chinese women in her book, thereby subjecting them to further indignity," Chang answered that "as a woman she had concerns about the pictures and had discussed the issue with her publishers, but had decided that rectifying the 'second rape' (Western ignorance of the Nanjing massacre) justified the risk of a 'third rape.'"[59] Rather than appealing to scientific method or civil liberties, Chang curiously reproduces the gendered narrative of China as a "raped woman" who can only be saved through "nationalist resistance."

Here we run into similar problems to those faced by journalists, academics, and activists who sought to document the "rape-warfare" activities of Serbs in the Bosnian war.[60] Much like in the Nanjing massacre six decades earlier, Serb soldiers took pictures and video of rapes to humiliate the women (and thus Bosnian nation) in ways that reinforced patriarchal nationalism. Moreover, there is evidence that these images were reproduced, distributed, and later used as pornographic "stimulants" for more rape warfare. The goal of feminist activists in the 1990s, like with the Nanjing massacre books and albums, was to give an accurate accounting and meaningful analysis of the atrocities.

However, unlike with the Nanjing massacre albums, these activists understood rape as an expression of power, and thus sought to avoid reproducing war pornography and patriarchal nationalism in their work. Hence, while criticizing "the murderous misogyny and rabid nationalism" of Serbian rape camps and rape videos, Allen states that her "challenge in representing them is to do so without repeating in any way the harm those atrocities have already perpetrated."[61] According to Enloe, "The challenge is to make visible women raped by men as soldiers without further militarizing those women in the process."[62] In this way "raped women" shifts from being a singular metaphor of national shame, which is reproduced again and again over the decades, to refer a group of specific people who need care and support, and hopefully legal justice rather than military revenge.

To accomplish this shift from military revenge to legal justice, it is necessary to rethink how we represent atrocities like the Nanjing massacre. Albums and exhibits of colonial photography, which contain pictures of half-naked "native" women taken by European men, have provoked similar questions. Like in the Nanjing massacre pictorials, these photographs now are reproduced as part of a critique of imperialism. But this criticism of colonial power also raises the familiar issue of the role of women in patriarchal nationalism. Although progressive in terms of geopolitics, the albums can be regressive for gender politics. In a discussion of such colonial photography, Mieke Bal explains how reproducing and recirculating these pictures risks "aestheticiz[ing] the images and thus to anesthetiz[ing] their conflicts."[63] The core problem of such pictorials and exhibitions, Bal argues, is "the combination of exuberant illustration with poverty of explanation."[64] The Nanjing massacre photo albums, with page after page of beheaded men and raped women, likewise risk being complicit in promoting the voyeuristic consumption of the rape photos as exotic erotica.

Rather than reproducing hundreds of photos, Bal suggests that we employ "a thoughtful, sparse use of visual material where every image is provided with an immediately accessible critique that justifies its use with specificity."[65] The visual texts of the Nanjing massacre do the opposite. They, thus, raise the now sadly familiar question of how to understand horrific images in a way that is respectful, but also critical. While the Nanjing massacre photos may not produce erotic desire, they certainly produce a desire for revenge – which like any desire, can never be satisfied. To resist complicity with exotic erotica and militant revenge, it is necessary to suspend, for a moment, the continual reproduction of the iconic Nanjing massacre images. To resist the linkage between women, war, and patriarchal nationalism it is necessary to change the subject, and reread the texts in a different way. Indeed, part of "resisting nationalism" here involves resisting the power of such photos.

Resisting Nationalism

A gendered view of the Nanjing massacre can provide openings for resistance to the dominant understanding of the War of Resistance, and the current militarization of Chinese identity. There is not much room for resistance in Chinese historical writing, which remains quite "monolithic": "categories such as gender and ethnicity have made little impact on what remains a masculine, Han Chinese narrative."[66] As we saw with Yuan Weishi's article in *Freezing Point*, it can be dangerous for historians in the PRC to directly criticize nationalist historiography. Chinese texts thus resist nationalist narratives largely by changing the subject, and thereby avoid reproducing categories such as "raped women" and "beheaded men" that tend to produce Japan and China as archenemies. The aim here is not to deny the atrocities, but to rewrite the history that gives them meaning in the twenty-first century. While the horrible photos tend to reproduce the hegemonic discourse of nationalism, a gendered view of identity provides an opening for critical space.

Upon second reading, we can find resistance to nationalism even within the Nanjing massacre books and photo albums. The books are very deliberately produced by local publishers in the city of Nanjing and Jiangsu province, rather than by the national publishers that produce and distribute tomes on the War of Resistance and the Century of National Humiliation.[67] The Nanjing massacre memorial likewise was primarily funded by local sources, rather than through national budgets like the other key war museums.[68] The message of the photo albums is also local: they healed the wounds of the Nanjing massacre by celebrating the modernization and development of Nanjing city, rather than the rise of China: for the people of Nanjing, prosperity is better than revenge.[69] Resisting any definition that looks to the mutilated bodies of the Nanjing massacre, photos at the end of the *Picture Collection* thus concentrate on wide-angle views of the physical infrastructure of this lively city (i.e., its regenerated municipal body): super-highways, skyscrapers, tree-lined boulevards, and landscaped parks (see Figure 6.3).[70] In this way, many of the Nanjing massacre media products construct a Nanjing identity that displaces (although not necessarily opposes) national identity.

The international aspect of the Nanjing massacre also leads us away from the hegemonic national narrative. As the Nationalist leadership was retreating from Nanjing in early December 1937, two dozen European and American residents marked off a four-square-mile section of the city as the neutral

Figure 6.3 "Nanjing under construction and development." Zhu Chenshan, *Nanjing datusha yu guoji dajiu jutuji*, 2002.

Nanjing Safety Zone to shelter Chinese refugees during the Japanese invasion.[71] While Maoist histories at times denounced this foreign activity, writers since 1978 have enthusiastically praised these Westerners for saving tens of thousands of Chinese lives.[72] This is remarkable because it goes directly against the narrative logic of the Century of National Humiliation. The Westerners who in humiliation history textbooks are commonly described as the worst imperialist devils – Christian missionaries and international capitalists – are transformed into angels in the Nanjing massacre books and albums. While the narrative strategies of national history work hard to differentiate between insiders as patriotic Chinese nationalists and outsiders as evil foreign invaders, the players here are more nuanced: while the Japanese are still devils, the Westerners of the Nanjing Safety Zone Committee are praised as angelic heroes.[73]

This visual narrative of Western angels became an international sensation in 2007 with *Nanking*, a feature-length documentary produced by former AOL Vice-Chairman Ted Leonis. To bring to life the horrors of the Nanjing massacre, *Nanking* weaves together archival photos and film, testimonies of survivors and Japanese soldiers, and staged readings of first-hand accounts from Westerners in the Nanjing Safety Zone. Inspired by Chang's *Rape of Nanking*, the film follows the general victim narrative seen in textbooks, pictorials, and museums, and uses many of the same photographs of beheaded men and raped women. Along with the international narrative of the massacre, it turns the tragedy into a triumph by showing, as Leonis tells us, the bravery of a handful of Westerners "who had the courage to stand up to an invading army to save lives."[74] *Nanking* was popular in both China and the United States: it was nominated for the Grand Jury Prize at the Sundance Film Festival (2007), and premiered at the National Political Consultative Auditorium in Beijing on July 3, 2007. In China it wowed the critics and conquered the market, becoming the best-selling foreign documentary of all time. The film's success confirms that the popular understanding in the PRC has shifted to include Westerners as heroes, while still targeting the Japanese as devils.

Writing alternative histories that look to local and international actors is a popular mode of resistance. But some authors choose to go outside official (and professional) history-writing to construct a different set of memories about Nanjing in 1937 and broader Sino-Japanese relations. In the preface to his novel, *Nanjing 1937: A Love Story*, Ye Zhaoyan confesses his confusion over the meaning of official history: "as a writer, I find myself unable to truly understand the history that historians call history. I see only shattered pieces, broken fragments, and a handful of melancholic stories destined to come to naught, all quietly playing out upon the grand stage of history."[75]

Xiao Hong's novel *Field of Life and Death* (1935) provides an interesting example of historical fiction that contests China's "nationalist resistance" history and its demonization of Japan. Although this novel was written before the Nanjing massacre, it addresses another violent episode in Sino-Japanese relations: Japan's conquest of Manchuria in 1931. While the Nanjing government refused to mobilize armed resistance to Japan, Chinese writers and artists still fought Japan through their creative work. Indeed, Xiao Hong's lover Xiao Jun wrote a novel that "epitomizes the ways nationalist discourse deploys gender during the war": its peasant widow character not only loses her family to the war, but "on top of all her bereavements, is raped by a Japanese soldier."[76] Xiao Hong's fiction, on the other hand, resisted the emerging patriarchal nationalism that was built on the mutilated bodies of women. Her character escapes being raped on the road by Japanese soldiers (by smearing her face with dirt to look old and ugly), only to be raped by a Chinese man once she enters the city.[77] Rather than Japan being demonized for a collective rape of China, Xiao Hong writes of the barbarity of Chinese toward each other, and especially toward women. Through this unexpected narrative twist, Xiao Hong highlights how rapes are important, not just in geopolitical conflict; they are a personal problem at home as well, especially since domestic violence tends to increase with the militarization of society. Like in other cases, here the politics of differentiation that sorts patriotic Chinese from barbaric Japanese breaks down because we are shown how harsh Chinese can be to each other.

In *Nanjing 1937: A Love Story*, Ye Zhaoyan contests the nationalist narrative of the Nanjing massacre in a different way. Although Ye consulted primary and secondary historical sources in his meticulous research for the novel, he chose to write a different story to challenge the hegemonic narrative of a patriarchal Chinese nation involved in an increasingly violent geopolitical conflict with Japan. Rather than a war story where Japan rapes China, Ye wrote a love story where a Chinese man romances a Sino-Japanese woman. There is plenty of violence in *Nanjing 1937*; Ding, the protagonist, is killed in the Japanese attack on Nanjing. But that happens on the last page – before then, all the violence is domestic: Chinese abusing, exploiting, raping, and killing each other.

However, the main narrative is not a war story, but a love story. At the beginning of 1937 Nanjing is a lively city, where Ding is an accomplished playboy who uses elaborate military language to plot his physical relations with women: "He continuously sought out different types of women, and once he achieved his conquest, he would immediately initiate his next campaign. He was like a general who had endured a hundred battles, charging forward amid a sea of women."[78] But when Yuyuan, the heroine, does not respond to Ding's standard strategies, he is forced to come to terms with the import of his "true love" for her. Ding gives up chasing women, and engages in a largely unrequited daily correspondence with Yuyuan; his romancing is not organized around the physical act of sex, but around new-found spiritual feelings expressed in writing. Over the course of hundreds of pages, Ye thus shifts the meaning of *Nanjing 1937* from the raw physical-ity of a brutal geopolitical rape to a deeply spiritual love between two people. Rather than focus on hating Japan, he stresses the importance of love – even love for a woman who is half-Japanese, a love that is largely unthinkable in China's national aesthetic.

While Ye's novel looks to an expanded and thoughtful notion of love (for the "other" – Japan), Xiao Hong's novel dwells on hatred – hatred of men, Japan, China, of everyone and everything: "I used to hate men only; now I hate the Japanese instead. Do I hate Chinese as well? Then there is nothing else for me to hate."[79] These two intensely self-reflective narrations of Chinese history and identity are remarkable because they are so risky for Chinese authors. Xiao Hong has been heavily censured by Chinese literary critics for her lack of patriotic fervor; soon after she published *Field of Life and Death*, she moved to Japan. Since *Nanjing 1937* can signify only one thing in contemporary China – www.nj1937.org is the official URL for the Nanjing Massacre Memorial Hall – Ye's sometimes satirical, sometimes critical, and certainly "unorthodox love story" constitutes a deliberate rewriting of Chinese identity away from official national history. In the novel's afterword, Ye recognizes the limits of censorship that he might face: "I write this novel without any regard for what the consequences might be; heaven only knows if anyone will read it."[80]

Conclusion

The Japanese army committed horrible war crimes in Nanjing, which should not be denied by Japanese politicians or in history textbooks. However, the Chinese textbooks, pictorials, museums, Web sites, films, and novels we have examined underline how the "history issue" concerns more than just revisionist voices in Japan. As we have seen, the Nanjing massacre and the War of Resistance are both central in the symbolic construction of China's pessoptimist national identity as a victim/victor. This close reading of written and visual texts has shown how successful both China's patriotic education policy and its history activists have been at setting the limits for the proper understanding of Japan – "hatred" is the common theme in books, photo albums, and memorials for the Nanjing massacre.

The interplay of the party-state's "edutainment" and history activists' multimedia products extends beyond the borders of the PRC. Overseas Chinese in North America have actively spread the horrible history of the Nanjing massacre to a global audience as a way of reaffirming their own transnational Chinese national identity. But overseas texts do not simply reproduce the official narrative; as we saw earlier, they have added the international aspect of Western angels to mainland understandings of the Nanjing massacre. Indeed, one of the new statues in the third phase of the Nanjing Massacre Memorial is of Iris Chang (who committed suicide in 2004) holding a book that says "Rape" in English. While adding a new cast of angels to the story, we must recognize that overseas Chinese under-standings of the Nanjing massacre often target Japanese as devils in even harsher terms. For the history activists in North America, discussions of Japanese atrocities are also discussions of what it means to be Chinese.

While I argue that "barbaric Japan" is embedded in China's identity politics, many analysts feel that China and Japan can reconcile their politi-cal differences through joint history projects that produce a "shared mem-ory" for the two countries.[81] A good example of such "shared memory" is *The Contemporary and Modern History of Three East Asian Countries: Facing the Future Using History as a Mirror, Building Together a New Framework of Peace and Friendship in East Asia* (2005). This regional history textbook was edited by a committee of young historians from China, Japan, and South Korea, and was published simultaneously in the three languages.[82] Its cumber-some title makes clear that "reconciliation" is the goal of this textbook. It is a milestone in the long process of forming a consensus view of the troubled past. But since it employs the "victim historiography" popular in China (and South Korea), the book is unlikely to attract a readership in Japan beyond the left-wing historians who wrote it.

In 2006, the Chinese and Japanese governments formed a more formal "China–Japan Joint History Research Committee" at their first bilateral summit in almost a decade.[83] By the beginning of 2009, this joint commit-tee of ten Chinese and ten Japanese scholars had met four times; but disagreements over how to understand events like the Nanjing massacre led them to conclude that they could not write a shared history – yet. The successes and failures of these shared history projects show how difficult it is for both sides to get around monolithic views of each other as the Other.

Although joint history projects are not paving the way for Sino-Japanese reconciliation, shared memory *is* emerging between China and the United States – about Japan. Ted Leonis's film *Nanking*, which was popular in both China and the United States, is a fascinating example of how a shared view of history is confirmed in the oddest places. While the Chinese censors are very careful about how Japan and the war are portrayed, Leonis reports that "We translated this film into Mandarin and not a word was touched, which doesn't often happen." Moreover, Leonis stressed that the story of the Western angels of "Nanking" is important in the twenty-first century, "at a time when we Americans are not popular around the world." To underline the film's part in fostering closer Sino-American relations, Leonis recounted how the Chinese president declared "China would never forget the acts of kindness of Westerners" in his toast at a recent White House state dinner.[84] The success of this cinematic diplomacy is miles away from the fantastic premier of *The Opium War* a decade earlier (discussed in Chapter 2), which targeted Westerners as imperialist barbarians.

The geopolitical meaning of *Nanking* is an example of China's triangular diplomacy where Beijing often creates new enemies in order to forge new alliances. Earlier we saw how Japan is targeted in Beijing's understanding of the War of Resistance as a way of promoting nationalist reunification with Taiwan. As the *Illustrated History of China's War of Resistance* concludes, World War II "aroused the Chinese people, filled them with a common hatred against the enemy, and enhanced their traditional national spirit as never before."[85] On the other hand, in 2002–3 Chinese calls for a *rapprochement* with Japan often downplayed the history issue by targeting "American hegemony" as a common foe.[86] China's triangular diplomacy thus is based more on shared enemies than on shared values. Like pessoptimistic politics in general, it is unstable; as we have seen throughout this book, the friend/enemy and civilization/barbarism distinctions can easily switch from positive to negative, and back again.

But strategic triangles that are built on self/other relations are not the only communities generated by the trauma of the Nanjing massacre. This chapter has argued that we need to understand the politics of the Nanjing massacre and Sino–Japanese relations on various levels: the photo albums and films may be progressive in terms of criticizing Japanese war crimes, but they tend to be problematic in other ways by promoting, for example, a militarized patriarchal Chinese nationalism. Perhaps the problem is not just "militarism" in China or Japan, but limiting our understanding of

global politics to inter*national* relations and state-led shared history projects. By looking to the local and the international communities generated
by the Nanjing massacre, the chapter showed how some people have
displaced the meaning of Nanjing 1937 from "devils" to "angels" and
from "hatred" to "love." When we shift from re-citing the iconic photos
to re-siting historical narratives, we can also shift from the hegemonic
narrative of "nationalist resistance" to a multitude of "resistances to nationalism," each of which has its own politics, possibilities, problems – and
answers to the question "Who is China?" This would multiply identity/
security politics and allow China to have a more fruitful engagement with
Japan, other countries, other peoples – and itself.

Chapter 7

Conclusion: How to Be Chinese in the Twenty-First Century

In many ways, now is the best time to be Chinese. Since Deng Xiaoping's economic reforms began in 1978, exciting social and cultural possibilities have opened up for the Chinese people. The People's Republic of China (PRC) has quite literally moved from the socialist planned economy's iron rice bowl to the market's golden chopsticks: China's growing variety of high-quality regional and international cuisine is compelling evidence of the country's prosperity and curiosity.

The festival surrounding the 2008 Olympics showed that Beijing is much more than an economic superpower. The capital's iconic new buildings – the National Stadium (i.e., the Bird's Nest), the National Aquatics Center (i.e., the Water Cube), the National Theater (i.e., the Egg), the new airport terminal, and the new China Central Television headquarters – show that China is now the global center of architectural innovation. Chinese art is likewise inspiring the world, and setting global trends. In 2008, Cai Guo-qiang's work was exhibited in top museums on three continents: the Guggenheim in New York, Beijing's National Museum, and then the Guggenheim in Bilbao, Spain. China's new middle class is broadening its horizons as well: more than 35 million travel abroad each year.[1]

Chinese foreign policy is also quite positive and optimistic. After being cast out of international society after the June 4th massacre in 1989, China has worked hard to engage with the international community as a responsible power. Beijing's foreign policy themes have wandered from "bide our time, while building up capability," to multipolarization, responsible power, peaceful rise, peaceful development, and now harmonious world. But the main objective has been quite constant – peace and development: a peaceful and cooperative international environment is necessary for China's domestic economic development. China's dream is to be strong, rich, equal, and respected – which are reasonable goals for a great power that is rising within the international system.

This is the "happy China" that Olympic imagineers worked hard to convey to the international audience; it is "the real China" that Chinese officials and netizens expect foreign journalists to report.[2]

Although many like to assume that American studies of Beijing's foreign policy engage in "demonizing" China as part of power politics, most recent analysis is quite optimistic too. The general conclusions are encouraging: China is not a threat. Rather than being an aggressive, renegade, or irredentist power that challenges the status quo, China has been socialized into the international system as a multilateral actor. Nationalism is an issue, but the negative emotions that we see in popular protests can (and should) be controlled by the Chinese state. The United States and China are enjoying their best relations since 1989; the only real risk of conflict is over Taiwan. However, this is the exception to the rule of China's peaceful rise, and it is under control, now that Beijing and Washington cooperate in constraining Taiwan's pro-independence voices. China thus is a normal status quo power – and should be treated as such.[3]

But this book goes against the grain of such analysis to question its sanguine view of China's rise. While there is much evidence for an optimistic understanding of China and its foreign policy, such interpretations only tell part of the story, generally ignoring or dismissing the negative side of "happy China."[4] In this book, on the other hand, we have seen that to understand China's dreams, we need to understand its nightmares. Alongside the positive images of China that point to 5,000 years of civilization and thirty years of economic growth, there is a very negative narrative of national humiliation that recalls China's modern history as an experience of suffering at the hands of foreign aggression.

Rather than finding a single correct core of "Chinese nationalism," we have seen how Chinese identity emerges through the interplay of positive and negative feelings. The widening of economic and cultural possibilities in China actually depends upon the narrowing of political space, especially when it comes to discussions of foreign relations. This positive/negative dynamic intertwines China's domestic and international politics because national security is closely linked to nationalist insecurities.

The heart of Chinese foreign policy thus is not a security dilemma, but an identity dilemma: who is China and how does it fit into the world?[5] "International status" certainly is one of China's main foreign policy issues;[6] but it is determined less by what Beijing does than by how the world sees China – and how China sees the world. Foreign policy thus goes beyond interstate diplomatic relations. Foreign affairs is a sovereignty performance that involves a broad range of Chinese people; it is a social activity where people divide friends from enemies, domestic from foreign, East from West, and patriots from traitors in everyday life. Because the multilateralism of the Foreign Ministry is not deeply embedded in Chinese society, we need to look beyond official policy to see how Chinese people relate to the world. Rather than only charting how China has been socialized into international society, we also need to appreciate how China socializes itself into a particular view of itself and the world.

To explain this complex mix of optimism and pessimism – what I call China's pessoptimism – I trace how identity and security are produced and consumed in various official and unofficial places: government documents and school textbooks, newspaper and academic articles, public and private museums, professional, pictorial, and popular books, feature films, television programs and novels, Web sites, blogs, bulletin boards, and online videos. I showed how China's relationship with itself and the world takes shape in the pessoptimist dynamics of patriotic education policy and the national humiliation curriculum, national days and national humiliation days, national maps and national humiliation maps, foreign brothers and domestic strangers, and Chinese patriots and foreign devils. Together the chapters demonstrate how the identity politics of Chinese nationalism produces the security politics of Chinese foreign policy. They show how the pessoptimist link between China's dream of civilization and its nightmare of humiliation is not fading away. While national humiliation discourse is not always obvious, it is ever-present in the background as a structure of feeling that guides China's national aesthetic. Indeed, these stories of China's civilization and humiliation are not only about past history; they provide the template of China's foreign relations that inflames popular feelings for future demonstrations, and primes the indignant youth for explosive protests.

To chart the trajectory of China's rise, the book thus shifts from examining the PRC's national interests to exploring China's national aesthetic. Rather than answering the standard social science question "what is China?" with statistics of economic and military power, this book asks "when, where, and who is China?" to explore the soft power dynamics of China's identity dilemma. While most see stability as the goal for China – stable answers for stable country in a stable world – this book has examined the contingencies of China as an unfinished project. China is a developing nation that has yet to complete its modernization program; and we have seen how it is also trying to complete various other identity projects, such as cleansing humiliations and recovering lost territories. The title of an academic article – "A Century of Anticipating the Unification of the Motherland" – gives a sense of aspirational China's mix of hope and fear.[7] While basking in the warm glow of global recognition of China as the next superpower, Chinese people want to make sure that they are not insulted, bullied, or humiliated by foreigners again. As a Chinese general recently explained, "China once made outstanding contributions to world civilization. But, in modern times, it has been bullied by foreign powers, and is still to some degree being bullied."[8]

Chinese identity and security thus emerge through a combination of modern humiliation and ancient civilization: China presents itself to the world as an innocent victim of foreign aggression. This official narrative of China's Century of National Humiliation leaves out important points: the Qing dynasty was a conquest empire that doubled Chinese territory, and in the last decades of the nineteenth century Beijing invaded, occupied, and exploited Korea in ways that should be described as national humiliations.[9] The national humiliation version of China's modern and contemporary history also excises catastrophic experiences like the Great Leap Forward and the Cultural Revolution that still haunt many Chinese people. But "learning truth from horrifying facts" is only one aspect of the national humiliation curriculum. Patriotic education is a moral campaign that teaches people how and what to *feel* – humiliation, hatred, and revenge are common themes.

The party-state appeals to this pessoptimist structure of feeling to narrow the possibilities for what it means to be Chinese. It does this by treating identity distinctions as moral categories: civilized/barbaric, domestic/foreign, modern/backward, East/West, and hero/traitor. National humiliation discourse thus acts as a paradigm of contentious international politics, which sets the template to frame foreigners as barbarians: the United States as the evil Hegemon, Japanese as devils, Taiwan as a renegade province, and the Dalai Lama as a ravenous wolf. As we have seen over the past decade, this foreign policy template has successfully produced mass demonstrations on the Web and on the street.

While this form of patriotic nationalism is now popular in China, we cannot take it for granted as the true expression of Chinese identity. National humiliation discourse itself has a history. It emerged after the First Sino-Japanese War (1894–5), and was the most popular way of expressing national identity between 1915 and 1940. However, with the founding of the PRC, "class struggle" displaced national humiliation as the main way to produce and consume Chinese identity. After a fifty-year hiatus, national humiliation days, history textbooks, and maps reappeared in the 1990s after Deng Xiaoping decided that the country's unruly youth needed to be taught how to be proper, patriotic Chinese.[10] Because the success of economic reform was not enough to legitimize the party-state, Deng instructed party workers to "Seize with both hands, with both hands holding tight" in order to cultivate political loyalty alongside economic prosperity. Thus, as economic and social opportunities have blossomed, possibilities for political identity have narrowed. As we have seen, this policy continues in the current Hu Jintao regime. It is not simply a negative act of state censorship; the Central Propaganda Department's multimedia patriotic education campaign productively generates a particular type of patriotism by outlining in detail who Chinese can be – and who they can't be.

But the current patriotic nationalist form of Chinese identity is much more than the outcome of an instrumental manipulation of cultural nationalism by the party elite. This expression of national pride and national humiliation flourishes because it resonates with a complementary structure of feeling – the civilization/barbarism distinction – that preceded the PRC. As we have seen throughout the book, the civilization/barbarism distinction keeps being reproduced in new ways to meet new political situations. While it is popular to see the state as the actor and the masses as the audience, we have seen how Chinese nationalism is produced and consumed in an interactive process where the actor is the audience, and the audience is the actor. It is common to assume that the state controls popular memory; but national humiliation days, textbooks and maps all emerged in civil society as criticisms of the Chinese state in the early twentieth century. The state then adopted, reworked, and redeployed this pessoptimistic discourse as a response to popular protest. Chinese identity thus grows out of a dynamic of reciprocal influence that integrates official policy and popular culture.

This interactive view of China's pessoptimist identity means that we need to rethink the role of the state and public opinion in Beijing's foreign policy-making. Many use the "history issue" to argue that Beijing's relations with Japan, Taiwan, and the United States are constrained by the "emotional nationalism" of public opinion. The solution to this problem of emotional public opinion is more (and better) state control over popular feelings that will promote a more pragmatic and reasonable nationalism.[11] Yet, this understanding of China's foreign policy dilemma neglects to recognize that official policy and popular feelings are already intertwined. The "problem" of emotional nationalism is actually a blowback from Beijing's own propaganda policy. After two decades of patriotic education that resonates with popular anxieties, China's pessoptimist nationalism is now beyond anyone's control.

Others see these patriotic demonstrations as the actions of a genuine grassroots movement.[12] But the protests are not an expression of a democratic opening; because they usually appeal to an even more extreme view of patriotism than the party-state, the protests entail a narrowing of political space. Instead of providing evidence of a growing civil society in China, the patriotic protests are often quite uncivil in their messages and tactics, which include "human flesh search engines." Rather than a sign of the liberalization of Chinese politics, mass movements in China are better understood as right-wing populist movements that further restrict political possibilities. Instead of evaluating Chinese popular opinion according to the procedural issue of whether it is "genuine" or not, it is time to focus on its content – and recognize that a rightwing nationalism that targets minorities at home and foreigners abroad is increasingly prevalent among Chinese. This combination of public opinion and popular protest is a growing domestic problem for Beijing; but China's pessoptimist nationalism is also a global issue because it animates official diplomacy and diasporic Chinese protests in North America, Europe, and Pacific Asia. China's diplomats exude national pride when times are good; but they quickly switch to national humiliation themes when China faces an international crisis. Ambassador Fu Ying's article in an English newspaper at the height of China's spring 2008 nationalist backlash is a prime example of such a dramatic shift. Fu is widely seen as the poster girl of China's rational multilateralism; but her article's response to the Olympic Torch relay's London protests uses emotional (and disrespectful) language to criticize British society.[13]

In many ways, this political problem comes from a disjuncture in China's view of itself; when China looks into the mirror, the "national image" it sees is both too small (a "poor developing country") and too large (the "next superpower"). Perceptions and capabilities are out of synch, which can warp both official policy and popular feelings.

While the global economic bubble inflated real estate and stock prices in China, the Chinese people have also experienced an inflated sense of self, especially with the success of the 2008 Olympics. This "propaganda bubble," which defines the twenty-first century as "China's century," generates a strong sense of entitlement among officials, intellectuals, and public opinion. According to this popular view, China's rise is not the outcome of a fortuitous combination of state policy and the global market; success is seen as China's "right," while China's rise is taken as "inevitable."

It is inevitable because Chinese power is figured as the telos of an "undeniable" historical process of fall and rise, humiliation and salvation: China fell from the heights of glorious civilization to the nadir of the Century of National Humiliation; the PRC's current success thus is seen as "the restoration" of China's natural status as a great power at the center of global politics. The goal of "the rejuvenation of China," according to strategist Yan Xuetong, is to "restore China's power status to the prosperity enjoyed during the prime of the Han, Tang and early Qing dynasties" when it was at the center of a hierarchical world order.[14]

This positive optimism also takes on negative forms; anything that gets in the way of China's inevitable rise is seen as an "obstacle" put there by foreigners whose nefarious schemes seek to "deny the right of a Chinese renaissance."[15] China's problems thus are not seen as the result of the growing pains of a country undergoing rapid economic and social change, but as the result of foreign conspiracies, which Beijing tells us "hurt the feelings of the Chinese people."

Complex international incidents thus are read according to a grand zero-sum East–West geopolitical logic. Foreign criticisms of Beijing's crackdown on Tibet in 2008, for example, convinced many Chinese scholars and policy-makers that the West "will use events like Tibet to smack down China and deny its standing on the international stage.... [Thus] the West is not ready to let China play a leading international role."[16] The fertile complexity of Chinese identity thus is reduced to stereotypes of East versus West.

There are many more examples of Chinese officials and scholars concluding that a particular criticism of a specific event involving China entails a general Western conspiracy to hold China down. This stems from the broader problem raised in the Preface: elites in China assume that as the PRC rises it will necessarily enjoy more friendship and respect. While China expects that its growing soft power will include greater control over how the world understands the PRC (as "the real China"), the opposite is more likely to ensue. As the experience of the United States shows, the more power a country has, the more scrutiny it faces. The more important a country is, the more commentary, including harsh and even unfounded criticism, it has to endure. Global power certainly can generate respect; but it also generates criticism simply because superpowers often become the target of the international media – as they should.

The Chinese government and many Chinese people continue to label foreign criticism as "disrespectful"; when foreigners "hurt the feelings of the Chinese people" they should expect negative consequences, we are

197

told. In his interview with *The Atlantic*, the head of China's sovereign wealth fund exemplifies these two mistaken assumptions: (1) that people are nice to superpowers, and (2) people will now be nice to China too: "You [Americans] are being treated nicely by everyone. . . . The simple truth today is that your economy is built on the global economy. And it's built on the support, the gratuitous support, of a lot of countries. So why don't you come over and . . . I won't say *kowtow*, but at least, *be nice* to the countries that lend you money."[17]

In early 2009, we are witnessing the burst of the propaganda bubble that described (and prescribed) China's inevitable rise. China is still certainly one of the top players in the global economics and politics. But its personalized notion of world politics, which is quick to take offense and demands a submissive style of respect, means that the early twenty-first century promises to be a rocky time.[18] As the more assertive nationalism exemplified by best-selling book *China is Unhappy* shows,[19] the problems of pessoptimist nation-alism are likely to become more acute as economic reversals lead to political protests that target China's leaders as traitors and foreigners as devils.

Ending the Century of National Humiliation

Is there a way out of pessoptimist nationalism? Or, to put it another way, how can China end its Century of National Humiliation, once and for all? As we have seen, people have tried to end this tragic century before. According to Chiang Kai-shek, it concluded in 1943 when Britain and the United States revised their unequal treaties with China: "It is our good fortune to witness this day the end of our humiliation and the beginning of a new stage in our struggle for independence and freedom."[20] For Mao Zedong, the Century of National Humiliation ended with the founding of the People's Republic in 1949: "Ours will no longer be a nation subject to insult and humiliation. We have stood up."[21] Jiang Zemin celebrated the eightieth anniversary of the founding of the Chinese Communist Party (CCP) in 2001 by declaring that China had "put an end to the history of national humiliation once and for all."[22] The return of Hong Kong (1997) and Macau (1999) are also seen as conclusions of the Century of National Humiliation, as is the 2008 Olympics (see Figure 7.1).[23]

But we have seen how "national humiliation" continues to be invoked in China to explain foreign relations, long after its century ended in the 1940s. In 2001, the collision of the Chinese fighter jet and the US surveillance plane was hailed as a new national humiliation; after Parisians protested against

Figure 7.1 "Cleanse the Century of National Humiliation," Guangzhou (1997). Courtesy of Yoshiko Nakano.

Olympic torch relay, France (and then the European Union) became the focus of pessoptimist nationalism. National humiliation thus has its own productive dynamic: new enemies generate new humiliations.

The most common way to resolve national humiliation, according to Chinese commentators, is *xuechi* – which literally means "cleanse humiliation" or "wipe away humiliation," but also means "revenge." A pessoptimist tension thus links *xuechi* as "avenging humiliation" in a militant zero-sum way and *xuechi* as "cleansing humiliation" in a cooperative positive-sum way. Chiang Kai-shek cleansed national humiliation in 1943 through a diplomatic agreement; but as his book *China's Destiny* shows, Chiang was still quite vengeful toward Britain and the United States. In 1949, Mao avenged national humiliation through the revolution's military victory; but he was more concerned with China's "liberation" than with revenge against Japan and the West.

The call for militant revenge against foreign devils was particularly strong in the early twentieth century. A declaration on the "Patriotic Map: National Humiliations and National Assets in One View" (1929) enjoins "all the millions of compatriots to unite . . . to seek revenge [*xuechi*] in the struggle for supremacy!"[24] A patriotic banner from World War II pictures a heroic Chinese soldier holding up a decapitated Japanese head as a trophy; its caption declares "To wipe out our humiliation with our enemy's blood"[25] (see figure 7.2).

Figure 7.2 "To wipe out our humiliation with our enemy's blood." Courtesy of William A. Callahan.

When national humiliation discourse returned in the 1990s, revenge and hatred also reappeared as major themes. A typical history textbook declares that its aim is "to help us understand that in China's modern history capitalist-imperialists invaded, tortured, and repressed the Chinese people. We should forever remember this tragic history of blood and tears, hatred and revenge."[26] Flashy pictorial histories likewise declare: "The Chinese nation's great humiliation and deep hatred can never be forgotten!"[27] Other books stress that China must prepare for war because national humiliation still continues in the present: "we want future generations to know that 'in times of peace, you must prepare for danger,' and remember that the motherland has endured galling shame and deep humiliation in the nation's history of blood and tears."[28]

For China's military, avenging humiliation remains a key goal. National Humiliation Day was revived in 2001 as National Defense Education Day. Its slogan in 2004 was "Do Not Forget the National Humiliation, Strengthen Our National Defense." A general took this opportunity to remind students that military strength needs to be a top priority: "While concentrating our efforts to develop the economy, we should at the same time strive to build a strong national defense and bolster the steel and iron Great Wall of the Republic. In this way, national defense education can thus enter all homes and families and embrace the entire society."[29] As we saw in Chapter 6, national humiliation discourse tends to militarize society and encourage a violent patriarchal form of national identity.

On the other hand, many of the national humiliation day commentaries from the early twentieth century are quite introspective. Rather than only blaming foreign imperialists, they argued that China also was responsible for its tragic situation; Chinese people first had to change themselves before they could expect international respect. A few writers in the twenty-first century are making similar points. For example, as we saw in Chapter 3, a recent newspaper commentary argued that Chinese must change how they understand Japan and World War II, shifting from seeking revenge to seeking justice.[30] This different approach to the past would have international as well as domestic implications: it could help transform Japan from China's eternal enemy into a friendly ally.

Jin Xide makes similar points in his discussion of how China can develop the proper "great power mentality":

> Regardless of what kind of psychological offensive the world may launch against us, we have nothing to be afraid of provided we are full of confidence and boast a strong national cohesiveness, at the

same time remaining open-minded. . . . We should adopt a neither-ob-sequious-nor-supercilious attitude toward international affairs. We should handle things calmly and keep our cool. This has profound significance for the rise of China.[31]

The goal here is not vengeance, but normality: China as a normal country in the family of nations.[32]

Since national humiliation is not merely political as we saw in Chapter 2, but economic, *xuechi* also has to address development issues. Long after its political victory united China in 1949, the CCP still needs to prove that it is better than previous "stupidly corrupt" regimes at achieving social and economic development.[33] National humiliation therefore can be cleansed through peaceful and cooperative economic development, as well as through militant revenge. Jiang Zemin thus celebrated China's economic achievements at the 15th Party Conference by declaring that living a "relatively comfortable life" also serves to cleanse national humiliation.[34] In other words, living well is the best revenge.

The more militant understanding of *xuechi* as revenge, though, rises to prominence whenever China has a crisis. In 1999, for example, outrage at America's bombing of China's Belgrade embassy was unanimous in the PRC. But there were mixed reactions about how to cleanse this new national humiliation. Legally, the bombing was a military strike on China's sovereign territory. Many popular demonstrations thus called for military vengeance, with signs that read *xixue guochi* – Avenge National Humiliation. Various semiofficial voices felt that this tragedy meant that China needed to "boost" its military strength: "China today is again facing self-imposed hardships in order to strengthen resolve to avenge a national humiliation. China should clearly realize that it is imperative to have powerful military strength."[35]

But China's leaders worked quickly to shift popular feelings away from demands for military revenge against the American hegemon. Jiang Zemin, for example, reinterpreted *xuechi* from vengeful violence to focus on economic development as the basis of Chinese power: "We must unswervingly take economic construction as the central task . . . This is the fundamental guarantee to the invincible position of socialist China."[36] The *People's Daily* rallied to this economic strategy as the proper "counterattack" on NATO and the United States: "As far as the 1.2 billion Chinese people are concerned, uniting under the leadership of the CCP, going all out to make the country strong, undergoing self-imposed hardships so as to strengthen resolve to wipe out national humiliation, and rejuvenating China – these represent the most effective counterattack."[37]

The call for economic development as *xuechi* also echoes Deng Xiaoping's guiding policy after the June 4th massacre: "bide our time, while building up capability" [*taoguang, yanghui*]. This important phrase is notoriously ambiguous, and its meaning remains a matter of debate among Chinese commentators. Most see it as part of Deng's "peace and development" strategy, which still guides policy in Beijing: China should lay low on the international stage in order to concentrate on building up its economic power. Yet the goal is still not clear. Is this a strategic policy that guides China's long-term cooperative development goals as part of international society? Or is it a short-term tactic that enables China to build its power as part of a long-term strategy that ultimately seeks revenge against rivals?

"Bide our time, while building up capability" here resonates with the classical idiom "sleeping on brushwood and tasting gall" [*woxin changdan*]. This phrase comes from an ancient story of humiliation and revenge: after a military defeat, King Goujian quietly suffered humiliation at the hands of his enemy, while working hard to increase the strength of his kingdom. But this is not simply a positive strategy of building up his kingdom's power; Goujian also used deception, trickery, lying, and bribery to weaken his rival economically, socially, militarily, and politically.

After ten years of building up economic strength, and another ten years of building up military strength, Goujian was finally able to attack and defeat his rival, and thus exact revenge. The lesson of this story, which is still popular in national humiliation texts, is clear: only when China endures humiliation and hard work will it be able to finally avenge its national humiliation.[38] As the English idiom puts it, revenge is a dish best served cold.

Many of the official and popular proclamations about the embassy bombing employ Goujian's style of *xuechi* as a tactic for revenge; as the *People's Daily* opined: Chinese must "go all-out to make the country strong, undergoing self-imposed hardships so as to strengthen resolve to wipe out [i.e., avenge] national humiliation." Jiang's response, which defused popular calls for revenge, could also mean that the time is not ripe – yet.

This mixture of contemporary and classical images shows how *xuechi* is a contingent concept with an unstable meaning. Even as some aim to cleanse humiliation through economic development, other calls for *xuechi* can at the same time point toward militant revenge once China has regained its international status. Beijing's foreign policy is often described as "pragmatic"; but we have to ask, pragmatic for what? What is the goal for China and its role in the world? While Beijing insists that China will peacefully develop as a responsible actor in international society, we have to recognize that other voices are promoting a more confrontational endgame.

The multicoded discourse of *xuechi* seems to be Beijing's pessoptimistic way of hedging against the possibility that China will be humiliated again. If this is the case, then the US and the EU also need to adopt a pessoptimistic strategy that simultaneously encourages cooperation with Beijing while preparing for China's revenge.

This is where hard and soft power come together. Through its growing international influence, Beijing is also exporting images of Japanese, Europeans, and Americans as foreign devils to audiences abroad; it thus sets a negative, soft-power agenda that can be coercive, as well as attractive. Taiwan remains a hot spot because it is widely seen in China as the key "lost territory" that Beijing needs to regain before it can be a truly great power. While Taiwanese public opinion overwhelmingly supports the status quo of separation, according to popular views in mainland China the United States is the main obstacle blocking the fulfillment of China's destiny; the United States thus is a target of popular indignation – and military planning.

Yet the main conclusion of this book is that we need to recognize that no one – not the party, the state, or the intellectual elite – can control pessoptimistic nationalism in China. The power of Western leaders is waning as well; in particular, the normative influence and soft power of the United States and the EU is largely negative in China. Even the "China model" is more negative than positive: it sees Russia, Europe, and the United States as models of what *not* to do.

But Western leaders and opinion-makers can better address China's global challenge if they see China for what it is, rather than what they want it to be. Much debate is polarized around diametrically opposing views of China; conservatives see China as a "communist threat" that needs to be contained, while liberals (especially in Europe) see it as a "socialist brother" that needs to be guided to democracy. But as this book has shown, China is neither communist nor socialist. It is best understood as a right-wing authoritarian party-state that gains legitimacy from a harsh form of capitalism and a primordial style of patriarchal nationalism. While the United States had some influence over right-wing dictatorships that were allies in the Cold War, it has little leverage over Beijing in the twenty-first century. It is unlikely that China's new middle class will push for political reform either; like in other countries undergoing political–economic transitions, they are benefiting from China's current hierarchical system – and actually fear any reforms that would spread political power to China's masses.

Because influence is limited, the United States and the EU should take a sober look at the issues they have with China – peace in the Taiwan straits, weapons nonproliferation, the environment, trade, human rights, democracy, and so on. Although diplomats and NGOs should certainly work in all these issue areas, it is important to recognize that it is not possible to succeed on all fronts. The United States and the EU need to prioritize these issues according to their values, formulate a set of objectives – and then stick to them.

In other words, we certainly need to understand how Chinese elites use national humiliation and Chinese civilization as a template to frame international politics. Yet, as we have seen, the "Century of National Humiliation" is less important as a set of facts than as a structure of feeling that guides a certain form of politics. So while we encourage China to move beyond national humiliation discourse, it is also necessary for Western commentators to avoid using the phrase "Century of National Humiliation," as many do, like it is a historical fact that can explain China's actions. We need to understand national humiliation, not because it is "true," but because understanding it is helpful for exiting this particular narrative of hostile international politics, which significantly narrows the possibilities for China and its relation with the world.

Deflating National Humiliation

Perhaps we are taking the vicious cycle of humiliation and revenge too seriously. Much like satirical treatments of national humiliation days in the 1920s to 1930s, Wang Shuo's novel *Please Don't Call Me Human* (1989) playfully satirizes the Century of National Humiliation's official themes and vocabulary.[39] The novel starts out with an international crisis; but the humiliation in question does not concern unequal treaties or foreign invasion. Rather, China has suffered a humiliating defeat to a Western wrestler in an international sports competition – a story that provides an interesting prelude for China's all-out quest for gold medals at the 2008 Olympics.

To cleanse this humiliation, a self-appointed "national" committee decides to recruit Yuanbao, a pedicab driver who comes from a martial arts family, to fight the Western wrestler. Although this seems far from China's foreign policy problems, we soon find out that the team's security dilemma is actually an identity dilemma. Yuanbao's intense training regime not only reshapes his body. Much like the continual recrafting of China's national image over the past decade, the new training regime reshapes Yuanbao's identity, remolding him again and again, from a pedicab driver into a martial artist, from a nativist Chinese into a Westernized man, into an intellectual, a TV actor, a ballet dancer, and a soldier. Rather than settle on a core Chinese identity, Wang describes how Yuanbao needs to try out various performances to see which one can best defeat his foreign enemy. Unfortunately for Yuanbao, before the big fight can take place the Western wrestler suddenly dies. Rather than mourning the death of a fellow athlete, the telegram back to the committee shows how Chinese see this untimely event as a victory to be celebrated: "FAT MAN LEARNED OF PLANS TO PIT HIM AGAINST A BILLION HOSTILE PEOPLE STOP . . . THIS MORNING COMMITTED SUICIDE . . . NATIONAL HUMILIATION AVENGED STOP HALLELUJAH STOP."[40]

But the committee can't be satisfied with this revenge. Since they created Yuanbao as a "commercial venture to beat the foreigners and make money,"[41] they can't stop here. Like in official national humiliation discourse, this farcical version sees cleansing in two areas. Although they have cleansed the humiliation of their sporting defeat, now they need to address economic development, which is transformed from national prosperity into their own semiprivate scam.

After looking for new opportunities, the committee finally decides that China's best chance for victory is in women's sports. Thus they reeducate Yuanbao one last time to train him in femininity – before his sex change operation. In the end, she wins an "Olympic" medal for China for "humiliation" in the International Endurance Competition by ripping off her own face. The one thing that Chinese excel at, Wang's novel tells us, is *enduring* national humiliation. Castration was not enough; China also needs to excel at losing face on the international stage.

Please Don't Call Me Human was originally published in late 1989, just as the patriotic education campaign was taking shape. Unfortunately, Wang's satirical critique did not gain much traction. Who knows, *Please Don't Call Me Human* might even have enabled national humiliation education.

Perhaps the best way to get out of the cycle of humiliation and revenge is to change the subject, and talk about something else. While it is common for Chinese leaders and scholars to see Hong Kong as "the epitome of the humiliation China suffered in modern history,"[42] Hong Kong-activist Feng Renzhao refuses to accept this burden: "We truly do not have to bear the cross of national humiliation created by an earlier generation. In fact, historically, neither the Nationalist Party nor the Communist regime has ever discharged its obligation to the Hong Kong people."[43] Ye Zhaoyan's novel *Nanjing 1937: A Love Story*, as we saw in Chapter 6, changes the subject from interstate hate to interpersonal love. At one point, even a character in *Please Don't Call Me Human* breaks out of China's pessoptimist hyperbole of national humiliation and national rejuvenation to declare, "National Salvation? Which Nation? Salvation from what? Our nation's doing just fine, thank you, and getting better."[44]

Beyond National Humiliation

I would like to end this book by looking beyond the tragedy of China's modern history to see how Chinese opinion-makers are thinking about their country's future – and the world's future. To get a better sense of where China is going, we need to look beyond the official orthodoxy promoted by the party-state to see what the rest of China is talking about.

Some Chinese intellectuals are thinking about how democracy and human rights can inspire China's next incarnation. In December 2008, 300 influential intellectuals signed a "Charter 08" that outlines a road for democratic change. While it is encouraging that this petition gathered seven thousand signatures in its first month, we should note that an anti-Japan petition gathered 22 million signatures over a similar time period in 2005.[45]

Rather than limit our understanding of public opinion to China's dissidents or its "indignant youth," it is necessary to see how other groups are increasingly guiding public feeling. Leading public intellectuals like philosopher Zhao Tingyang, filmmakers Zhang Yimou and Ang Lee, and artist Cai Guoqiang are interesting because their work gives a good sense of current debates over China's past, present, and future. Rather than promote a singular vision of China's trajectory, they offer a complex range of possibilities and opportunities that go beyond being simply pro- or anti-China. In this way, they provide different views of Chinese identity, China's future, and the world's future. These public intellectuals are important because they engage a broad audience, while also generating official interest. In addition to being popular in China, many are also hugely successful on the world stage; Lee and Cai actually live in New York, and are prominent examples of the global impact of Sinophone (i.e., Chinese-speaking) culture.

As we have seen throughout the book, such public intellectuals are important beyond their professional fields because their creative work reflects discussions taking place among a broad group of opinion-makers and policy-makers. Even though they are not the usual sources for ideas about China's grand strategy, such cultural figures are influential because their work focuses on the big issues of war and peace, world order, and world institutions, and civilization and barbarism. In other words, these public intellectuals elaborate on this book's main topic: what it means to be Chinese, and how China fits into the world.

Zhao, Zhang, Lee, and Cai are typical of a new breed of intellectual in China who do more than simply promote or criticize the party line. They actually operate in a social space that blurs the distinction between official and dissident work. So while engaging in utopian theory and experimental art, they also have ties to the party-state: Zhao works at China's largest think tank, while Zhang and Cai created the official ceremonies of Beijing's 2008 Olympics. Because they play for both state and non-state audiences, they are best understood as "nonofficial intellectuals."[46]

While some Chinese writers and artists hope to profit from official censorship by marketing their creative work to a foreign audience as "packaged dissent,"[47] these nonofficial intellectuals are important because they are playing for both a global audience and a Chinese audience. By using distinctly "Chinese" ideas to address universal questions they profitably engage in what could be called "patriotic cosmopolitanism." These nonofficial intellectuals thus can help us decode the meaning of Beijing's foreign policy narrative of "harmonious world," as well as its slogan for the 2008 Olympics: "One World, One Dream."

Zhao's Chinese-style Utopia

In the past decade, a group of theorists has emerged that looks beyond modernization – which they criticize as "Westernization" – to see how Chinese concepts are necessary for the twenty-first century, which they see as China's century. Zhao Tingyang's book *The Tianxia System: The Philosophy for the World Institution* (2005) is a prominent example of this trend.[48] Zhao works at the Philosophy Institute at the Chinese Academy of Social Sciences; but his goal is to reach a broad audience to tackle problems, not only in political philosophy, but also in public policy. And Zhao has been very successful, both in China and abroad: officials use similar concepts to talk about China's "harmonious world" foreign policy; *China Security* recently commissioned Zhao to write an essay for its special section "Debating China's Future."[49]

Chinese people need to discuss China's worldview, according to Zhao, because to be a true world power, China needs to excel not just in economic production, but in "knowledge production." To be a knowledge superpower, the PRC needs to stop importing ideas from the West, and exploit its own indigenous "resources of traditional thought." To be a world power, therefore, China must "create new world concepts and new world structures."[50]

To do this, Zhao looks to the traditional concept of Tianxia, which literally means All-under-Heaven, but also means Empire, the World, and even "China" itself. As the earlier chapters have shown, Tianxia is very popular as a policy concept among Chinese officials and intellectuals. Zhao aims to use Tianxia to solve global problems in a global way; thinking *through* the world in an "all-inclusive" way, rather than thinking *about* the world from an inferior national or individual perspective. He appeals to Chinese philosophy for answers, and bases his argument on a passage from Laozi's *Daode Jing*: "use the world [Tianxia] to examine the world [Tianxia]." World unity, for Zhao, leads to world peace and world harmony.[51] Tianxia thus is a utopia that sets up the analytical and institutional framework that is necessary for solving the world's problems.

The Tianxia system prescribes a global unity that is geographical, psychological, and institutional. Since there are no physical or ethical borders in Zhao's Tianxia, the main task in this all-inclusive system is to transform enemies into friends. Since it is a utopia, Zhao does not provide many details of his Tianxia system. However, he argues that imperial China's hierarchical tributary system, which employed the "civilization/barbarism distinction," is a good model for transforming enemies into friends not just in the past, but in the future. Zhao thus provides the Tianxia system as the solution to the world's problems; it is a new interpretation of Confucianism's hierarchical system that values order over freedom, ethics over law, and elite governance over democracy and human rights.

But Zhao's argument that Tianxia is all-inclusive seems to miss the point that not everyone wants to be included: some people want to stay different and outside. In Zhao's Tianxia system, however, any difference risks being seen as a barbarian enemy that needs to be converted into a civilized friend – otherwise you risk being branded as a terrorist, as we have seen in Beijing's recent dealings with Xinjiang and Tibet.

While Beijing says that China will peacefully rise as a responsible power within the present international system, the success of *The Tianxia System* shows that there is a thirst in China for "Chinese solutions" to world problems, especially when they promote a patriotic form of cosmopolitanism. While most notions of cosmopolitanism are suspicious of nations and states, Zhao's aspirational project looks to a China for a model of world order. As he says, Tianxia is a utopia with practical applications. In many ways, the Tianxia system is the theoretical and institutional plan for "One World, One Dream."[52]

Zhang and Lee's Cinematic World Orders

Zhang Yimou's *Hero* [*Yingxiong*] (2002) and Ang Lee's *Crouching Tiger, Hidden Dragon* [*Wo hu cang long*] (2000) also address the grand issue of world order in terms of the problems of war and peace, identity, and difference. These two films are exemplary cases because they were popular and critical successes both at home and abroad. *Hero* grossed $185 million worldwide, while *Crouching Tiger* grossed $215 million; each was nominated for numerous Academy Awards (*Crouching Tiger* won Best Foreign Film and two others).

These two films also are related in the sense that *Hero* was a reaction to *Crouching Tiger*: after Lee's success on the world market, Zhang was encouraged to direct a martial arts epic for the first time – his previous films were about village and family life. *Hero* then opened new doors for Zhang: after the success of the film he was appointed to organize the 2008 Olympics ceremonies because China's leaders felt that Zhang's cinematic aesthetic promoted their national aesthetic.

While Zhao's *Tianxia System* is about world order and world institutions, *Hero* is about war and peace, order and chaos, conquest and surrender. Again, the focus here is on the state and state power. The film's narrative is based on a historical story about the unification of China under the first emperor of the Qin dynasty in 221 BC. It is actually topical for international relations because the film is about the transition in China from the multi-centric Warring States period – which has been compared to the Westphalian world order – to the universal empire of Tianxia.[53] As we saw with Zhao, the goal for many Chinese intellectuals is to find a way back to China's ethical Tianxia system that was destroyed in the nineteen century by the Westphalian system's immoral violence.

Tianxia itself is mentioned throughout the film in ways that are strikingly similar to Zhao's *Tianxia System*: the film concludes with the assassin being transformed into a hero when he decides *not* to kill the emperor, which is much like Zhao's goal of transforming enemies into friends. The lesson is clear: the individual has to sacrifice himself and his kingdom for the greater good of the Tianxia empire, because as the hero reasons, "Only the King of Qin can stop the chaos by unifying Tianxia" through conquest. The individual person – and individual nations – thus have to sacrifice everything for the greater good of universal empire. Once again, unity defines security, and diversity is seen as a security threat: the goal is "One World, One Dream" rather than a multiplicity of worlds and dreams.[54]

Conversely, in Ang Lee's *Crouching Tiger, Hidden Dragon* civilization and barbarism collide when two characters, Jiaolong and Xiaohu, meet in China's northwest borderlands. This is not just an issue of identity politics: Central Asia's premier security forum, the Shanghai Cooperation Organization, was founded to control the flow of such "national minority" populations across international borders. The encounter is instructive because it states the traditional civilization/barbarian distinction seen in Zhao's *Tianxia System*, before blurring it through sex, love, and finally mutual respect.

This narrative starts with a journey from the civilized center of Beijing to the wilderness of China's Northwest borderlands. The trail literally leads the caravan of Chinese officials through a desert, prompting Jiaolong's mother to ask: "Will I ever see a tree again? Why couldn't your father get an appointment closer to civilization?" The uncivilized nature of the terrain is confirmed when the caravan is attacked by barbaric bandits, whose leader, Xiaohu, steals Jiaolong's jade comb – which is a symbol of civilization.

The second meeting, where Jiaolong seeks to recapture her civilized comb, leads to another confrontation with Xiaohu – which in time transforms from a violent struggle into an erotic encounter. Indeed, the standard categories of civilization and barbarism are undermined as Xiaohu shows that he is a (civilized) gentleman by looking away while Jiaolong bathes; Jiaolong's bad manners, on the other hand, show that she is quite barbaric. After wandering around the beautiful desert together, Jiaolong and Xiaohu come to love and respect not just each other, but also each others' way of life.

Still, Jiaolong decides to go back to her family and civilization, because neither Jiaolong nor Xiaohu could meaningfully live in the other's space. Xiaohu later pursues her to the center of civilization in Beijing, but she rejects him. They can only come together again far away from both the civilized center and the barbaric borderlands in the alternative space of a martial arts academy that sits atop an isolated mountain. The ending is ambiguous: it is not clear how and where the lovers can be together.

This fruitful ambiguity provides an interesting solution to China's enduring problem of civilization/barbarian relations, where the aim is not to convert barbarianism to civilization by turning enemies into friends, but to allow space to appreciate different ways of life. Rather than asserting a cultural or an institutional unity like *The Tianxia System* or *Hero*, *Crouching Tiger* helps us to question the limits of any singular understanding of political identity. Indeed, here Chinese identity is not located in the imperial capital of Beijing, but in various translocal centers of activity.

Lee's work thus challenges the idea that China's strength lies in unity, because violence is converted into respect by encouraging difference. Indeed, while *Crouching Tiger* was popular in Greater China and around the world, many critics in the PRC panned it for not being "Chinese enough" – especially since Lee is originally from Taiwan. However, if we widen the scope of analysis to include the global Sinophone community, can't we take *Crouching Tiger* as an alternative way of understanding China's search for respect in the world? Doesn't it provide an alternative solution that encourages difference and love, rather than unity and hate?

Cai's Explosive Art

Our last public intellectual, Cai Guoqiang, is celebrated in both the Chinese and the global art scenes because his "creative transgressions and cultural provocations have literally exploded the accepted parameters of art-making in our time."[55] Indeed, Cai's work has geopolitical significance: both Chinese and Western critics draw a parallel between the Rise of China and the rise of Cai.[56] Cai, thus, is a key example of a nonofficial intellectual who is outside China's intellectual bureaucracy, and still occasionally works with

Figure 7.3 "Project to Extend the Great Wall" (1993). Courtesy of Cai Guo-Qiang.

the Chinese state: while his solo exhibit was showing in New York at the Guggenheim Museum in early 2008, Cai was busy creating visual effects for Beijing's Olympic ceremonies.

Cai's explosive impact is not just metaphorical: he is famous for using gunpowder creatively. In his early career in China, he experimented with gunpowder in painting to explode the conventions of traditional literati art. More recently, Cai has tried to get out of the art gallery by experimenting with fireworks in public events at places like China's Great Wall (see Figure 7.3). Since he came to the United States in 1995, Cai has created massive explosion events that evoke joy and wonder for huge audiences, including a pyrotechnic tornado on the Potomac River in Washington DC for the Kennedy Center's "Festival of China" in 2005. Many of these "explosion projects" are part of political events in China as well: in October 2001, Cai's official fireworks display celebrated China's hosting of the Asia-Pacific Economic Cooperation (APEC) meeting in Shanghai.

Since September 11, Cai has acted as both a showman and a shaman – the Chinese word for fireworks literally means "fire medicine." By directly deploying fireworks in a pyrotechnics of hope and mourning, Cai worked to heal the wounds of terrorist attacks in *Transient Rainbow* (2002) for New York and *Black Rainbow* (2005) for Spain after the Madrid train bombing. Cai's art thus is creative destruction, where fireworks perform a sort of nonviolent violence. The explosion – complete with fantastic light and sound – does not destroy its target; the fireworks actually enhance its value.

So like Zhao whose Tianxia system challenges Eurocentric international relations theory, Cai's work challenges the art system by adding a critical non-Western eye to the global art world. Cai's combination of beauty and danger mesmerizes critics who declare that he uses explosive techniques "to suspend, provoke, and challenge our habits of the mind," and thus open up space for the "contemplation of alternative, co-existing, or multiple realities."[57]

But just what is the target of Cai's criticism? While Cai's art opens up space for different interpretations, there are two main ways of understanding its message. In the West, Cai's work is praised for providing a different view that challenges the "stereotypes" that we use to understand China and Asia. He plays with "China threat" alarmism, for example, in works like *Cry Dragon/Cry Wolf: The Ark of Genghis Khan* (1996), which evokes European memories of Mongol conquest in the past, and Western worries about Japan's "economic invasion" more recently.[58]

While Cai is an active part of a multicultural art scene in the West that values outsiders' critique, in China his art is seen as patriotic in familiar

Figure 7.4 "The Century with Mushroom Clouds" (1996). Courtesy of Cai Guo–Qiang and Hiro Ihara.

ways: Cai shows how a Chinese intellectual can succeed on the world stage by criticizing the West.

Cai's first major work in America, *The Century with Mushroom Clouds* (1996), is telling (see Figure 7.4). As a way to explore the United States after he arrived in 1995, Cai traveled around the country detonating home-made, hand-held explosives at iconic sites, including a nuclear test site in Nevada and by lower Manhattan where a "small, almost delicate 'mushroom cloud'" is framed by the Statue of Liberty and the Twin Towers.[59]

When asked to choose his favorite book soon after September 11, he picked *Unrestricted Warfare: War and Strategy in the Globalization Era*. Although art historians might not be familiar with this book, it is well known among international relations specialists as a call by a pair of People's Liberation Army colonels for Beijing to use asymmetrical warfare, including terrorism, to attack the United States.[60] The centerpiece of Cai's solo exhibit at the Guggenheim, "Inopportune: Stage One," continues this theme of blowing up Americans. Cai simulates a car bomb explosion to ask "his viewers to appreciate some kind of redeeming beauty in terrorist attacks and warfare."[61] While cultural critic Wang Hui tells us that Cai's work deploys "art as a substitute for weapons,"[62] Cai's creative destruction not only transforms physical violence into art – it also risks celebrating the transformation of art into physical violence.

We saw this on September 11, which was not only planned to blow up the Twin Towers; it was designed as a "spectacular" for a global audience – which it was, and continues to be. The beginning of the Iraq war was similarly designed in aesthetic terms to "Shock and Awe" not only Baghdadis, but a global news-watching audience. Indeed, "Shock and Awe" is the title of an art journal's recent interview with Cai.[63]

While he blows up Western icons, Cai embellishes China's sacred space. His explosive project at the Great Wall does not destroy this nationalist symbol; it actually extends the Great Wall by another ten kilometers. In

Figure 7.5 Cai's New York exhibit commemorated on a Chinese stamp. Courtesy of William A. Callahan.

2008, this project was celebrated again when Beijing issued a special stamp of the Great Wall that is embellished with gunpowder art to recognize Cai's success in America (see Figure 7.5).

According to Wang Hui, Cai's public art at APEC (2001) ushered in a new era by "display[ing] the dynamism of China."[64] Cai thus was invited to direct the visual effects of the 2008 Olympics because his art is "palatable to this group of leaders and the way they want their national project to be seen."[65] A Chinese art critic puts it simply: Cai is "very patriotic, and it shows in the Olympics work."[66] As the world saw in August 2008, Cai's fireworks show at the Olympics was a celebration of China's state power, just as his APEC fireworks were seen as an "event symbolizing a trans-formed global order."[67]

More to the point, when Cai faces political criticism from China, he backs off: *Rent Collection Courtyard* (1999), which reinterpreted a famous Cultural Revolution-era sculpture at the Venice Biennale, generated fero-cious controversy in China. But it wasn't included when Cai's Guggenheim exhibit moved to the National Museum in Beijing after the Olympics because, as Cai explains, it "is still forbidden in China."[68]

Recent Chinese experimental art shares Cai's "fascination with various kinds of destruction." But while others use their explosive art to engage in a critique of China's domestic problems,[69] much of Cai's art is seen as a celebration of the rise of China on the world stage. Rather than exploring the pleasures and pains of a common humanity, or criticizing power in both China and the West, Cai sees identity (and security) in terms of difference.[70] The meaning of Cai's art thus is multilayered: while it engages in a radical critique of Western values and the global art system, it celebrates Chinese icons. He is cosmopolitan as the voice of China on the world scene; in the PRC, however, he is quite patriotic. Cai is thus a prime example of patriotic cosmopolitanism.

Cai's work is quite stunning, and is much more than simply martial or militaristic art. Yet, regardless of our aesthetic judgments about his work we need to appreciate how the violence of Cai's art is going in the opposite direction from Beijing's official policy that celebrates China's peaceful rise as a responsible stakeholder. Unlike Zhao and Zhang, Cai is not directly talking about the Chinese state or foreign policy. But he is part of a national aesthetic that takes shape not only through cultural debates, but also in national and global institutions.

Does Cai's aesthetic of creative destruction provide us with a different under-standing of China and its relation to the world? Does a Chinese-style harmo-nious world order actually require both peaceful rises and explosive falls?

Identity and Security in China

When we hear slogans like "One World, One Dream," it is necessary to ask which world, and which dream. We have to be careful, of course, not to over-interpret the meaning of a particular work, or the influence of a particular public intellectual. That is why it is important to explore a broad group of nonofficial intellectuals, while highlighting the pivotal work of China's top thinkers, directors, and artists.

Certain themes definitely emerge in this sampling of academic, popular, and artistic culture – and they go in different directions from how China's Foreign Ministry talks about China and the world. These works generally focus on identity as difference in a zero-sum game that distinguishes civilization from barbarism, and China from the rest of the world. They thus redeploy stark cold war-style divisions between East and West, not just in terms of policy (which is changeable), but in terms of civilization (which is enduring). Their cosmopolitanism doesn't appeal to global themes of common humanity so much as to patriotic themes that envision China as the model of world order. These nonofficial intellectuals also show a fascination with power as the exercise of control through violence, where unity is the goal, and diversity is seen as a security threat. Living abroad does not necessarily temper these views: as we saw, Cai's work celebrates violence and conflict even more than the others.

While it is common to understand China's recent outbursts of aggressive nationalism by looking to the activities of China's "indignant youth," these nonofficial intellectuals are all middle-aged. They are a part of China's elite generation that entered university when schools reopened after the Cultural Revolution in 1978. These opinion-makers are noteworthy because their group will supply the next generation of China's leaders. Their thoughts and dreams are important because we now need to look beyond the party-state to see what semi-independent nonofficial intellectuals have to say, especially when their unorthodox ideas provide an alternative view of China's future – and the world's future.

Such examples confirm that the anger and sense of injustice seen in China goes beyond youthful exuberance. It is necessary therefore to look beyond official texts and violent outbursts to carefully analyze and understand this enduring anger, which is seen as righteous rage in China.

Ang Lee's film is interesting because it is the exception to the rule of state violence found in the work of the other public intellectuals: it converts enmity into amity through personal engagement, rather than through a grand explosion or a universal institution. Rather than focusing on national hate and humiliation, Lee's characters find happiness through mutual love and respect.

As we saw in Chapter 1, the Chinese government employed the Beijing Olympics to make foreigners "love China, desire China...and see that Chinese people are happy."[71] Yet, it is fascinating that hope appears in *Crouching Tiger* only when we leave the imperial capital and repair to a remote mountain. This suggests that students of Chinese foreign policy also need to get out of Beijing more, to explore what the rest of China is thinking and feeling.

Notes

Chapter 1

1. See Liu Hongbo in "Zhang Yimou and State Aesthetics," *China Digital Times*, August 6, 2008; also see Wu Hung, "Ruins, Fragmentation, and the Chinese Modern/Postmodern," in *Inside Out: New Chinese Art*, edited by Gao Minglu (San Francisco: San Francisco Museum of Modern Art, 1998), 59–67.
2. Joseph Kahn, "Chinese Unveil Mammoth Arts Center," *International Herald Tribune*, December 24, 2007.
3. See Chris Alden, *China in Africa* (London: Zed Press, 2007).
4. David Leheny, "A Narrow Place to Cross Swords: 'Soft Power' and the Politics of Japanese Popular Culture in East Asia," in *Beyond Japan: The Dynamics of East Asian Regionalism*, edited by Peter J. Katzenstein and Takashi Shiraishi (Ithaca, NY: Cornell University Press, 2006), 223.
5. Zhao Tingyang, *Tianxia tixi: Shijie zhidu zhexue daolun* [The Tianxia system: A Philosophy for the World Institution] (Nanjing: Jiangsu jiaoyu chubanshe, 2005), 2, 3.
6. See Martin Fletcher, "The Chinese Dream has replaced America's," *The Times* (London), 22 August 2008; Joshua Cooper Ramo, *Brand China* (London: Foreign Policy Centre, 2007).
7. Cited in Ian Johnson, "World Seeks a Label to Define the Beijing Games," *Wall Street Journal*, August 8, 2008.
8. "Interview with Zhang Jigang, Deputy Director of the Beijing Olympics Opening Ceremony," *Liberation Daily*, 1 August 2008, translated for *China Digital Times*, August 6, 2008.
9. Jim Yardley, "China's Leaders Try to Impress and Reassure World," *New York Times*, August 9, 2008.
10. Chen Qigang, interview on China Central Television, August 11, 2008, translated on *China Digital Times*.
11. Zhang Ying and Xia Zhen, "Zhang Yimou liangwan yan xishu kaimushi muhou gushi" [Zhang Yimou's 20,000 word statement tells inside story of the opening ceremony], *Nanfang zhoumo*, 14 August 2008, translated as Zhang Yimou, "The Way Art Works" and "Only China Can Produce This," *China Digital Times*, August 17, 2008.
12. Cited in Yardley, "China's Leaders Try to Impress."

13. Cited in Jim Yardley, "China's Leaders Are Resilient in Face of Change," *New York Times*, August 6, 2008.
14. Zhang and Xia, "Zhang Yimou's 20,000 word statement."
15. Ye Hailin, "Games Proves Validity of the China Model," *China Daily*, September 23, 2008; for a more aggressive anti-Western argument see the Chinese version: Ye Hailin, "Beijing Aoyun chongji Xifang jiazhi zixin" [Beijing Olympics are a blow to self-confidence of Western values], *Guoji xianqu daobao*, August 28, 2008.
16. Jing Zhang, "A View from Beijing: 'Proud to be Chinese,'" *New York Times*, August 8, 2008.
17. Wang Huaiqi, *Guochi jinian ticao* [National humiliation gymnastics] (Shanghai: Zhongguo tixue chubanshe, 1929).
18. Xu Guoqi, *Olympic Dreams: China and Sports, 1895–2008* (Cambridge, MA: Harvard University Press, 2008), 1–29, 225–52; Susan Brownell, *Beijing's Games: What the Olympics Mean to China* (Boulder, CO: Rowman & Littlefield, 2008), 19.
19. "Interview with Zhang Jigang," *China Digital Times*.
20. Jin Xide, "China Must Adopt a Great-power Mentality, Make Psychological Change Part of its Modernization," *Beijing huanqiu shibao* (September 12, 2002), translated in FBIS CPP20020927000153.
21. "The Chinese Celebrate Their Roaring Economy, as They Struggle with Its Costs: Near Universal Optimism about Beijing Olympics," Pew Global Attitudes Project (July 22, 2008), 1.
22. Xie Chuanjiao, "China's Suicide Rate Among World's Highest," *China Daily*, September 11, 2007.
23. Song Xiaojun et al., *Zhongguo bu gaoxing: Da shidai, da mubiao, ji women de neiyou waihuan* [China is Unhappy: The Great Era, Grand Objective, and Our Domestic Troubles and Foreign Calamities], (Nanjing: Jiangsu renmin chubanshe, 2009). Also see Austin Ramzy, "A New Book Reveals Why China Is Unhappy," *Time*, March 20, 2009.
24. "Interview with Xu Guoqi—Author of Olympic Dreams," Play the Game for Open Journalism Web site, http://playthegameforopenjournalism.org/china-and-the-olympics/olympic-dreams-xu-guoqi.html.
25. See David Shambaugh, "International Schizophrenia," *China Security* 4:2 (2008): 16–17; David Shambaugh, "China's Competing Nationalisms," *International Herald Tribune*, 5 May 2008.
26. The phrase "structure of feeling" comes from Raymond Williams's many writings.
27. See Evan Osnos, "Angry Youth: The New Generation's Neocon Nationalists," *The New Yorker* (July 28, 2008).
28. Yong Deng, *China's Struggle for Status: The Realignment of International Relations* (New York: Cambridge University Press, 2008), 8.

29. See Jia Qingguo, "Disrespect and Distrust: the External Origins of Contemporary Chinese Nationalism," *Journal of Contemporary China* 14:42 (2005): 11–22.
30. Bates Gill, *Rising Star: China's New Security Diplomacy* (Washington, DC: Brookings Institution Press, 2007); Evan S. Medieros and M. Taylor Fravel "China's New Diplomacy," *Foreign Affairs* 82:6 (2003): 23–35.
31. Gill, *Rising Star*, 7; Deng, *China's Struggle for Status*, 291; Medieros and Fravel "China's New Diplomacy"; also see Jim Yardley, "After Glow of Games, What Next for China?," *New York Times*, August 25, 2008.
32. Allen Carlson, *Unifying China, Integrating with the World: Securing Chinese Sovereignty in the Reform Era* (Stanford, CA: Stanford University Press, 2005); Alastair Iain Johnston, *Social States: China in International Institutions, 1980–2000* (Princeton: Princeton University Press, 2008); Gill, *Rising Star*.
33. Johnston, *Social States*, 210–12.
34. Susan Shirk, *China: Fragile Superpower* (New York: Oxford University Press, 2007); David M. Lampton, *The Three Faces of Chinese Power: Might, Money, and Minds* (Berkeley, CA: University of California Press, 2008).
35. See Suisheng Zhao, *A Nation-State by Construction: Dynamics of Modern Chinese Nationalism* (Stanford, CA: Stanford University Press, 2004); Peter Hays Gries, *China's New Nationalism: Pride, Politics and Diplomacy* (Berkeley, CA: University of California Press, 2004).
36. Robert Zoellick, "Whither China: From Membership to Responsibility?," Remarks to National Committee on U.S.–China Relations, New York City, September 21, 2005.
37. Qin Yaqing, "Guoji guanxi lilun Zhongguo pai shengcheng de keneng he biran" [The Chinese School of International Relations Theory: Possibility and Necessity], *Shijie jingji yu zhengzhi* no. 3 (2006): 7–13, on 13; also see Jin, "China Must Adopt a Great-power Mentality."
38. Cheng Shiwei et al., eds., *Wuwang guochi* [Never forget national humiliation] (Changchun: Jilin wenshi chubanshe, 1998), 1.
39. See He Yu, *Bainian guochi jiyao* [A Summary of the Century of National Humiliation] (Beijing: Beijing Yanshan Press, 1997).
40. Zhongguo geming bowuguan [Revolutionary History Museum of China] ed., *Zhongguo: Cong quru zouxiang huihuang, 1840–1997*, vol. 1 [China: From Humiliation to Glory, 1840–1997, vol. 1] (Beijing: Chinese National Photography Press, 1997); Guo Qifu, ed., *Wuwang guochi: Zaichuang huihaung* [Never Forget National Humiliation: Recreating the Glory] (Wuhan: Wuhan daxue chubanshe, 1996).
41. Robert Kagan and William Kristol, "A National Humiliation," *The Weekly Standard Magazine* 6:30 (16–23 April 2001): Web edition. For an analysis of China's politics of apology, see Gries, *China's New Nationalism*, 86–115.
42. Dominique Moïsi, "The Clash of Emotions," *Foreign Affairs* (January/February 2007): 8–12; Gerrit W. Gong, "The Beginning of History: Remembering

and Forgetting as Strategic Issues," *The Washington Quarterly* (Spring 2001): 45–57.

43. See, for example, Sheila Miyoshi Jager, "On the Uses of Cultural Knowledge," Strategic Studies Institute (Carlisle Barracks, PA: US Army War College, November 2007).

44. See, for example, Robert E. Harkavy, "Defeat, National Humiliation, and the Revenge Motif in International Politics," *International Politics* 37 (2000): 345–68; Edward Weisband, "Discursive Multilateralism: Global Benchmarks, Shame, and Learning in the ILO Labor Standards Monitoring Regime," *International Studies Quarterly* 44 (2000): 643–66; Evelin Lindner, *Making Enemies: Humiliation and International Conflict* (Westport, CT: Praeger, 2006).

45. *Liji Jijie* [The Book of Rites, Critical Edition] (Beijing: Zhonghua Shuju, 1998), 1262.

46. Mao Zedong, *Selected Works of Mao Zedong*, Vol. 5 (Beijing: Foreign Languages Press, 1977), 17.

47. *Jindai Zhongguo bainian guochi ditu* [Maps of the Century of National Humiliation of Modern China] (Beijing: Renmin chubanshe, 1997/2005).

48. Michael Yahuda, "Hong Kong: A New Beginning for China?," in *Hong Kong's Transitions, 1842–1997*, edited by Judith M. Brown and Rosemary Foot (London: Macmillan, 1997), 209; Gong, "The Beginning of History," 47; Orville Schell, "Prisoner of its Past," *Salon* (8 June 1999): www.Salon.com.

49. Chiang Kai-shek, *China's Destiny* (New York: Roy Publishers, 1947 [Chinese edn., 1943]), 44–75; also see Liu Zhen, *Guochi shigang* [Outline History of National Humiliation] (Taibei: Zhengzhong Press, 1974).

50. Hou Hongjian, 'Guoxue, guochi, laoku sanda zhuyi biaolie' [Three Principles: National studies, National humiliation and Hard work], *Jiaoyu zazhi* 7:7 (1915): 21–4.

51. See Zhao, *The Tianxia System*; Chen Liankai, "Zhongguo, huayi, fanhan, zhonghua, zhonghua minzu: Yige neizai lianxi fazhan bei renshi de guocheng [One method for recognizing the developmental relations between the terms Zhongguo, Huayi, Fanhan, Zhonghua, Zhonghua minzu], in *Zhonghua minzu de duoyuan yiti geju* [The pluralistic unity structure of Chinese nationalism], edited by Fei Xiaotong (Beijing: Zhongyang minzu xueyuan chubanshe, 1989), 72–113; Ma Rong, "Lijie minzu guanxi de xinselu: xiaoshu zuqun wenti de 'qu zhengzhihua'" [New perspectives on nationalities relations: the "depoliticization" of the ethnic minority question], *Beijing daxue xuebao* 41:6 (Nov. 2004): 122–33; David C. Kang, *China Rising: Peace, Power and Order in East Asia* (New York: Columbia University Press, 2007).

52. Li Shaojun, *Guoji zhengzhixue gailun* [An Introduction to International Politics] (Shanghai: Renmin chubanshe, 2002), 526–34; Yan Xuetong "The Rise of China in Chinese Eyes," *Journal of Contemporary China* 10:26 (2001): 33–40; Zhang Tiejun, "Chinese Strategic Culture: Traditional and Present Features," *Comparative*

Strategy 21:2 (2002): 73–80; Liu Zhiguang, *Dongfang heping zhuyi: yuanqi, liubian ji zouxiang* [Oriental Pacificism: Its Origins, Development and Future] (Changsha, Hunan: Hunan chubanshe, 1992).

53. Zheng Bijian, "China's 'Peaceful Rise' to Great-Power Status," *Foreign Affairs* (Sept/Oct 2005), 22.

54. "Anniversary highlights China's peaceful growth," *China Daily*, 12 July 2005; also see Sheldon H. Lu, *Chinese Modernity and Global Biopolitics: Studies in Literature and Visual Culture* (Honolulu: University of Hawai'i Press, 2007), 191.

55. See Geoffrey Wade, "The Zheng He Voyages," *Journal of the Malaysian Branch of the Royal Society of Asiatic Studies* 78:1 (2005): 37–58 on 44–51.

56. See Kirk W. Larsen, *Tradition, Treaties, and Trade: Qing Imperialism and Choson Korea, 1850–1910* (Cambridge, MA: Harvard University Press), 1–22.

57. See James Holmes and Toshi Yoshihara, "Soft Power Goes to Sea," *The American Interest* (March–April 2008): 69–70.

58. See Zhao, *The Tianxia System*; Ma, "New Perspectives on Nationalities Relations."

59. William A. Callahan, *Contingent States: Greater China and Transnational Relations* (Minneapolis: University of Minnesota Press, 2004), 25–55.

60. See, for example, Emma Jinhua Teng, *Taiwan's Imagined Geography: Chinese Colonial Travel Writing and Pictures, 1683–1895* (Cambridge, MA: Harvard University Press, 2004), 11–13; Li Dalong, "Chuantong Yi-Xia guanyu Zhongguo jiangyu de xingcheng" [The Traditional Barbarian–Civilization View and the Formation of China's Territory], *Zhongguo bianjiang shidi yanjiu* 14:1 (2004): 5, 11–12.

61. See William Connolly, *Identity\Difference: Democratic Negotiations of Political Paradox* (Ithaca, NY: Cornell University Press, 1991), 36–63; R. B. J. Walker, *Inside/Outside: International Relations as Political Theory* (Cambridge: Cambridge University Press, 1993); Tzvetan Todorov, *The Conquest of America: The Question of the Other* (New York: Harper Collins, 1984).

62. Jiang Tingfu, *Zhongguo jindai shi* [Modern History of China] (Beijing: Tuanjie chubanshe, 2005), 1.

63. Arthur Waldron, *The Great Wall of China: From History to Myth* (Cambridge: Cambridge University Press, 1990), 190.

64. See Chen, "One Method"; Lien-sheng Yang, "Historical Notes on the Chinese World Order," in *The Chinese World Order: Traditional China's Foreign Relations*, edited by John King Fairbank (Cambridge, MA: Harvard University Press, 1968), 20–33; Li, "The Traditional Barbarian–Civilization View and the Formation of China's Territory."

65. Yang, "Historical Notes," 20.

66. Chen, "One Method," 82.

67. *Zuozhuan* cited in Yang, "Historical Notes," 25.

68. See, for example, Lydia H. Liu, *The Clash of Empires: The Invention of China in Modern World Making* (Cambridge, MA: Harvard University Press, 2004).

69. Cited in Chen, "One Method," 80.
70. Cited in Leibold, *Reconfiguring Chinese Nationalism*, 30.
71. *Fu Qing Mie Yang*. A picture of a Boxer holding this banner was part of "The Rise of Modern China: A Century of Self-Determination" exhibit, Hong Kong Museum of History, October 1999.
72. Jane Geaney, "Shame and Sensory Excess in Chinese Thought," presented at the Eighth East-West Philosophers' Conference (January 2000), Honolulu.
73. Chen, "One Method," 82.
74. See "A Significant and Urgent Strategic Task—First Commentary for Establishing Socialist View of Honor and Shame," *Renmin Ribao*, 21 March 2006, trans. in FBIS 200603211477.1_6835016a6683d71f.
75. Cited in Keith Bradsher, "Feeling the Heat, Not Breathing Fire," *New York Times*, August, 2007.
76. For a critique of such culturalist analysis of the exotic Orient see Edward Said, *Orientalism*, (New York: Vintage Books, 1979).
77. Walter Benjamin, "Theses on the Philosophy of History, VII," in *Illuminations: Essays and Reflections* (New York: Schocken Books, 1968), 256–7.
78. See Daniel Bertrand Monk, *An Aesthetic Occupation: The Immediacy of Architecture and the Palestine Conflict* (Durham, NC: Duke Press, 2002).
79. See Elizabeth J. Perry, "Challenging the Mandate of Heaven: Popular Protest in Modern China," *Critical Asian Studies* 33:2 (2001), 175, 178; Carma Hinton, Geremie R. Barmé, and Richard Gordon, producers and directors, *Morning Sun* [Bajiudian zhong de taiyang] (Brookline, MA: Longbow Group, 2005).
80. See William A. Callahan, "War, Shame, and Time: Pastoral Identity Politics in England and America," *International Studies Quarterly* 50:2 (2006): 395–419.
81. Irvine Welsh, *Trainspotting* (New York: Norton, 1996), 78.
82. Geremie R. Barmé, *In the Red: On Contemporary Chinese Culture* (New York: Columbia University Press, 1999), 90.
83. Cited in Keith Bradsher, "Feeling the Heat, Not Breathing Fire," *New York Times*, August 3, 2007. The *Times* reports that this blog was soon blocked. Also see James Fallows, "The $1.4 Trillion Question," *The Atlantic Monthly* (January–February 2008).
84. On the political impact of crises on Chinese politics see Elizabeth J. Perry, "Studying Chinese Politics: Farewell to Revolution?," *The China Journal* no. 57 (Jan 2007): 11; Yan Xuetong, "The Rise of China and its Power Status," *Chinese Journal of International Politics* 1:1 (2006): 5–33.
85. Shirk, *China: Fragile Superpower*.
86. Jiang Zemin quoted in Anne-Marie Brady, *Marketing Dictatorship: Propaganda and Thought Work in Contemporary China*, (New York: Rowman & Littlefield Publishers, Inc., 2008), 50.
87. Peter Hessler, "Wheels of Fortune," *The New Yorker* (November 26, 2007): 104–14 (on 107–8).

88. See "Full Text of Jiang's Speech at CPC Anniversary Gathering (IV)," *People's Daily* (July 1, 2001).

Chapter 2

1. Deng Xiaoping, "Address to the Officers at the Rank of General and Above in the Command of the Troops Enforcing Martial Law in Beijing, June 9, 1989," http://english.peopledaily.com.cn/dengxp/vol3/text/c1990.html.
2. Deng Xiaoping, "We Are Confident That We Can Handle China's Affairs Well (September 16, 1989)," http://english.peopledaily.com.cn/DengXP/Vol3/text/d1040.html.
3. David Shambaugh, "China's Propaganda System: Institutions, Processes and Efficacy," *The China Journal* 57 (January 2007): 25–58 on 27.
4. Anne-Marie Brady, *Marketing Dictatorship: Propaganda and Thought Work in Contemporary China* (New York: Rowman & Littlefield Publishers, 2008), 30.
5. Brady, *Marketing Dictatorship*, 50.
6. Michael Schoenhals, *Doing Things with Words in Chinese Politics: Five Studies* (Berkeley, CA: Institute of East Asian Studies, University of California, 1992), 3.
7. See Bates Gill, *Rising Star: China's New Security Diplomacy* (Washington, DC: Brookings Institution Press, 2007), 4–5.
8. See Zheng Bijian, *China's Peaceful Rise* (Washington, DC: Brookings Institution Press, 2005).
9. See, for example, Ling Dequan, "'Heping jueqi' gangju muzhang" [Explaining "Peaceful Rise"], *Liaowang* 5 (February 2, 2004), 6.
10. "Interview with Zhang Jigang, Deputy Director of the Beijing Olympics Opening Ceremony," *Liberation Daily*, August 1, 2008, translated for *China Digitial Times*, August 6, 2008.
11. See Brady, *Marketing Dictatorship*, 9–33.
12. Shambaugh, "China's Propaganda System," 30.
13. See Jonathan Unger, ed., *Using the Past to Serve the Present: Historiography and Politics in Contemporary China* (Armonk, NY: M. E. Sharpe, 1993); Geremie R. Barmé, "A Year of Some Significance," *China Digital Times*, April 20, 2006.
14. "Jiang Zemin tongzhi zhixin Li Tieying, He Dongchang tongzhi, qiangdiao jinxing Zhongguo jinxiandaishi he guoqing jiaoyu" [General Secretary Jiang Zemin's Letter to Li Tieying and He Dongchang stresses to conduct education on Chinese modern and contemporary history and national conditions], *Renmin ribao* (March 9, 1991); "Zhongxiaoxue jiaqiang Zhongguo jindai, xiandaishi ji guoqing jiaoyu de zongti gangyao (chugao) de tongzhi" [General outline on strengthening Chinese modern and contemporary history and national conditions in primary and secondary education], *National regulations and documents* (August 29, 1991).
15. See Hou Hongjian, "Guoxue, guochi, laoku sanda zhuyi biaolie" [Three Principles: National studies, National humiliation and Hard work], *Jiaoyu zazhi* 7:7

(1915): 21–4; Lü Simian, *Guochi xiaoshi* [A short history of national humiliation] (Shanghai: Zhonghua shuju, 1929); Jiang Gongsheng, *Guochi shi* [History of national humiliation] (Shanghai: Xinhua shuju, 1927); Cao Zengmei and Huang Xiaoxian, eds. *Xinbian Guochi Xiaoshi* [A short history of national humiliation: new edition] (Shanghai: Commercial Press, 1932). Also see Zhang Mianhong, "Minguo qianqi xuexiao guochi jiaoyu de xingqi yu fazhan [The appearance and development of national humiliation education in schools in the early Republican period]," *Guangxi shehui kexue* 12 (2006):192–4.

16. Lü Simian, *Baihua benguo shi: zixiu shiyong* [A vernacular history of China, revised] (Shanghai: Shangwu, 1926); Lü, *A Short History of National Humiliation*.

17. Chiang Kai-shek, *China's Fate* (New York: Roy Publishers, 1947 [Chinese edn., 1943]).

18. See, for example, Guangdong Provincial Culture And Education Office, *Aiguo zhuyi jiaoyu cankao ziliao* [Patriotic education reference materials] (Guangzhou: Huanan renmin chubanshe, 1951); Yu Teli et al., *Lun aiguo zhuyi jiaoyu* [On patriotic education] (Beijing: Qunzhong shudian, 1951).

19. "Aiguo zhuyi jiaoyu shishi gangyao" [Outline for Implementing Patriotic Education], *Renmin ribao* (September 6, 1994), 3; Suisheng Zhao, *A Nation-State by Construction: Dynamics of Modern Chinese Nationalism* (Stanford, CA: Stanford University Press, 2004), 219.

20. Wei Pizhi, Qu Qingrong, Xiang Wancheng, eds., *Aiguo zhuyi jiaoyu shiyong dadian* [Practical Dictionary of Patriotic Education] (Beijing: Dianzi kezhi daxue chubanshe, 1997), 581–938. This dictionary was republished in 2006.

21. Deng Xiaoping, "We Are Working to Revitalize the Chinese Nation, April 7, 1990," http://english.peopledaily.com.cn/dengxp/vol3/text/d1140.html.

22. Liu Jisheng, *Guochi fen* [The Indignation of National Humiliation] (Ji'nan, Shandong: Ji'nan chubanshe, 1990), 284.

23. Wu Zijiao, "Zeyang jinxing guochi jiaoyu? " [How can we conduct national humiliation education?], *Anhui jiaoyu* 6 (June 1990), 22–3; on 22.

24. He Dongchang, "Xu" [Preface], in *Wuwang guochi* [Never forget National Humiliation, edited by the National Education Committee, Elementary Education section (Tianjin: Xinlei chubanshe, 1991), 1.

25. Wei Yunhong, "Qianghua guochi guonan yanjiu he jiaoyu" [Strengthen National Humiliation and National Crisis Research and Education], *Liaowang* 37 (September 13, 2004): 35.

26. See Zheng Wang, "National Humiliation, History Education, and the Politics of Historical Memory: Patriotic Education Campaign in China," *International Studies Quarterly* 52 (2008): 783–806, on 792.

27. Hou Jiefu and Dang Dexin, eds., *Guochi hen yu Zhonghua wei: Bainian lai Zhongguo renmin fanqinlue douzheng jishi* [National humiliation, hatred and the soul of China: A Record of a century of China's people's struggle against invasion] (Shenyang: Liaoning Education Press, 2001), 1.

28. See Jiang, *History of National Humiliation*. The title's translation is from the copy in the Hamilton Library at the University of Hawaii at Manoa.

29. Zhou Shan and Zhang Chunbo, eds., *Guochi lü: Tushuo Zhonghua bainian* [A Record of National Humiliation: Pictures and Stories of China's Century] (Lanzhou: Gansu qingnian chubanshe, 1998). For a similar organization of national humiliation history in the early twentieth century see Jiang, *History of National Humiliation* (1927), Lü, *A Short History of National Humiliation* (1929), and Cao and Huang, *A Short History of National Humiliation* (1932).

30. Paul A. Cohen, *History in Three Keys: The Boxers as Event, Experience and Myth* (New York: Columbia University Press, 1997), 14.

31. "Jiang Zemin's Letter to Li Tieying and He Dongchang."

32. An Zuozhang, "Xu" [Preface], in *Guochi: Zhongguo renmin bu gai wangji* [National Humiliation: Chinese People Should Never Forget], edited by Che Jixin (Ji'nan: Shangdong youyi shushe, 1992), 1.

33. Cheng Shiwei et al., eds., *Wuwang guochi* [Never Forget National Humiliation] (Changchun: Jilin wenshi chubanshe, 1998), 4–5.

34. Dou Benwei and Shen Xiaomei, *Wuwang guochi* [Never Forget National Humiliation] (Shenyang: Liaoning renmin chubanshe, 2002), 1; also see Cheng, *Never Forget National Humiliation*, 1.

35. Cheng, *Never Forget National Humiliation*, 2. Also see Liang Zhanjun, *Jindai Zhonghua guochi lü* [A Record of the National Humiliation of Modern China] (Beijing: Beijing chubanshe, 1994), 70; Dou and Shen, *Never Forget National Humiliation*, 1.

36. Cheng, *Never Forget National Humiliation*, 5. Also see Liang, *A Record of the National Humiliation*.

37. Cheng, *Never Forget National Humiliation*, 4.

38. Cheng, *Never Forget National Humiliation*, 39–41, 47–9, 60–1.

39. See Kirk W. Larsen, *Tradition, Treaties, and Trade: Qing Imperialism and Choson Korea, 1850–1910* (Cambridge, MA: Harvard University Press), 1–22; Peter C. Perdue, *China Marches West: The Qing Conquest of Central Eurasia* (Cambridge, MA: Harvard University Press, 2004).

40. Cheng, *Never Forget National Humiliation*, 23.

41. Liang, *A Record of the National Humiliation*, 74.

42. See Lydia H. Liu, *The Clash of Empires: The Invention of China in Modern World Making* (Cambridge, MA: Harvard University Press, 2004), 31–69.

43. Liang, *A Record of the National Humiliation*, 2; also see Cheng, *Never Forget National Humiliation*, 24.

44. For a patriotic education book organized around this Monument see Lu Denglai, *Renmin yingxiong jinian bei shihua* [Stories of the Monument to People's Heroes] (Shanghai: Shanghai jiaoyu chubanshe, 1980).

45. Feng Cai and Li Deyuan, eds., *Yichilü: Maiguo qiurongzhe de xiachang* [A Record of a Shameful Legacy: The Fate of Those Who Betray the Nation for Personal Gain] (Beijing: Junshi kexue chubanshe, 1990), 1.

46. See Shi Yun, *Zhongguo jindai aiguo yingxiong* [China's Modern Patriotic Heroes] (Beijing: Beijing kexue zhishu chubanshe, 1995).

47. Liang, *A Record of the National Humiliation*, 107–8.

48. Feng and Li, *A Record of a Shameful Legacy*, 1.

49. Baogang He and Yingjie Guo, *Nationalism, National Identity and Democratization in China* (Aldershot: Ashgate Publishing, 2000), 79–105; also see Geremie R. Barmé, "History for the Masses," in *Using the Past to Serve the Present: Historiography and Politics in Contemporary China*, edited by Jonathan Unger (Armonk, NY: M. E. Sharpe, 1993), 260.

50. Guo Qifu, ed., *Wuwang guochi: Zaichuang huihaung* [Never Forget National Humiliation: Recreating the Glory] (Wuhan: Wuhan daxue chubanshe, 1996), 126.

51. Mao Zedong, "On New Democracy (January 1940)," http://www.marxists.org/reference/archive/mao/selected-works/volume-2/mswv2_26.htm.

52. Cheng, *Never Forget National Humiliation*, 16, 17.

53. Cheng, *Never Forget National Humiliation*, 2.

54. Hou and Dang, *National Humiliation, Hatred and the Soul of China*, 1.

55. Liang, *A Record of the National Humiliation*, 108.

56. An, "Preface," 1.

57. Jiang Tingfu, *Zhongguo jindai shi* [Modern Chinese History] (Beijing: Tuanjie chubanshe, 2005), 2.

58. Qin Yaqing, "Guoji guanxi lilun Zhongguo pai shengcheng de keneng he biran" [The Chinese School of International Relations Theory: Possibility and Necessity], *Shijie jingji yu zhengzhi* 3 (2006): 7–13, on 13; also see Jin, "China Must Adopt a Great-Power Mentality."

59. For an analysis of the discourse of modernization and backwardness in China's national strategy see Elena Barabantseva, "Marginality and Nation: Overseas Chinese and Ethnic Minorities in China's National Project," manuscript, 2008.

60. An, "Preface," 2.

61. Zhao Rongchang and Wu Jialin, *Wuwang bainian guochi*, vol. II [Never Forget the Century of National Humiliation, vol. II] (Beijing: Zhongguo renmin daxue chubanshe, 1992), 358.

62. Dai Yi, *Xuyan* [Preface], in Liu, *The Indignation of National Humiliation*, 1–3; Dai Yi, "Xuyan" [Preface], in *Guochi shidian: 1840–1949* [Dictionary of National Humiliation: 1840–1949], edited by Zhuang Jianping (Chengdu: Chengdu chubanshe, 1992), 1–6.

63. Huang Baozhang, "Xu" [Preface], in *Wuwang guochi, Yi shi yu ren: Nongmin Ren Dianjue zifei chuangban Rijun QinHua xuixing zhan jishi* [Never Forget National Humiliation, Use History to Teach the people: Peasant Ren Dianjue's Self-financed and Organized Exhibit on the Crimes of the Japanese Invasion], edited by Liu Xinduan, Peng Xunhou, and Sun Huijun (Beijing: Zhongguo wenshi chubanshe, 2003), 1–4.

64. Zhang Haipeng, Deng Hongzhou, and Zhao Yishun, *Guochi Baitan* [100 events of National Humiliation] (Beijing: Zhonghua Shuju, 2001).

65. Chen Chengxiang, Jiang Yihao, and Jiang Jian, eds., *Jianming Guochi Cidian* [Simple Dictionary of National Humiliation] (Beijing: Changchun chubanshe, 1993).

66. See Zheng Xunian, *Wuwang guochi: Zhongguo jindai lishi duben* [Never Forget National Humiliation: A Popular Reader of Modern Chinese History] (Beijing: Zhongguo shehui kexueyuan chubanshe, 2000), 1; Zhang, *100 Talks on National Humiliation*, 1–3; Jiang, *Modern Chinese History*.

67. Liu et al., eds., *Never Forget National Humiliation, Use History to Teach the People: Peasant Ren Dianjue's Self-Financed and Organized Exhibit on the Crimes of the Japanese Invasion.* For a discussion of the role of "private museums" see James Reilly, "China's History Activism and Sino-Japanese Relations," *China: An International Journal* 4:2 (2006): 189–216.

68. Xie Jin, Dir., *The Opium War* (Chengdu: Sichuan Films, 1997).

69. For a discussion of the film's logistics see Rebecca E. Karl, "The Burdens of History: *Lin Zexu* (1959) and *The Opium War* (1997)," in *Whither China: Intellectual Politics in Contemporary China*, edited by Xudong Zhang (Durham, NC: Duke University Press, 2001), 229–62; on 231–2; Zhiwei Xiao, "Nationalism in Chinese Popular Culture: A Case Study of The Opium War," in *Exploring Nationalisms of China: Themes and Conflicts*, edited by C. X. George Wei and Xiaoyuan Liu (Westport, CN: Greenwood Press, 2002), 41–54, on 47–8. For reports on the premier see "China: Xinhua Feature on 1898 Signing of Hong Kong Lease," Beijing: Xinhua, 10 June 1997, FBIS-CHI-97-161; Andrew Higgins, "China's Epic Exorcism: Britain is the Arch-Villain of a Film to Purge the Imperial Legacy," *The Guardian*, June 12, 1997.

70. See Xiao, "Nationalism in Chinese Popular Culture."

71. Ironically, the film's English subtitles misspell Denton's name as "Danton."

72. Jiang Zemin, "Speech Commemorating Hong Kong's Return," in *Xianggang huigui diyitian* [The First Day of the Return of Hong Kong], edited by Xinhua News Agency Hong Kong Office (Beijing: Xinhua, 1997), 2.

73. "Outline for Implementing Patriotic Education," 3.

74. Liang, *A Record of the National Humiliation*, ii.

75. Dou and Shen, *Never Forget National Humiliation*, 2.

76. Yuan Weishi, "Xiandaihua yu lishi jiaokeshu" [Modernization and History Textbooks], *Bingdian* weekly supplement to *Zhongguo qingnian bao* (January 11, 2006). For the original Chinese and an English translation see http://www.zonaeuropa.com/20060126_1.htm.

77. Jin Xide, "China Must Adopt a Great-power Mentality, and Make Psychological Change Part of its Modernization," *Beijing huanqiu shibao* (September 12, 2002), translated in FBIS CPP20020927000153.

78. Richard Curt Kraus, *The Party and the Arty in China: The New Politics of Culture* (Boulder, CO: Rowman & Littlefield, 2004), 232.

79. Joseph Kahn, "Where's Mao? Chinese Revise History Books," *New York Times*, 1 September 2006.

80. Gill, *Rising Star*, 7.

81. *Huangyan yu zhenxiang: toushi 3.14 Lasa baoli shijian* [Lies and Truth: A Clear View of the March 14th Lhasa riot] (Beijing: Sanlian shudian, April 4, 2008); also see Fu Ying, "Western Media has 'Demonised' China," *Sunday Telegraph* (London), April 13, 2008.

82. "Understanding Another World: How to Criticize China," Peace in Tibet Web site, May 8, 2008, http://www.peaceintibet.com; also see [Anonymized], "Truth in Tibet: The Truth I Can Tell You," personal email correspondence, April 18, 2008.

83. See "Tibet WAS, IS, and ALWAYS WILL BE a part of China," YouTube, 15 March 2008, http://www.youtube.com/watch?v=x9QNKB34cJo.

84. See Brady, *Marketing Dictatorship*, 125–74.

85. See Laura Hein and Mark Selden, eds., *Censoring History; Citizenship and Memory in Japan, Germany, and the United States* (Armonk, NY: M. E. Sharpe, 2000).

86. See "Russia's Past: The Rewriting of History," *The Economist*, 8 November 2007.

87. David Campbell, *Writing Security*, rev. ed. (Minneapolis, MN: University of Minnesota Press, 1998), 170–90.

Chapter 3

1. See "National Day Celebrated All Over China," *People's Daily*, October 2, 2002.

2. "Festive mood pervades Tiananmen Square," *China Daily*, October 1, 2007.

3. This description comes from notes from my fieldwork visit to Beijing in autumn 1999, and from Bruce Kennedy, "So Close, Yet So Far: Watching China's National Day Parade from a Tantalizing Distance," CNN Interactive (October 1, 1999); James Miles, "Analysis: Jiang's Day of Glory," BBC (October 1, 1999).

4. "China's Public Holidays: Golden Weeks or Silver Days?," *The Economist*, November 22, 2007; "Top 10 Domestic News Events in 2007," Xinhua, December 30, 2007.

5. *Zhonghua renmin gongheguo guofang jiaoyu fa* [National Defense Education Law of the People's Republic of China], April 28, 2001, articles 12, 20. "China Fails to Designate National Humiliation Day," Beijing: Xinhua, April 28, 2001, FBIS-CHI-2001-0428; *Renmin ribao*, September 16, 2001; Feng Chunmei, "Jintian shi diyige quanmin guofang jiaoyuri" [Today is the First Nationwide National Defense Education Day], *Zhongguo qingnian bao*, September 15, 2001; "CPC, State Council Suggestions for Improving Ideological Building of Young Adults," Xinhua Domestic Service, March 22, 2004, translated in FBIS: CPP20040322000249.

6. See Jiang Xianghai, "Wuwang guochi, qiang wo guofang" [Never Forget National Humiliation, Strengthen Our National Defense], *Zhongguo minbing* 9 (September 2004), 1; *Jiefangjun bao* (September 19, 2004), FBIS-CHI-2004–0920.

7. See William A. Callahan, "War, Shame, and Time: Pastoral Identity Politics in England and America," *International Studies Quarterly* 50:2 (2006): 395–419.

8. Jeffrey N. Wasserstrom, *Student Protest in Twentieth Century China: The View from Shanghai* (Stanford University Press, 1991), 3–4, 9–10.

9. Mona Ozouf, *Festivals and the French Revolution* (Cambridge, MA: Harvard University Press, 1988), 161.

10. Henrietta Harrison, *The Making of a Republican Citizen: Political Ceremonies and Symbols in China: 1911–1929* (Oxford University Press, 2000), 14ff; also see Robert Culp, *Articulating Citizenship: Civic Education and Student Politics in Southeastern China, 1912–1940* (Cambridge, MA: Harvard University Press, 2007).

11. *Zhonghua mingguo yuannian lishu* [Almanac of the First Year of the Republic of China] (Hunan yanshuo zongke yin, 1912).

12. See, for example, Che Jixin, ed., *Guochi: Zhongguo renmin bu gai wangji* [National Humiliation: Chinese People Should Never Forget] (Ji'nan: Shangdong youyi shushe, 1992), 1; He Yu, *Bainian Guochi Jiyao* [A Summary of the Century of National Humiliation] (Beijing: Beijing Yanshan Chubanshi, 1997), 43.

13. Sun Xiangmei, "Minguo shiqide guochi jinianri" [National Humiliation Commemoration Days in the Republican Era], *Zhongshan fengyu* 4 (2007): 16–19; Paul A. Cohen, "Remembering and Forgetting: National Humiliation in Twentieth-Century China," *Twentieth-Century China*, 27:2 (April 2002): 1–39; Luo Zhitian, "National Humiliation and National Assertion: the Chinese Response to the Twenty-one Demands," *Modern Asian Studies* 27:2 (1993): 297–319.

14. See *Guochi* [National Humiliation] (Shanghai) 1:1 (June 1915); Zhichi she (Psued., Sense of Shame Association), ed., *Guochi* [National Humiliation] (Shanghai: Zhichi she, 1915). Also see Sun, "National Humiliation Days in the Republican Era," 17.

15. Karl Gerth, *China Made: Consumer Culture and the Creation of the Nation* (Cambridge, MA: Harvard University Asia Center, 2003), 137.

16. See Hou Hongjian, "Guoxue, guochi, laoku sanda zhuyi biaolie" [Illustrative charts displaying the three great principles: National studies, national humiliation and hard work], *Jiaoyu zazhi* 7:7 (July 1915): 21–4.

17. Sun, "National Humiliation Days in the Republican Era," 18. Also see Culp, *Articulating Citizenship*.

18. See Chiang Kai-shek, *China's Destiny* (New York: Roy Publishers, 1947), 44–75. (This book was originally published in Chinese in 1943.)

19. Cited in Liang Xin, *Guochi shiyao* [History of national humiliation] (Shanghai: Rixin yudi xueshi, 1931), 1, 6. Also see "China to observe 25 'Humiliation Days,'" *New York Times*, September 16, 1928, 60.

20. Xiu Jun, "Wujiu zhi wo jian" [My view of May 9th], *Shenbao*, May 9, 1921, 18; *North China Herald*, May 18, 1925, 271.

21. Cheng Zhizheng, "Wuhu wuyue" [Alas, May], *Shenbao*, May 9, 1928, 21.

22. *North China Herald*, May 8, 1928, 189.

23. "Zhongyang feichu wujiu jinian" [Central government cancels May 9th commemoration], *Shenbao*, May 7,1940, 4.

24. Chen Xinde, "Yi shi wai jing, wuwang guochi: jinian jiu yiba shibian 70 zhounian" [Use History as a mirror, Never Forget National Humiliation: Commemorate the 70th Anniversary of the Event of 9–18], *Guangxi dangshi* 5 (2001).

25. Zhang Wen, "Laoji '7.7' guochi, fengfa jiangguo fumin" [Remember the National Humiliation of 7.7 to Make the Nation Strong and the People Rich], *Lantai shijie* 7 (1997), 30; Zhu Chenshan, ed., *Nanjing datusha yu guoji dajiu jutuji* [Picture Collection of the Nanjing Massacre and the International Rescue] (Nanjing: Jiangsu guji chubanshe, 2002), 184.

26. Chen Yunjie, "Qing shi 'guochi ri'" [Please Establish 'National Humiliation Day'] *Jiaoyu yu zhili* 4 (1995), 22; Su Zhiliang, "Wuwang guochi, wo de sandian jianyi" [Never Forget National Humiliation, My Three Proposals]," *Tansuo yu zhengwu* 12 (2000), 9–11.

27. Chen, "Please establish 'National Humiliation Day,'" 22.

28. Liu Jichang, "Guochi wei jing, guoxing wei di: aiguo zhuyi jiaoyu xin guanjiao" [National Humiliation as the Mirror, National Renaissance as the Meaning: A New Approach to Patriotic Education], *Guizhou wenshicongkan* 3 (2002), 47–50, 50; also see (Editorial), "The Eve of Pearl Harbor," *New York Times*, December 6, 1943, 22. There is a persistent misreading of Pearl Harbor Day as National Humiliation Day in Chinese texts. This perhaps comes from a mistranslation of "a day that will live in infamy" from President Roosevelt's declaration of war speech.

29. Feng, "Today is the First Nationwide National Defense Education Day," 2001.

30. "China Fails to Designate National Humiliation Day," *Peoples Daily*, April 28, 2001.

31. "China Fails to Designate National Humiliation Day," *Peoples Daily*, April 28, 2001.

32. See Luo "National Humiliation and National Assertion," 310–12, Cohen, "Remembering and Forgetting," 26.

33. The 1946 National Humiliation Day marked Chiang Kai-shek's signing of the China–US Treaty of Friendship and Commerce, which the CCP saw as a new "unequal treaty." See *Jinian xin guochi* [Commemorate New National Humiliation] (Xingtai: Taixing quncong shudian, 1947); Tillman Durdin, "China Reds Mourn U.S. Trade Accord," *New York Times* January 26, 1947), 39.

34. "Chinese Lawmaker Proposes to Mark Japanese Invasion with National Humiliation Day," Xinhua, March 15, 2007, FBIS: 200703151477.1_7ca40042a6e9f19f. In 2006, the director of the September 18th museum in Shenyang also urged the NPC

to declare it National Humiliation Day. ("Chinese Cities Sound Sirens To Commemorate Japanese Invasion of 1931," Xinhua, September 18, 2006, FBIS: 200609181477.1_ade10078c8454909).

35. "Jiu-yiba wuwang guochi ri guochan shouji tuijian" [September 18th, Never Forget National Humiliation Day, a Plan to Recommend National Products], http://www.sina.com.cn, September 18, 2008; also see a posting on the Never forget national humiliation Web site, which includes a petition to sign "Wuwang guochi; jinian jiu yiba; sheli guochiri!" [Never Forget National Humiliation, Commemorate September 18th, Establish National Humiliation Day!], http://www.wwgc.cc/qianming/default.asp, last accessed on September 18, 2008; "Remember History, Never Forget National Humiliation!], http://bbs.myspace.cn/t/3912664.html, last accessed on September 18, 2008.

36. See Liu, "National Humiliation as the Mirror," 48.

37. Ozouf, *Festivals and the French Revolution*, 175, 180.

38. Ah Yuan, "Ba ziji de rizi guohao" [Happily Pass Your Days], *Liaowang* 38 (September 19, 2005), 6.

39. Cited in Harrison, *The Making of a Republican Citizen*, 112.

40. (Editorial), "Feizhi wujiu jiniande yiyi" [The Meaning of the Cancellation of May 9th Commemoration], *Shenbao*, May 8, 1940, 4; also see Li Lichen, "Heyi yao you jinian shi" [How Should We Commemorate?], *Shenbao*, May 9, 1921, 18.

41. For a vivid description of activities, including flirting with girls at the demonstrations, see Liao Guofang, "Yongyuan buwang: guochi jinian xiaoshuo" [Never Forget: A National Humiliation Commemorative Story], *Shenbao*, May 9, 1928, 21.

42. Wasserstrom, *Student Protest in Twentieth Century China*, 86, 64; Sun, "National Humiliation Days in the Republican Era," 18–19.

43. See *Shenbao*, May 9, 1919, 1.

44. See *Hua-Si xinbao* [Chino-Siamese Daily News], May 8, 1925, 2.

45. "Jinri zhongyang dahuitang zhi guochi jinianhui" [Today the Central Convention Center Holds a National Humiliation Commemoration Meeting], *Shenbao*, May 9, 1925, 13; also see Wasserstrom, *Student Protest in Twentieth Century China*, 78–9.

46. "Yong gongxuezhi guochi jinian" [National Humiliation Commemoration at Yong Public School], *Shenbao*, May 9, 1925, 13.

47. Wang Huaiqi, *Guochi jinian ticao* [National Humiliation Commemorative Gymnastics] (Shanghai: Zhongguo tixue chubanshe, 1929).

48. "12,000 Chinese Here in Protest Parade," *New York Times*, May 10, 1938, 14.

49. "Guochi ri yi" [Things One Should Do on National Humiliation Day], *Shenbao*, May 9, 1922, 17.

50. Feng Shuren, "Wufenzhong redude fenxi" [An Analysis of Five Minutes of Enthusiasm], *Shenbao*, May 9, 1924, 18.

51. "Beixinjing wuqi jinian dahui ji" [The Meeting to Commemorate May 7th in Beixinjing], *Shenbao*, May 9, 1927, 9.

52. "Jinri guochi jinian fanwei" [The Limits of Today's National Humiliation Commemoration], *Shenbao*, May 9, 1929, 13.

53. "Jinri wujiu guochi jinian" [Today's May 9th National Humiliation Commemoration], *Shenbao*, May 9, 1930, 13; "Jingshi jinri juxing" [Meeting Held in the Capital Today], *Shenbao*, May 9, 1935, 5.

54. Liang Yiqun et al., *Yibaige guochi jinianri* [100 National Humiliation Days] (Beijing: Zhongguo qingnian chubanshe, 1995).

55. Liu Jisheng, *Guochi fen* [The Indignation of National Humiliation] (Jinan, Shandong: Ji'nan chubanshe, 1990), 284.

56. Thanks to Yinan He for raising this point.

57. Committee Of Leaders Of The Moral Education In Primary And Secondary Schools Of Dongcheng District [Beijing], "Huanqing Xianggang huigui, xixue bainian guochi" [Welcome Back Hong Kong, Cleanse the Century of National Humiliation], *Beijing jiaoyu* 22 (1997), 7–8.

58. Suisheng Zhao, *A Nation-State by Construction: Dynamics of Modern Chinese Nationalism* (Stanford: Stanford University Press, 2004), 241.

59. Wang Guangjue and Wang Liansu, "Jingyuxian shenjiju kaizhan 'wuwang guochi, zhenxing Zhonghua' de aiguo zhuyi jiaoyu" [Jingyu County Auditing Department Opens 'Never Forget National Humiliation, Rejuvenate China' Patriotic Education], *Dangdai shenji* 5 (2001), 43.

60. (Editorial), "Yinghuigui xueguochi jiancai gongye yao da er qiang" [Welcome Back, Cleanse National Humiliation, the Construction Materials Industry Must Be Great to Be Strong], *Zhongguo jiancai* 7 (1997), 4.

61. Wang Xiuying, "Guochi buneng wangque, kangri jingshen yongcun" [National Humiliation Cannot Be Forgotten, the Anti-Japanese Spirit Endures], *Zhongguo fuyun* 8 (1995), 47.

62. "China: Xinhua Feature on 1898 Signing of Hong Kong Lease," Beijing: Xinhua, June 10, 1997, FBIS-CHI-97-161.

63. Yan Cun, "Wuwang guochi zhenxing Zhonghua" [Never Forget National Humiliation, Rejuvenate China], *Jiangsu tongji* 7 (1997), 35.

64. Wang Juchang, *Guochi shihua* [Ode to National Humiliation] (Shanghai: Xinjiyuan chubanshe, 1947), 85.

65. "Chinese Lawmaker Proposes To Mark Japanese Invasion With National Humiliation Day," Xinhua, March 15, 2007; "Chinese Cities Sound Sirens To Commemorate Japanese Invasion of 1931," Xinhua, September 18, 2006; "PRC: Shenyang Marks 70th Anniversary of Outbreak of War With Japan," Xinhua, September 19, 2001, FBIS-CHI-2001-0919.

66. Ah Yuan, "Happily Pass Your Days," 6.

67. "PRC Couples Refuse to Hold Wedding Ceremonies on 'Day of National Humiliation,'" Xinhua, September 14, 2005, FBIS: 200509141477.1_600 70038d76dd4e1.

68. Yuan Xiaoming, "9–18, buneng chengle chiru de baofu" [September 18th Doesn't Have to Become a Humiliating Burden], *Huanqiu ribao*, September 18, 2007. *Huanqiu ribao* is a *People's Daily* tabloid.

69. "Jinri guochi jinian," [Today Commemorate National Humiliation], *Shenbao*, May 9, 1927, 9.

70. See G. John Ikenberry and Michael Mastanduno, eds., *International Relations Theory and the Asia-Pacific* (New York: Columbia University Press, 2003); Gerrit W. Gong, ed. *Memory and History in East and Southeast Asia: Issues of Identity in International Relations* (Washington, DC: The CSIS Press, 2001).

71. See Wu Xinbo, "Memory and Perception: The Chinese Thinking on Japan," in *Memory and History in East and Southeast Asia*, edited by Gerrit W. Gong (Washington, DC: The CSIS Press, 2001), 65–85.

72. *Shenbao*, May 9, 1925, 13.

73. See Gerth, *China Made*, 365. For a discussion of the links between the national products movement and national humiliation day see Gerth, *China Made*, 133–49.

74. Figure 3.4 source: *Shenbao*, May 9, 1925, 1.

75. Anne-Marie Broudehoux, *The Making and Selling of Post-Mao Beijing* (New York: Routledge, 2004), 65–8; Geremie R. Barmé (Editorial) "Yuanming Yuan, The Garden of Perfect Brightness," *China Heritage Quarterly*, 8 (December 2006); Erik Eckholm, "A Glorious Ruin and a Face-Lift Furor," *New York Times*, August 10, 1999, A4; Shang Guanfeng et al., *Yuanming yuan yizhi gongyuan* [Yuanmingyuan park: An Eternal Monument] (Beijing: Xin shijie chubanshe, 2002), 5–7.

76. Young-tsu Wong, *A Paradise Lost: The Imperial Garden Yuanming Yuan* (Honolulu: University of Hawaii Press, 2001), 194.

77. See Broudehoux, *The Making and Selling of Post-Mao Beijing*, 45, 76–7, 82–4; *China Daily*, October 19, 1990, 1; Barmé, "Yuanming Yuan."

Chapter 4

1. "Chinese Cartography: China Beat Columbus to It, Perhaps," *The Economist*, January 12, 2006, http://www.economist.com/displaystory.cfm?story_id=5381851. Gavin Menzies has adopted this map, which he calls the "1418 Map," and posted it on his "1421: The Year When China Discovered the World" Web site, http://www.1421.tv/assets/images/maps/1418_map_download.jpg (accessed on January 15, 2008).

2. Walter D. Mignolo, *The Darker Side of the Renaissance: Literacy, Territoriality, and Colonization* (Ann Arbor: University of Michigan Press, 1995), 219–313.

3. Wang Xiaodong, Fang Ning, and Song Qiang, *Quanqiuhua yinxiang xiade Zhongguo zhi lu* [China's Road under the Shadow of Globalization] (Beijing: Shehui kexue chubanshe, 1999).

4. See, for example, Joseph Kahn, "Storm over 1418 Map: History or Scam?," *International Herald Tribune*, January 17, 2006. Menzies's argument that China discovered America in 1421 is also seen as a hoax by most historians. Gavin Menzies, *1421: The Year When China Discovered the World* (New York: Perennial, 2003).

5. See Roger Des Forges and Luo Xu, "China as a Non-Hegemonic Superpower? The Uses of History among the *China Can Say No* Writers and Their Critics," *Critical Asian Studies* 33 (2001): 498, 507.

6. See, for example, Chen Gaoji, preface to *Zhongguo xin yutu* [New Atlas of China] (Shanghai: Commercial Press, 1925).

7. Zhao Dachuan, "Shiji qipan zuguo tongyi" [A Century of Anticipating the Unification of the Motherland], *Ditu* [Cartography] 2 (2000): 39–44.

8. Thongchai Winichakul, *Siam Mapped: A History of the Geo-body of a Nation* (Honolulu: University of Hawai'i Press, 1994), 17. See also Benedict Anderson, *Imagined Communities: Reflections on the Origin and Spread of Nationalism*, new ed. (New York: Verso, 2006), 170–8.

9. Lü Yiran, ed., *Zhongguo jindai bianjie shi*, 2 vols. [History of China's Modern Borders] (Chengdu: Sichuan renmin chubanshe, 2007), I:1–2; for a more critical view see Huang Donglan, "Lingtu, jiangyu, guochi: Qingmo Minguo dili jiaokeshu de kongjian biaoxiang" [Territory, Domain and National Humiliation: Concepts of Space in Geography Textbooks from the late Qing and Republican Periods], in *Shenti, xinxing, quanli* [Body, Mind and Power], edited by Huang Donglan (Hangzhou: Zhejiang People's Press, 2005), 77–9.

10. This argument is summarized from Thongchai, *Siam Mapped*, 147–8.

11. Johannes Putsch, *La Vergine Europa* [Europe as a Virgin], 1592.

12. Mignolo, *The Darker Side of the Renaissance*, 218; also see J. B. Harley, "Deconstructing the Map," *Cartographica* 26 (1989): 1–20; Gearóid Ó Tuathail, *Critical Geopolitics* (Minneapolis: University of Minnesota Press, 1996), 1–20.

13. Untitled map (1743), British Library. The most famous "Huayi tu" (1136) is inscribed on a stone stele now housed in Xi'an, China. For a rubbing of this map, see the Library of Congress Web page.

14. See Li Dalong, "Chuantong Yi-Xia guanyu Zhongguo jiangyu de xingcheng" [The Traditional Barbarian–Civilization View and the Formation of China's Territory], *Zhongguo bianjiang shidi yanjiu* 14:1 (2004): 1–14.

15. For a critical discussion of the conventions of premodern Chinese maps, see the chapters by Cordell Yee in *The History of Cartography, Vol. II, Book II, Cartography in the Traditional East and Southeast Asian Societies*, edited by J. B. Harley and David Woodward (University of Chicago Press, 1994), 35–230; Richard J. Smith, *Chinese Maps: Images of 'All Under Heaven'* (Oxford: Oxford University Press, 1996); Richard J. Smith, "Mapping China's World: Cultural Cartography in

Late Imperial Times," in *Landscape, Culture and Power in Chinese Society*, edited by Wen-hin Yeh (Berkeley: Institute of East Asian Studies, University of California, 1998), 52–105; Peter C. Perdue, "Boundaries, Maps, and Movement: Chinese, Russian, and Mongolian Empires in Early Modern Central Eurasia," *The International History Review* 20 (1998): 263–86; William A. Callahan, *Contingent States: Greater China and Transnational Relations* (Minneapolis, MN: University of Minnesota Press, 2004), 78–90.

16. Iwo Amelung, "New Maps for the Modernizing State: Western Cartographic Knowledge and Its Application in Nineteenth and Twentieth Century China," in *Graphic and Text in the Production of Technical Knowledge in China: The Warp and the Weft*, edited by Francesca Bray, Vera Dorofeeva-Lichtmann, and Georges Métailié (Leiden: Brill, 2007), 34; Ding Wenjiang, Weng Wenjing, and Zeng Shiying, *Zhonghua minguo xin ditu* [New Map of the Republic of China] (Shanghai: Shenbao guan, 1934).

17. Mignolo, *The Darker Side of the Renaissance*, 253–4; Huang, "Territory, Domain and National Humiliation."

18. John Hay, "The Body Invisible in Chinese Art?," in *Body, Subject and Power in China*, edited by Angela Zito and Tani E. Barlow (Chicago: University of Chicago Press, 1994), 52.

19. Anonymous historical geographer, interview by author in Beijing, July 16, 2007.

20. *Zhonghua mingguo yuannian lishu* [Almanac of the First Year of the Republic of China] (Hunan yanshuo zongke yin, 1912).

21. *The Constitutional Compact of the Chung Hua Min Kuo* [bilingual edn.], *Peking Daily News* (May 1, 1914), Chapter 1, Article 3. The ROC's 1923 Constitution obscures this transition by axiomatically declaring that "The territory which originally belonged to the Republic shall be the territory of the Republic of China" (*Constitution of the Republic of China* (Peking: The Commission on Extraterritoriality, 1924), Chapter 3, Article 3).

22. In addition to the Untitled map (1743), see "Da Qing wannian yitong dili quantu" [Complete Universal Map of the Unified Great Qing Empire], 1816. An image of this map is posted on the Library of Congress Web page.

23. "Zhonghua guochi ditu" [Map of Chinese national humiliation] (Shanghai: Central cartographic society, 1916); "Zhongguo guochi ditu" [Map of China's National Humiliation] in *Zuixin Zhonghua minguo gaizao quantu* [The Atlas of the Republic of China, with the Latest Corrections], compiled by Bai Meichu (Beiping: Jianshe tushuguan, 1930), map 2.

24. For color versions of these maps see William A. Callahan, "The Cartography of National Humiliation and the Emergence of China's Geobody," *Public Culture* 21: 1 (2009): 153–4. For other examples of a white and blank China surrounded by lost territories marked with red slashes, see "Zhonghua guochi ditu" [Map of Chinese National Humiliation] (Henan provincial government,

1922); "Zhonghua guochi ditu" [Map of Chinese National Humiliation] (Industry and Commerce Association of Hebei Province, 1929); and "Aiguo ditu: Guochi yu guochan yilan," [Patriotic map: National humiliations and national assets in one view] (Meeting of the Central Government, Wuhan Branch meeting, 1929).

25. Huang uses geography textbooks to make a similar argument about an expanding popular view of lost territories in the early twentieth century China (Huang, "Territory, Domain and National Humiliation," 90).

26. Bai, "Preface" to *The Atlas of the Republic of China*, 1.

27. See a description of the "Map of Chinese National Humiliation" in Zhu Jingmei, "30 niandai bianzhe chubande 'Zhonghua guochi ditu'" [The 'Map of Chinese National Humiliation' published in the 1930s], *Minguo chunqiu* 3 (2000): 36. The map in question is "Zhonghua guochi ditu" [Map of Chinese National Humiliation] (Wuchang: Yaxin Geographical Society, 1931).

28. "Zhongguo guochi ditu, zaiban" [Map of China's National Humiliation, reprint] (Shanghai: Zhonghua shuju, February 1927).

29. For similar maps of concentric circles and lost territories see "Zhongguo jianming guochi yutu" [Simple Map of China's National Humiliation] (Jiangsu army surveying department, 1928); "Zhongguo guochi ditu" [Map of China's National Humiliation], in Gu Yijun, *Zhongguo guochi dilixue* [Geography of China's National Humiliation] (Beiping: Wenhua xueshe yinxing, 1930); "Zhongguo sangshi lingtu linghai tu" [Map of China's Lost Land and Maritime Territories], in Xie Bin, *Zhongguo sangdi shi* [The History of China's Lost Territories] (Shanghai: Zhonghua shuju, 1925).

30. See Zhu "The 'Map of Chinese National Humiliation' Published in the 1930s," 35.

31. Gu, *Geography of China's National Humiliation*, 1.

32. *Jindai Zhongguo bainian guochi ditu* [Maps of the Century of National Humiliation of Modern China] (Beijing: Renmin chubanshe, 1997).

33. *Maps of the Century of National Humiliation*, 25–6.

34. *Maps of the Century of National Humiliation*, 47–8.

35. *Maps of the Century of National Humiliation*, 49.

36. See Peter C. Perdue, *China Marches West: The Qing Conquest of Central Eurasia* (Cambridge, MA: Harvard University Press, 2004); Kirk W. Larsen, *Tradition, Treaties, and Trade: Qing Imperialism and Choson Korea, 1850–1910* (Cambridge, MA: Harvard University Press, 2008).

37. Joanna Waley-Cohen, "Changing Spaces of Empire in Eighteenth-Century Qing China," in *Political Frontiers, Ethnic Boundaries and Human Geographies in Chinese History*, edited by Nicola Di Cosmo and Don J. Wyatt (London: RoutledgeCurzon, 2003), 333. Also see "Universal Map of the Unified Great Qing Empire," 1816.

38. Emma Jinhua Teng, *Taiwan's Imagined Geography: Chinese Colonial Travel Writing and Pictures, 1683–1895* (Cambridge, MA: Harvard University Press, 2004), 7, 251. See, for example, Li, "The Traditional Barbarian-Civilization View and the Formation of China's Territory."

39. Robert Culp analyzes geography textbooks to make a similar point in *Articulating Citizenship: Civic Education and Student Politics in Southeastern China, 1912–1940* (Cambridge, MA: Harvard University Press, 2007), 72–96.

40. *Zuixin xiangxi Zhonghua minguo diyu quantu* [The Latest Detailed Complete Map of the Republic of China] (n.p., 1923).

41. "Patriotic Map: National Humiliations and National Assets in One View," 1929. I studied this fascinating map at Beijing's National Library. Unfortunately, my request for a copy was denied because the map is very fragile.

42. *Maps of the Century of National Humiliation*, 86; also see Zhang Haipeng, *Zhongguo jindaishi guo dituji* [Atlas of Modern Chinese History] (Shanghai: Ditu chubanshe, 1984).

43. Lü, *History of China's Modern Borders*, I:1–8, 264, 276, 324, 342, 352. This edited volume is the result of a major research project by the Center for the Study of Borderland History and Geography at the Chinese Academy of Social Sciences. According to a scholar at this center, the book was written to set the standard for border studies for the next few decades (Anonymous historical geographer, interviewed by author in Beijing, July 17, 2007).

44. Zhao Ming, ed., *Baige aiguo zhuyi jiaoyu shifan jidi dituji* [Atlas of One Hundred Patriotic Education Sites] (Beijing: China Cartographic Press, 1999).

45. M. Taylor Fravel, *Strong Borders, Secure Nation: Cooperation and Conflict in China's Territorial Disputes* (Princeton, NJ: Princeton University Press, 2008), 3, 10; also see Maria Chang, "Chinese Irredentist Nationalism," in *Return of the Dragon* (Boulder, CO: Westview, 2001), 205–26.

46. Old Secretariat, *Chinese Aggression in Maps: Nine Maps, with an Introduction and Explanatory Notes* (Delhi: Publications Division, 1962); the Southeast Asian concern is cited in Greg Austin, *China's Ocean Frontier: International Law, Military Force and National Development* (Sydney: Allen & Unwin, 1998), 331.

47. See Allen Carlson, *Unifying China, Integrating with the World: Securing Chinese Sovereignty in the Reform Era* (Stanford, CA: Stanford University Press, 2005), 49–91, 231; Fravel, *Strong Borders, Secure Nation*.

48. For China's territorial disputes between 1949 and 2005 see Fravel, *Strong Borders, Secure Nation*, 46–7, table 1.3.

49. Carlson, *Unifying China, Integrating with the World*, 50.

50. Carlson, *Unifying China, Integrating with the World*, 65. Fravel's argument that China characteristically gives up more than half of disputed territories also assumes an expansive view of Chinese territory.

51. See Mark C. Elliott, "The Limits of Tartary: Manchuria in Imperial and National Geographies," *Journal of Asian Studies* 59 (2000): 603–46.

52. "BaoRi qiangzhan woguo dongbei guochi tu" [The Map of National Humiliation: Japan's Violent Occupation of Our Country's Northeast] (Shanghai: n.p, ca. 1932).

53. Zhang Qingmin, "Global Challenges, Domestic Pressures, and the Making of China's Foreign Policy," presented at the British Inter-university China Center launch conference, Oxford, June 2007, 12; e-mail correspondence with Zhang, July 29, 2007.

54. In Chinese the area is usually called Outer Northeast (*wai dongbei*) and in English, Outer Manchuria. But the Web site makes clear that they are both referring to the same lost territory. (http://baike.baidu.com/view/173829.htm; accessed March 10, 2008). Also see the Chinese Wikipedia site, which is even more detailed and has a colored map that marks lost territories in red. (http://zh.wikipedia.org/wiki/%E5%A4%96%E6%9D%B1%E5%8C%97; accessed March 10, 2008).

55. See Zhonghua Bantu Wang [China Map Net] (http://www.uc321.net/bbs/view-thread.php?tid=3303&extra=page%3D1), and Taizhou Qingnian Luntan [Taizhou Youth Discussion Forum] (http://www.tz94.com/bbs/read.php?tid=46943); (accessed March 10, 2008).

56. See John Garnaut, "Russia on Edge as China Grows," *Sydney Morning Herald*, June 9, 2008, http://business.smh.com.au/business/Russia-on-Edge-as-China-Grows; Mikhail Alexseev, "The 'Yellow Peril' Revisited: The Impact of Chinese Migration in Primorskii Krai," Program on New Approaches to Russian Security (PONARS), Policy Memo series, 94 (October 1999), 2–3; Alexander Lukin, *The Bear Watches the Dragon: Russia's Perceptions of China and the Evolution of Russian-Chinese Relations Since the Eighteenth Century* (London: M. E. Sharpe, 2002).

57. Peter Hays Gries, "The Koguryo Controversy, National Identity, and Sino-Korean Relations Today," *East Asia* 22 (2005), 3; Larsen, *Tradition, Treaties, and Trade*, 26; Yonson Ahn, "Competing Nationalisms: The Mobilization of History and Archeology in the Korea-China Wars over Koguryo/Gaogouli," *Japan Focus* (February 9, 2006); Austin Ramzy, "Rewriting History," *Time* (August 16, 2004); "China's Ancient Koguryo Kingdom Site Added to World Heritage List," *People's Daily*, July 2, 2004.

58. See "China's Claims for Korean History Revealed," *Chosun Ilbo*, June 4, 2007.

59. Gries, "The Koguryo Controversy," 3–4; Ramzy, "Rewriting History." There are numerous Chinese publications on Koguryo from the Northeast Asia project. For discussions on Chinese claims to the Koguryo Kingdom as a vassal, see Ma Dazheng and Jin Xizheng, eds., *Gaoguli Bohai lishi wenti yanjiu lunwenji* [Essays on the History of Koguryo and Parhae] (Yanji, Jilin: Yanbian daxue chubanshe, 2004).

60. Park Woo-Jung, "'Goguryeo, China' and 'Dokdo, Japan'?," *The Hankyoreh* (January 12, 2004), translated in *Korea Focus* (Jan–Feb 2004): 38.

61. Park Young-sun, "China's 'Northeast Asia Project': Launch of a 'History War'?," *Korean Historical Review*, translated in *Korea Focus* (Sept–Oct 2004).

62. "Map Hints Chinese Territory as Ancient Korean," *Korea Times*, November 21, 2007; "Goguryeo Kingdom (B.C. 37–A.D. 668)," http://Kokuryo.com (accessed March 10, 2008).

63. Anonymous international relations specialist, interview by author in Beijing, July 13, 2007; Gries, "The Koguryo Controversy," 5–6; Park, "China's 'Northeast Asia Project'"; Larsen, *Tradition, Treaties, and Trade*, 293.

64. See, for example, *How Thailand Lost Her Territories to France* (Bangkok, Department of Publicity, 1940). The maps in this official book come from World War II when imperial France could not protect its Indochinese colonies, which were occupied by Japan and Thailand. Bangkok was forced to return this territory after the war. But such views of expansive Thai space continue to inspire unofficial Pan-Thai movements in the twenty-first century.

65. The photograph of the carpet was taken by Ablimit Baki at a weaving collective in Hotan, 2005.

66. Dung Kai Cheung [Dong Qizhang], *Dituji: Yige xiangxiangde chengshide kaoguxue* [The Atlas: The Archeology of an Imaginary City] (Taibei: Lianhe wenxue, 1997).

67. See Mignolo, *The Darker Side of the Renaissance*, 259.

68. "Huan ge jiaodu kan Taiwan" [Change the Perspective to View Taiwan], compiled by the Geography Department, National Taiwan University (Taipei: Council for Cultural Affairs, 2004).

69. "Interview with Zhang Jigang, Deputy Director of the Beijing Olympics Opening Ceremony," *Liberation Daily*, August 1, 2008, translated for *China Digitial Times*, August 6, 2008.

70. See "Tibet WAS, IS, and ALWAYS WILL BE a part of China," YouTube, March 15, 2008, http://www.youtube.com/watch?v=x9QNKB34cJo. For a description of how such patriotic videos are produced see Evan Osnos, "Angry Youth: The New Generation's Neocon Nationalists," *The New Yorker* (July 28, 2008).

71. This map by an anonymous activist is reproduced in Robert Barnett, "Thunder from Tibet," *New York Review of Books* 55:9 (May 29, 2008), http://www.nybooks.com/articles/21391 (accessed on November 8, 2008).

72. See Joel Martinsen, "Mapping the Hurt Feelings of the Chinese People," December 11, 2008, http://www.danwei.org/foreign_affairs/a_map_of_hurt_feelings.php.

73. The 1999 map of China disintegrating (Figure 4.2) seems to be adapted from the Dalai Lama's autobiography (see *Freedom in Exile*, HarperCollins, 1990, x–xi). Thanks to Richard Rigby for this reference.

74. Dan Gillmor, cited in Miguel Helft, "Citizen Cartographers Reshape the World Online," *International Herald Tribune*, July 26, 2007, 11.

75. R. B. J. Walker, "The Subject of Security," in *Critical Security Studies*, edited by Keith Krause and Michael C. Williams (Minneapolis, MN: University of Minnesota Press, 1997), 71–2.

Chapter 5

1. For a detailed description of the Tibetan unrest, see Robert Barnett, "Thunder from Tibet," *New York Review of Books* 55:9 (29 May 2008). Ethnic Hui merchants were also a target of violence on 14 March.

2. Wang Lixiong, Liu Xiaobo, et al., "Guanyu chuli Xizang jushi de shi'er ge yijian" [Twelve Suggestions for Dealing with the Tibetan Situation by Some Chinese Intellectuals], 22 March 2008.

3. Mao Zedong, "Address to the Preparatory Meeting of the New Political Consultative Conference, 15 June 1949"; Mao Zedong, "Proclamation of the Central People's Government of China [October 1, 1949]," in *Renmin ribao*, 2 October 1949 [*Collected Works of Mao Tse-tung* (1917–49), vol. 9].

4. See, for example, Central Party School, *Yishi weijing, mianxiang weilai: jinian Zhongguo renmin kangRi zhanzhengji* [Take History as a Mirror to Guide the Future: Commemorate China's War of Resistance Against Japan] (Beijing: Zhonggong dangxiao chubanshe, 2005), 1.

5. Mao, "Proclamation."

6. Dru C. Gladney, *Dislocating China: Reflections on Muslims, Minorities and Other Subaltern Subjects* (Chicago, IL: The University of Chicago Press, 2004), 15.

7. Dru C. Gladney, *Ethnic Identity in China: The Making of a Muslim Minority Nationality*, (New York: Harcourt Brace College Publishers, 1997), p. 171.

8. Information Office of the State Council of the People's Republic of China, "China's National Defense in 2008," January 2009, Beijing, section 1.

9. See, for example, Fei Xiaotong, "Plurality and Unity in the Configuration of the Chinese People," in *Tanner Lectures on Human Values*, Vol. 11, edited by Grethe B. Peterson (Salt Lake City, UT: University of Utah Press, 1990), pp. 165–221; Chen Liankai, "Zhongguo, huayi, fanhan, zhonghua, zhonghua minzu: Yige neizai lianxi fazhan bei renshi de guocheng [One Method for Recognizing the Developmental Relations Between the Terms Zhongguo, Huayi, Fanhan, Zhonghua, Zhonghua minzu], in *Zhonghua minzu de duoyuan yiti geju* [The Pluralistic Unity Structure of Chinese Nationalism], edited by Fei Xiaotong, (Beijing: Zhongyang minzu xueyuan chubanshe, 1989):72–113; Li Dalong, "Chuantong Yi-Xia guanyu Zhongguo jiangyu de xingcheng" [The Traditional Yi-Xia View and the Formation of China's Territory], *Zhongguo bianjiang shidi yanjiu* [Historical Geography of China's Borderland] 14:1 (2004): 1–14.

10. Jiang Rong, *Lang tuteng* [Wolf totem], (Wuhan: Changjiang wenyi chubanshe, 2004).

11. Gladney, *Ethnic Identity in China*, 160.

12. William Schue, "Tizang yu xindi de minzu chishi" [The Discriminatory Complex in Our Sub-consciousness], posted on Achilles' Heel blog, July 8, 2008,

translation on *China Digital Times*, July 9, 2008. Pan-Han includes non-Han groups who have been assimilated.

13. Evan Osnos, "Angry Youth: The New Generation's Neocon Nationalists," *New Yorker*, July 28, 2008.

14. Ma Rong, "Ethnic Relations in Contemporary China: Cultural Tradition and Ethnic Policies Since 1949," *Policy and Society* (Sydney) 25:1 (2006): 85. Although Ma is Hui, he would be included as pan-Han.

15. See Lieg-sheng Yang, "Historical Notes on the Chinese World Order," in *The Chinese World Order: Traditional China's Foreign Relations*, edited by John King Fairbank (Cambridge, MA: Harvard University Press, 1968), 20–33; Li, "The Traditional Barbarian–Civilization View," 2.

16. Li, "The Traditional Barbarian–Civilization View," 4–5; Ma, "Ethnic Relations in Contemporary China," 85.

17. Xiaoyuan Liu, *Frontier Passages: Ethnopolitics and the Rise of Chinese Communism, 1921–1945* (Washington DC: Woodrow Wilson Center Press and Stanford, CA: Stanford University Press, 2004), 8, 7.

18. Yang, "Historical Notes," 20.

19. Cited in Li, "The Traditional Barbarian–Civilization View," 4.

20. Yang, "Historical Notes," 27.

21. *Zuozhuan* cited in Yang, "Historical Notes," 25.

22. *Zuozhuan* cited in Frank Dikötter, *The Discourse of Race in Modern China* (Stanford, DA: Stanford University Press, 1992), 3.

23. *Mencius*, trans. by D. C. Lau (London: Penguin, 1970), 3A/4.

24. Li, "The Traditional Barbarian–Civilization View," 6, 4.

25. See Fei, "Plurality and Unity"; Li, "The Traditional Barbarian–Civilization View."

26. Li, "The Traditional Barbarian–Civilization View," 6; Yang, "Historical Notes," 33.

27. James Leibold, *Reconfiguring Chinese Nationalism: How the Qing Frontier and Its Indigenes Became Chinese* (New York: Palgrave Macmillan, 2007), 22ff; Yang, "Historical Notes."

28. Cited in Leibold, *Reconfiguring Chinese Nationalism*, 30.

29. Leibold, Reconfiguring Chinese Nationalism, 30, 32.

30. Sun Yat-sen, "The Three Principles of the People (1919)," in *Prescriptions for Saving China: Selected Writings of Sun Yat-sen*, edited by Julie Lee Wei, Ramon H. Myers, and Donald G. Gillin (Stanford, CA: Hoover Institution Press, 1994), 225.

31. See Sun Yat-sen, *Three People's Principles* in F. W. Price, *San Min Chu Yi: Three Principles of the People* (Shanghai: China Committee, Institute of Pacific Relations, 1927), 11–12.

32. Sun Yat-sen, *Memoirs of a Chinese Revolutionary* (New York: Ams Press, 1970), 229.

33. Gladney, *Ethnic Identity in China*, 163.

34. Chiang Kai-shek, *China's Destiny & Chinese Economic Theory* (New York: Roy Publishers, 1947), 30, 40. The original Chinese version was published in 1943.
35. Cao Zengmei And Huang Xiaoxian, eds., *Xinbian guochi xiaoshi* [A Short History of National Humiliation, new ed.] (Shanghai: Commercial Press, 1932), 98–151.
36. See Xie Bin, *Zhongguo sangdi shi* [The History of China's Lost Territories] (Shanghai: Zhonghua shuju, 1925); Xie Bin, *Xizang wenti* [The Tibet Problem] (Shanghai: Zhonghua shuju, 1926).
37. Lü Simian, *Guochi xiaoshi*, 2 vols. [A Short History of National Humiliation, 2 vols.] (Shanghai: Zhonghua shuju, 1929), 2:36.
38. *Constitution of the People's Republic of China*, adopted on 4 December 1982, Preamble.
39. Information Office Of The State Council, "National Minorities Policy and its Practice in China," Beijing (June 2000): Section I; Fei, "Plurality and Unity."
40. Fei, "Plurality and Unity," 167–8.
41. Chih-yu Shih, *Autonomy, Ethnicity and Poverty in Southwestern China: The State Turned Upside Down* (New York: Palgrave MacMillan, 2007), 1–2.
42. Edgar Snow cited in Gladney, *Dislocating China*, 11.
43. Cited in Gladney, *Dislocating China*, 11.
44. See Schein, *Minority Rules*, 68.
45. "National Minorities Policy," 2000: Section III.
46. Fei Hsiao Tung [Fei Xiaotong], *Toward a People's Anthropology* (Beijing: New World Press, 1981), 22.
47. "National Minorities Policy," Section I.
48. Ma, "A New Perspective in Guiding Ethnic Relations," 200, 207.
49. Fei, *Toward a People's Anthropology*, 60.
50. See Fei, *Toward a People's Anthropology*, 60–77.
51. Table 2.1 in *Zhongguo 2000 nian renkou pucha ziliao* [Tabulation of the 2000 Population Census of the People's Republic of China] (Beijing: Zhongguo tongji chubanshe, 2002), 299.
52. Schein, *Minority Rules*, 82.
53. Liu, *Frontier Passages*, 171.
54. Gladney, *Ethnic Identity in China*, 159, 168.
55. Gladney, *Dislocating China*, 20.
56. Schein, *Minority Rules*, 97.
57. Fei, "Plurality and Unity," 216.
58. Schein, *Minority Rules*, 84.
59. Fei, "Plurality and Unity," 181, 214.
60. Elena Barabantseva, "Development as Localization: Ethnic Minorities in China's Official Discourse on the Western Development Project," *Critical Asian Studies* 41:2 (2009): 225–54.
61. Fei, "Plurality and Unity," 218.

62. Gladney, *Dislocating China*, 13.
63. Jiang Zemin, *Jiang Zemin lun shehuizhuyi jingshen wenming jianshe* [Jiang Zemin on the Construction of Socialist Spiritual Civilization], (Beijing: Central Committee Documents Press, 1999): 8–12.
64. Shih, *Autonomy, Ethnicity and Poverty*, 233.
65. Schue, "The Discriminatory Complex."
66. Shih, *Autonomy, Ethnicity and Poverty*, 1–2.
67. Cited in Michael Sheridan, "Olympic Crackdown: China's Secret Plot to Tame Tibet," *Sunday Times* (London), 13 July 2008.
68. See Barnett, "Thunder from Tibet."
69. Gladney, *Dislocating China*, 18.
70. See Andrew Martin Fischer, "Reaping Tibet's Whirlwind," *Far Eastern Economic Review* (March 2008).
71. The following paragraphs are a summary of Ma Rong, "Lijie minzu guanxi de xinselu: xiaoshu zuqun wenti de 'qu zhengzhihua'" [New perspectives on nationalities relations: the "depoliticization" of the ethnic minority question], *Beijing daxue xuebao* 41:6 (2004): 122–33; Ma Rong, "A New Perspective in Guiding Ethnic Relations in the Twenty-first Century: 'Depoliticization of Ethnicity in China," *Asian Ethnicity* 8:3 (2007): 199–217; Ma, "Ethnic Relations in Contemporary China."
72. Ma, "A New Perspective in Guiding Ethnic Relations," 202–3.
73. Ma, "A New Perspective in Guiding Ethnic Relations," 216–17; also see Ma, "Ethnic Relations in Contemporary China," 105.
74. In the United States, for example, these issues are now typically framed in terms of "racial politics" rather than "ethnic minorities." See Michael Hanchard And Erin Aeran Chung, "From Race Relations to Comparative Racial Politics," *Du Bois Review* 1:2 (2004): 319–43.
75. Cited in Joe Studwell, *The China Dream* (New York: Grove Press, 2003), 70.
76. See Wang Gungwu, *China and the Chinese Overseas*, (Singapore: Times Academic Press, 1991), 216, 236, 253.
77. Wang Gungwu, *The Chinese Overseas: From Earthbound China to the Quest for Autonomy* (Cambridge, MA: Harvard University Press, 2000), 43; Adam Mckeown, "Conceptualizing Chinese Diasporas, 1842 to 1949," *Journal of Asian Studies* 58:2 (1999), 323.
78. Ren Guixiang and Zhao Hongying, *Huaqiao Huaren yu guogong guanxi* [Overseas Chinese and Nationalist Party-Communist Party Relations] (Wuhan: Wuhan daxue chubanshe, 1999), 2.
79. Ren and Zhao, *Overseas Chinese*, 53.
80. Wang, *The Chinese Overseas*, 47.
81. Wang, *The Chinese Overseas*, 43.
82. For more details about the life of this businessman-turned-official, Hiapsoon Kasemsap, see Thani Phansaeng, *Botbat Dan Setakit Lae Kanmuang kong Chao Jin*

nai ket thesaban muang Rot-et, 2398–2540 [The Political and Economic Role of Chinese in Rot-et Municipality, 1855–1997], a scholarly paper for an MA in Thai Studies, Mahasarakham University, Thailand, May 2001, 36.

83. Ren and Zhao, *Overseas Chinese*, 380–1, 1.

84. Shen Jinglin, "Foreword," in *Zhongguo: cong quru zouxiang huihuang, 1840–1997*, vol. 1 [China: From Humiliation to Glory, 1840–1997, vol. 1], edited by Revolutionary History Museum of China, (Beijing: Zhongguo minzu sheying yishu, 1997), 5; Yang Wanxiu, "Zhongguo jindaishi kaiduan yu huaqiao" [Overseas Chinese and the Start of Modern History in China], *Bagui qiaoshi*, 9 (1991): 47.

85. Chen Weiren, *Guli miaoyi: Guaipan lulue Huagong de zui'e goudang* [The Coolie Trade: The Criminal Activities of the Abduction and Pillage of Overseas Chinese Laborers] (Beijing: China Overseas Chinese Press, 1992).

86. Cheng Shiwei et al., eds., *Wuwang guochi*, (Changchun: Jilin wenshi chubanshe 1998), 25–8.

87. Liang Zhanjun, *Jindai Zhonghua guochi lü* [A Record of the National Humiliation of Modern China] (Beijing: Beijing chubanshe, 1994), 82–5. Also see Jiang Gongsheng, *Guochi shi* [History of National Humiliation] (Shanghai, Xinhua shuju, 1927).

88. Zhou Shan and Zhang Chunbo, eds., *Guochi lü: Tushuo Zhonghua bainian* [A Record of National Humiliation: Pictures and Stories of China's Century] (Lanzhou: Gansu qingnian chubanshe, 1998), 2.

89. Cited in Dikötter, *The Discourse of Race in Modern China*, 158.

90. Chen, "One Method," 76.

91. Ren and Zhao, *Overseas Chinese*, 380.

92. Cited in Wang, *The Chinese Overseas*, 68–9.

93. Ren and Zhao, *Overseas Chinese*, 8–9.

94. McKeown, "Conceptualizing Chinese Diasporas," 326; Yang, "Overseas Chinese," 45.

95. Erik Eckholm, "For Many Expatriates, Olympics Signal China's Arrival," *New York Times*, 11 August 2008.

96. Liang Zhiwen, ed., *Wuwang guochi* [Never Forget National Humiliation] (Jilin: Jilin wenshi, 1999), 25–31; Jiang Gongsheng, *Guochi shi* [History of National Humiliation], (Shanghai: Xinhua shuju, 1927), 281–93; Yang, "Overseas Chinese," 43.

97. Interview, December 2007 in Bangkok.

98. The following section is based largely on Elena Barabantseva, "Marginality and Nation: Overseas Chinese and Ethnic Minorities in China's National Project," manuscript, 2008; Barabantseva, "Trans-Nationalising Chinese *Nation-state* Overseas Chinese in the PRC's Modernisation Strategies," *ASIEN*, 96 (2005): 7–28. Also see Liu Hong, "New Migrants and the Revival of Overseas Chinese Nationalism," *Journal of Contemporary China*, 14:43 (2005): 291–316.

99. Barabantseva, "Trans-Nationalising Chinese Nation-State," 11.
100. Richard P. Suttmeier, "State, Self-Organization and Identity in the Building of Sino-U.S. Cooperation in Science and Technology," *Asian Perspective* 32:1 (2008): 5–31.
101. Zhao Hongying, cited in Barabantseva, "Marginality and Nation," Chapter 5.
102. Liu Hong, "New Migrants and the Revival of Overseas Chinese Nationalism."
103. Cited in Barabantseva, "Marginality and Nation," Chapter 5.
104. Cited in Barabantseva, "Marginality and Nation," Chapter 5.
105. Shen Jinglin, "Foreword," in *Zhongguo: cong quru zouxiang huihuang, 1840–1997* [China: From Humiliation to Glory, 1840–1997], edited by the Revolutionary History Museum of China (Beijing: Zhongguo minzu sheying yishu, 1997), 7.
106. Barabantseva, "Marginality and Nation," Chapter 5.
107. Anne-Marie Brady, *Marketing Dictatorship: Propaganda and Thought Work in Contemporary China* (New York: Rowman & Littlefield Publishers, Inc., 2008), 163.
108. Bernard Keane, "Torch Watch: Chinese Out in Force; Others Stay Away"; Geremie R. Barmé, "Torching the Relay," *The China Beat*, 4 May 2008.
109. CNN, 27 April 2008.
110. Sang-hun Choe, "Chinese Clash with Protesters at Seoul Torch Rally," *New York Times*, 27 April 2008.
111. "Expert: China's Sovereignty over Tibet Proved by History," Xinhua, 22 April 2008.
112. "Overseas Chinese Groups, Chinese-language Media Condemn Riots in Tibet," Xinhua, 20 March 2008.
113. Ian Buruma, "The Joys and Perils of Victimhood," *New York Review of Books*, 8 April 1999, 4.
114. "Russia and China 'Approval Down'," BBC News, February 6, 2009.
115. Jiang, *Lang tuteng*.
116. Jiang Rong, *Wolf Totem*, trans. by Howard Goldblatt (New York: Penguin, 2008); "2007 Man Asian Literary Prize Winner Announced," November 10, 2007, http://www.manasianliteraryprize.org/2008/2007winner.php (viewed on 17 November 2008).
117. Jiang, *Lang tuteng*, 364–408.
118. See Barry Lopez, *Of Wolves and Men* (New York: Scribner Classics, 1978).
119. Yuan Weishi, "Xiandaihua yu lishi jiaokeshu" [Modernization and History Textbooks], *Bingdian* weekly supplement to *Zhongguo qingnian bao* (January 11, 2006).
120. Jiang, *Lang tuteng*, 298.
121. Jiang, *Wolf Totem*, 217–18.
122. Jiang, *Wolf Totem*, 303.
123. Jiang, *Lang tuteng*, 399–402.

124. Wang Hui, *China's New Order: Society, Politics, and Economy in Transition*, edited by Theodore Huters, (Cambridge, MA: Harvard University Press, 2003), 170.

Chapter 6

1. See "US-China Trade Statistics and China's World Trade Statistics," US-China Business Council, http://www.uschina.org/statistics/tradetable.html (accessed on December 21, 2008).
2. See Yinan He, "Remembering and Forgetting the War: Elite Mythmaking, Mass Reaction, and Sino-Japanese Relations, 1950–2006," *History and Memory* 19:2 (2007): 43–74; James Reilly, "China's History Activism and Sino-Japanese Relations," *China: An International Journal* 4:2 (2006): 189–216; Caroline Rose, *Sino-Japanese Relations: Facing the Past, Looking to the Future?* (London: Routledge-Curzon, 2005).
3. Cited in Hu Sheng, *Imperialism and Chinese Politics* (Beijing: Foreign Languages Press, 1955), 126.
4. See Wu Xinbo, "Memory and Perception: The Chinese Thinking of Japan," in *Memory and History in East and Southeast Asia: Issues of Identity in International Relations*, edited by Gong, Gerrit W. (Washington, DC: The CSIS Press, 2001), 65–85.
5. Iris Chang, *The Rape of Nanking: The Forgotten Holocaust of World War II* (New York: Penguin Books, 1997).
6. See Claudia Schneider, "The Japanese History Textbook Controversy in East Asian Perspective," *Annals of the American Academy of Political and Social Science*, 617 (2008): 107–22; John K. Nelson, "Tempest in a Textbook: A Report on the New Middle-School History Textbook in Japan," *Critical Asian Studies* 34:1 (March 2002): 129–48.
7. See the Web site of the International Institute for Strategic Studies, http://www.chinaiiss.org/data/img/more.asp. Also see a Web site called 'Soldier' (http://www.junren.org). (Accessed on February 28, 2006).
8. Cited in Peter Hays Gries, "China's 'New Thinking' on Japan," *The China Quarterly* 184 (2005), 835.
9. Joseph Fewsmith and Stanley Rosen, "The Domestic Context of Chinese Foreign Policy: Does 'Public Opinion' Matter?," in *The Making of Chinese Foreign and Security Policy in the Era of Reform, 1978–2000*, edited by David M. Lampton (Stanford: Stanford University Press, 2001), 162.
10. Wang Renzhi, "Zongxu" [General preface], in *Nanjing datusha shiliaoji*, vol. 28: *Lishi tuxiang* [Historical materials of the Nanjing Massacre, vol. 28: Historical images], edited by Cao Bihong (Nanjing: Jiangsu renmin chubanshe, 2006), 1–2.
11. See for example, Saburo Ienaga, "The Glorification of War in Japanese Education," *International Security*, 18:3 (1993/94): 113–33; Honda Katsuichi,

The Nanjing Massacre: A Japanese Journalist Confronts Japan's National Shame, trans. by Karen Sandness (Armonk, NY: M. E. Sharpe, 1999 [1987]).

12. The sexual violence in Nanjing was not an isolated event, but was an extreme example of how the Japanese military treated women during the war, especially with the forced prostitution of the "comfort women" in occupied territories (See George L. Hicks, *The Comfort Women: Japan's Brutal Regime of Enforced Prostitution in the Second World War* (New York: W. W. Norton & Company, 1997).)

13. Schneider, "The Japanese History Textbook Controversy," 111.

14. See Rey Chow, *The Age of the World Target: Self-Referentiality in War, Theory, and Comparative Work* (Durham, NC: Duke University Press, 2006), 25–43.

15. Beverly Allen, *Rape Warfare: The Hidden Genocide in Bosnia-Herzegovina and Croatia* (Minneapolis, MN: University of Minnesota Press, 1996), xvii.

16. Shi Young and James Yin, *The Rape of Nanjing: An Undeniable History in Photographs*, 2nd ed. (Chicago, IL: Innovative Publishing Group, 1997), 108.

17. Geremie R. Barmé, "History for the Masses," in *Using the Past to Serve the Present: Historiography and Politics in Contemporary China*, edited by Jonathan Unger (Armonk, NY: M. E. Sharpe, 1993), 260; also see Geremie R. Barmé, "A Year of Some Significance," *China Digital Times*, April 20, 2006.

18. For more discussion of the shift in official historiography see Rana Mitter, "Old Ghosts, New Memories: China's Changing War History in the Era of Post-Mao Politics," *Journal of Contemporary History* 38:1 (2003): 117–31, on 118–21; He, "Remembering and Forgetting the War"; Peter Hays Gries, *China's New Nationalism: Pride, Politics and Diplomacy* (Berkeley, CA: University of California Press, 2004), 69–85.

19. Mitter, "Old Ghosts, New Memories," 120.

20. For another view of the historiographies of the Nanjing massacre see Joshua A. Fogel, ed., *The Nanjing Massacre in History and Historiography* (Berkeley, CA: University of California Press, 2000); Takashi Yoshida, *The Making of the 'Rape of Nanking': History and Memory in Japan, China and the United States* (Oxford: Oxford University Press, 2006).

21. Che Jixin, ed., *Guochi: Zhongguo renmin bu gai wangji* [National Humiliation: Chinese People Should Never Forget] (Ji'nan: Shangdong youyi shushe, 1992).

22. An Zuozhang, "Xu" [Preface], in Che, *National Humiliation*, 1–2.

23. Zuo Yi'na, "Nanjing datusha" [Nanjing Massacre], Che, *National Humiliation*, 427–31.

24. Zuo, "Nanjing Massacre," 427.

25. Zuo, "Nanjing Massacre," 427–8.

26. Zuo, "Nanjing Massacre," 428–9.

27. Zuo, "Nanjing Massacre," 430.

28. Zuo, "Nanjing Massacre," 431.

29. Wang Xinhua, "KangRi zhanzheng bu dengtong yu guochi" [The War of Resistance Against Japan is Not the Same as National Humiliation], *Wenming* 7 (2005), 8–9.

30. Central Party School, *Yishi weijing, mianxiang weilai: jinian Zhongguo renmin kangRi zhanzhengji* [Take History as a Mirror to Guide the Future: Commemorate China's War of Resistance Against Japan] (Beijing: Zhonggong dangxiao chubanshe, 2005), 1.

31. Zhang Chengjun and Liu Jianye, *An Illustrated History of China's War of Resistance Against Japan* (Beijing: Foreign Languages Press, 1995), 39.

32. Museum Of The Chinese People's War Of Resistance Against Japan, eds., *Zhongguo renmin kangRi zhanzheng jinianguan* [Museum of the Chinese People's War of Resistance against Japan] (Beijing: Zhongguo heping chubanshe, 1998), 24–5.

33. La La, "Wuwang guochi, fafen tuqiang [Never Forget National Humiliation, Work to Make the Country Strong]," *Xiaoxuesheng shidai* 7/8 (2005), 10–17, on 13–5.

34. Zhang and Liu, *An Illustrated History of China's War of Resistance*, 3, 1; also see Central Party School, *Take History as a Mirror*, 2; Wang, "The War of Resistance," 9.

35. La, "Never Forget," 10; Zhang and Liu, *An Illustrated History of China's War of Resistance*, 2.

36. Central Party School, *Take History as a Mirror*, 2; also see Wang, "The War of Resistance," 8–9; Museum of the Chinese People's War of Resistance against Japan, 1.

37. Wang, "The War of Resistance," 8–9.

38. Liu Ye and Bo Liechen, eds., *Nanjing datusha tuzheng* [Photographic Evidence of the Nanjing Massacre] (Changchun: Jilin renmin chubanshe, 1995); *Nanjing datusha* [The Nanjing massacre] (Hong Kong: Wide Angle Press, 1995); China News Daily, "WWW Memorial Hall of the Victims in the Nanjing Massacre"; Young and Yin, *The Rape of Nanjing: An Undeniable History in Photographs*, 1997; Zhu Chenshan, ed., *Nanjing datusha yu guoji dajiu jutuji* [Picture Collection of the Nanjing Massacre and the International Rescue] (Nanjing: Jiangsu guji chubanshe, 2002); Li Guojiang and Zhang Peixin, *Nanjing datusha* [The Nanjing Massacre] (Hong Kong: Hong Kong Activities Committee for Commemorating the 60th Anniversary of the Victory in the War of Resistance Against Japan, 2005); Zhu Chengshan and Zhang Qingbo, eds., *Qinhua Rijun Nanjing datusha jinianguan chenzhan tuji* [Collected images of exhibitions of the Memorial Hall of the Victims of the Nanjing Massacre by the Invading Japanese Army], (Beijing: Changcheng chubanshe, 2008); Cao Bihong, ed., *Nanjing datusha shiliaoji*, vol. 28: *Lishi tuxiang* [Historical Materials of the Nanjing Massacre, vol. 28: Historical Images] (Nanjing: Jiangsu renmin chubanshe, 2006); "The Memorial Hall for Compatriots Killed in the Nanjing Massacre by Japanese Invaders," http://www.nj1937.org/english/default.asp.

39. Liu and Bo, *Photographic Evidence*, 45–8; Zhu, *Picture Collection*, 26.

40. See Zhu and Zhang, *Collected Images of Exhibitions of the Memorial Hall*; Zhu, *Picture Collection*, 30ff; Young and Yin, *The Rape of Nanjing*, 217–40; Chang, *The Rape of Nanking*, 105–39.

41. Liu and Bo, *Photographic Evidence*, 93, 132; also see Zhu, *Picture Collection*, 46–97; Cao, *Historical Materials of the Nanjing Massacre*, vol. 28: *Historical Images*, 246.

42. Young and Yin, *The Rape of Nanjing*, 107–56, 168.

43. Qi Kang, *QinHua Rijun Nanjing datusha yunan tongbao jinianguan* [The Monument Hall to Compatriots Murdered in the Japanese Military Invasion of China] (Shenyang: Liaoning daxue kexue jishu chubanshe, 1999), 12.

44. Qi, *The Monument Hall*, 13.

45. Qi, *The Monument Hall*, 16.

46. Qi, *The Monument Hall*, 17.

47. Qi, *The Monument Hall*, 17.

48. This description comes from my 2 May 2009 visit to the Nanjing Massacre Memorial Hall; much of the museum exhibit is reproduced in Zhu and Zhang, *Collected Images of Exhibitions of the Memorial Hall*. Also see Jeff Kingston, "Nanjing's Massacre Memorial: Renovating War Memory in Nanjing and Tokyo," *Japan Focus*, (22 August 2008).

49. Lydia H. Liu, "The Female Body and Nationalist Discourse: Manchuria in Xiao Hong's *Field of Life and Death*," in *Body, Subject and Power in China*, edited by Angela Zito and Tani E. Barlow (Chicago: University of Chicago Press, 1994), 157–77, on page 161.

50. See Susan Brownmiller, *Against Our Will: Men, Women and Rape* (New York: Penguin Books, 1976), 31–113.

51. Cynthia Enloe, *Bananas, Beaches and Bases: Making Feminist Sense of International Politics*, updated edn. (Berkeley CA: University of California Press, 2000), 44.

52. *Richou baoxing shilü* [A Faithful Record of the Atrocities of the Japanese invaders] (Political Department of the Military Committee of the Guomindang, 1938); also see Zhu, *Picture Collection*, 165.

53. Cao Bihong, "Bence shuoming" [Introduction to This Volume], in Cao, *Nanjing Massacre Historical Materials*, 28:2; "The Memorial Hall for Compatriots Killed in the Nanjing Massacre."

54. Liu and Bo, *Photographic Evidence*, xi, 294–5.

55. Daqing Yang, "The Challenges of the Nanjing Massacre: Reflections on Historical Inquiry," in Fogel, ed., *The Nanjing Massacre in History and Historiography*, 133–79, on 145–6. Yang notes that prominent Chinese historians have also criticized the cavalier way that photographs are used in Chinese texts, including Liu and Bo's *Photographic Evidence of the Nanjing Massacre*.

56. Liu and Bo, *Photographic Evidence*, 93, 126–36.

57. Liu and Bo, *Photographic Evidence*, 95; Zhang and Liu, *An Illustrated History*, 39; Young and Yin, *The Rape of Nanjing*, 165–6, 169; also see Cao, *Historical Materials of the Nanjing Massacre*, vol. 28: *Historical Images*, 247–52.

58. Young and Yin, *The Rape of Nanjing*, 108.
59. Gries, *China's New Nationalism*, 82–3.
60. Alexandra Stiglmayer, ed., *Mass Rape: The War Against Women in Bosnia-Herzegovina* (Lincoln, NE: University of Nebraska Press, 1993).
61. Allen, *Rape Warfare*, xii, 30.
62. Cynthia Enloe, *Maneuvers: The International Politics of Militarizing Women's Lives* (Berkeley, CA: University of California Press, 2000), 109.
63. Mieke Bal, "The Politics of Citation," *Diacritics* 21:1 (1991), 31.
64. Bal, "The Politics of Citation," 38.
65. Bal, "The Politics of Citation," 41–2.
66. Mitter, "Old Ghosts, New Memories," 129.
67. See Zhu *Picture Collection*; Cao, *Historical Materials of the Nanjing Massacre*, vol. 28: *Historical Images*; Ye Zhaoyan's *Nanjing 1937: A Love Story* was originally published by Jiangsu Arts and Literature Press in 1996 (Ye Zhaoyan, *Nanjing 1937: A Love Story*, trans. by Michael Berry (London: Faber and Faber, 2003).)
68. Qi, *The Monument Hall*, 12, 132; Liu and Bo, *Photographic Evidence*, 278; Zhu, *Picture Collection*, 169; "Nanjing daxue wei kuojian Nanjing datusha jinianguan yongyue," [Nanjing University Eagerly Contributes Funds to the Expansion of the Nanjing Massacre Museum], *Renmin wang* (March 7, 2005), http://news.sina.com.cn/e/2005-03-07/23145292223s.shtml (accessed on December 10, 2008).
69. Zhu, *Picture Collection*, 198–203.
70. Zhu, *Picture Collection*, 200.
71. For a contemporary discussion of the invasion and the safety zone, see F. Tillman Durdin, "Butchery Marked Capture of Nanking," *New York Times*, December 18, 1937; Timothy Brook, ed., *Documents on the Rape of Nanking* (Ann Arbor, MI: University of Michigan Press, 1999).
72. Zhu, *Picture Collection*, 126.
73. See Zhu and Zhang, *Collected Images of Exhibitions of the Memorial Hall*; Zhu, *Picture Collection*, 30ff; Young and Yin, *The Rape of Nanjing*, 217–40; Chang, *The Rape of Nanking*.
74. "Respond to 'Nanking' with Humanity, Respect, Tears and Applause: Interview [with Ted Leonis]," *People's Daily*, July 25, 2007.
75. Ye, *Nanjing 1937*, 1.
76. Liu, "The Female Body and Nationalist Discourse," 161. The following discussion is informed by Liu's analysis of Xiao Hong's novel.
77. Hsiao Hung [Xiao Hong], *The Field of Life and Death and Tales of Hulan River*, trans. by Howard Goldblatt and Ellen Yeung (Bloomington, IN: Indiana University Press), 89, 98–9.
78. Ye, *Nanjing 1937*, 36.
79. Xiao Hong, *The Field of Life and Death*, 100.
80. Ye, *Nanjing 1937*, 392, 394.

81. See Yinan He, *The Search for Reconciliation: Sino-Japanese and German-Polish Relations Since World War II* (New York: Cambridge University Press, 2009); Rose, *Sino-Japanese Relations*.

82. *Dongya sanguo de jinxiandai lishi: Yi shi wei jing, mainxiang weilai gong gong jianshi heping yu youhao de dongya keju* [The Contemporary and Modern History of Three East Asian Countries: Facing the Future Using History as a Mirror, Building Together a new Framework of Peace and Friendship in East Asia] (Beijing: Shehui kexue wenxian chubanshe, 2005).

83. China–Japan Joint Press Communiqué, October 8, 2006, http://www.fmprc.gov.cn/eng/wjdt/2649/t276184.htm.

84. "An American Conversation: Ted Leonis and the Making of NANKING," National Archives, Washington, DC (March 5, 2008).

85. Zhang and Liu, *An Illustrated History of China's War of Resistance*, 1.

86. See Gries, "China's 'New Thinking' on Japan," 831, 839–40.

Chapter 7

1. See Nicolai Ouroussoff, "In Changing Face of Beijing, a Look at the New China," *New York Times*, July 13, 2008; Jonathan Fenby, *The Penguin History of Modern China: The Fall and Rise of a Great Power, 1850–2008* (New York: Penguin, 2008), xxxi–xlvii.

2. "Interview with Zhang Jigang, Deputy Director of the Beijing Olympics Opening Ceremony," *Liberation Daily*, August 1, 2008, translated for *China Digitial Times*, August 6, 2008; Fu Ying, "Chinese Ambassador Fu Ying: Western Media Has 'Demonised' China," *Daily Telegraph*, April 13, 2008.

3. See, for example, M. Taylor Fravel, *Strong Borders, Secure Nation: Cooperation and Conflict in China's Territorial Disputes* (Princeton, NJ: Princeton University Press, 2008); Bates Gill, *Rising Star: China's New Security Diplomacy* (Washington, DC: Brookings Institution Press, 2007); Allen Carlson, *Unifying China, Integrating with the World: Securing Chinese Sovereignty in the Reform Era* (Stanford, CA: Stanford University Press, 2005); Alastair Iain Johnston, *Social States: China in International Institutions, 1980–2000* (Princeton, NJ: Princeton University Press, 2008); David M. Lampton, *The Three Faces of Chinese Power: Might, Money and Minds* (Berkeley, CA: University of California Press, 2008); Yong Deng, *China's Struggle for Status: The Realignment of International Relations* (New York: Cambridge University Press, 2008); Suisheng Zhao, "China's Pragmatic Nationalism: Is It Manageable?," *The Washington Quarterly* 29:1 (2005–6): 131–44; Evan S. Medieros and M. Taylor Fravel "China's New Diplomacy," *Foreign Affairs* 82:6 (2003): 23–35; David Shambaugh, ed., *Power Shift: China and Asia's New Dynamics* (Berkeley, CA: University of California Press, 2006); Eric Hagt, "Debating China's Future," *China Security* 4:2 (2008): 2–26. For a less sanguine view see Avery Goldstein, *Rising to the Challenge: China's Grand Strategy and International*

Security (Stanford, CA: Stanford University Press, 2004); Christopher R. Hughes, *Chinese Nationalism in the Global Era* (London: Routledge, 2006); Susan Shirk, *China: Fragile Superpower* (New York: Oxford University Press, 2007); Minxin Pei, *China's Trapped Transition: The Limits of Developmental Autocracy* (Cambridge, MA: Harvard University Press, 2008).

4. See, for example, Deng, *China's Struggle for Status*, 291; Lampton, *The Three Faces of Chinese Power*, 260; Gill, *Rising Star*, 7; Medieros and Fravel "China's New Diplomacy"; Shambaugh, *Power Shift*, 25.

5. See Qin Yaqing, "Guoji guanxi lilun Zhongguo pai shengcheng de keneng he biran" [The Chinese School of International Relations Theory: Possibility and Necessity], *Shijie jingji yu zhengzhi* 3 (2006): 7–13.

6. Deng, *China's Struggle for Status*.

7. Zhao Dachuan, "Shiji qipan zuguo tongyi" [A Century of Anticipating the Unification of the Motherland], *Ditu* no. 2 (2000): 39–44.

8. Pan Zhenqiang in Eric Hagt, "Debating China's Future," *China Security* 4:2 (2008): 2–26, on 19.

9. Peter C. Perdue, *China Marches West: The Qing Conquest of Central Eurasia* (Cambridge, MA: Harvard University Press, 2004); Kirk W. Larsen, *Tradition, Treaties, and Trade: Qing Imperialism and Choson Korea, 1850–1910* (Cambridge, MA: Harvard University Press), 1–22.

10. Deng Xiaoping, "We Are Confident That We Can Handle China's Affairs Well (September 16, 1989)," http://english.peopledaily.com.cn/DengXP/Vol3/text/d1040.html.

11. Zhao, "China's Pragmatic Nationalism"; Deng, *China's Struggle for Status*.

12. See Peter Hays Gries, *China's New Nationalism: Pride, Politics and Diplomacy* (Berkeley, CA: University of California Press, 2004).

13. Fu, "Western Media Has 'Demonised' China"; also see Shirk, *China: Fragile Superpower*, 109–10.

14. Yan Xuetong, "The Rise of China and its Power Status," *Chinese Journal of International Politics* 1 (2006): 5–33, on 13.

15. Deng, *China's Struggle for Status*, 272.

16. John Hamre in Hagt, "Debating China's Future," 25; also see Deng, *China's Struggle for Status*.

17. James Fallows, "Be Nice to the Countries That Lend You Money," *The Atlantic* (December 2008).

18. See Anne-Marie Slaughter, "Fears of an Angry Dragon," *Newsweek*, December 15, 2008.

19. Song Xiaojun et al., *Zhongguo bu gaoxing: Da shidai, da mubiao, ji women de neiyou waihuan* [China is Unhappy: The Great Era, Grand Objective, and Our Domestic Troubles and Foreign Calamities] (Nanjing: Jiangsu renmin chubanshe, 2009).

20. Chiang Kai-shek, *China's Destiny* (New York: Roy Publishers, 1947 [Chinese edn., 1943]), 106.

21. Mao Zedong, *Selected Works of Mao Zedong*, vol. 5 (Beijing: Foreign Languages Press, 1977), 17.

22. See "Full Text of Jiang's Speech at CPC Anniversary Gathering (IV)," *People's Daily* (July 1, 2001), http://english.peopledaily.com.cn/200107/01/eng20010701_73929.html.

23. Alan Knight And Yoshiko Nakano, eds., *Reporting Hong Kong: Foreign Media and the Handover* (London: Curzon, 1999), p.81.

24. "Aiguo ditu: Guochi yu guochan yilan," [Patriotic Map: National Humiliations and National Assets in one View] (Meeting of the Central Government, Wuhan Branch meeting, 1929).

25. The caption is in English and Chinese. This silk poster was painted at the Chinese Communist Party's Lu Xun Academy of Art and Literature in Yan'an. The picture was taken at "The Rise of Modern China: A Century of Self-determination" exhibit, Hong Kong Museum of History, October 1999.

26. Liang Yiqun, et al., *Yibaige guochi jinianri* [100 National Humiliation Days] (Beijing: Zhongguo qingnian chubanshe, 1995), 12.

27. Zhou Shan and Zhang Chunbo, eds., *Guochi lü: Tushuo Zhonghua bainian* [A Record of National Humiliation: Pictures and Stories of China's Century] (Lanzhou: Gansu qingnian chubanshe, 1998), 2.

28. Jiang Siyi, "Yi tu zheng shi, wuwang guochi" [Document History with Maps, Never forget national humiliation (Preface)], in *Jindai Zhongguo bainian guochi ditu* [Maps of the Century of National Humiliation of Modern China] (Beijing: Renmin chubanshe, 1997), 1.

29. Xun Xiaoming and Du Xianzhou, "Taking Part in Capital's National Defense Education Day Activities, Cao Gangchuan Stresses Need to Continue Promoting In-depth Development of Cause of National Defense Education," *Jiefangjun Bao* (September 19, 2004), FBIS-CHI-2004–0920.

30. Yuan Xiaoming, "9–18, buneng chengle chiru de baofu" [September 18th Doesn't Have to Become a Humiliating Burden], *Huanqiu ribao*, September 18, 2007.

31. Jin Xide, "China Must Adopt a Great-Power Mentality, and Make Psychological Change Part of its Modernization," *Beijing huanqiu shibao*, September 12, 2002, FBIS CPP20020927000153.

32. "People's Observations: China's International Status and Foreign Strategy After the Cold War – Speech by Pang Zhongying at the Qinghua University on April 16, 2002," *Renmin ribao* (May 5, 2002), FBIS CPP20020506000022.

33. Guo Qifu, ed., *Wuwang guochi: Zaichuang huihaung* [Never Forget National Humiliation: Recreating the Glory] (Wuhan: Wuhan daxue chubanshe, 1996), 126.

34. Jiang Zemin, "Report to the 15th Party Conference," BBC Summary of World Broadcasts (September 15, 1997).

35. "China Must Boost Military Strength," *Ta Kung Pao* (Hong Kong) (May 11, 1999), FBIS-CHI-1999–0511.

36. Jiang Zemin in BBC/SWB (May 15, 1999): G2.

37. "Renmin Ribao Hails PRC Anti-NATO 'Counterattack,'" *Renmin ribao* (May 14, 1999), FBIS-CHI-1999-0514.

38. See Paul A. Cohen, *Speaking to History: The Story of King Goujian in Twentieth-Century China* (Berkeley, CA: University of California Press, 2009), 1–35, 266. For a discussion of how Chinese strategists use *woxin changgan* and *taoguang yanghui* see Michael Pillsbury, *China Debates the Future Security Environment* (Washington, DC: National Defense University Press, 2000).

39. Wang Shuo, *Please Don't Call Me Human*, Howard Goldblatt, trans. (London: No Exit Press, 2000), 253; also see Geremie R. Barmé, *In the Red: On Contemporary Chinese Culture* (New York: Columbia University Press, 1999), 89–95.

40. Wang, *Please Don't Call Me Human*, 186. I have changed the translation from "cleansed" to "avenged."

41. Wang, *Please Don't Call Me Human*, 182.

42. Jiang Zemin, 'Speech Commemorating Hong Kong's Return,' in *Xianggang huigui diyitian* [The First Day of the Return of Hong Kong] (Beijing: Xinhua, 1997), 2.

43. Feng Renzhao, "The Hongkongnese: Who are the Hongkongnese?," *Chinese Sociology and Anthropology* 30:3 (1998): 39.

44. Wang, *Please Don't Call Me Human*, 11.

45. "China's Charter 08," trans. by Perry Link, *New York Review of Books* 56:1 (January 15, 2009); David Stanway, "Beijing Strikes at Dissidents," *The Observer* (London), January 4, 2009; Joseph Kahn, "If 22 Million Chinese Prevail at U.N., Japan Won't," *New York Times*, April 1, 2005.

46. "Nonofficial intellectuals" has been taken from Barmé's analysis of "nonofficial artists" (Barmé, *In the Red*, 202).

47. See Barmé, *In the Red*, 179–200.

48. Zhao Tingyang, *Tianxia tixi: Shijie zhidu zhexue daolun* [The Tianxia system: The Philosophy for the World Institution] (Nanjing: Jiangsu jiaoyu chubanshe, 2005).

49. Zhao Tingyang "All Under Heaven," in Hagt, "Debating China's Future," 15.

50. Zhao, *The Tianxia System*, 2, 3.

51. Zhao, *The Tianxia System*, 108, 40.

52. For a more detailed analysis see William A. Callahan, "Chinese Visions of World Order: Post-hegemonic or a New Hegemony?," *International Studies Review* 10 (2008): 749–61.

53. See Victoria Ti-Or Hui, *War and State Formation in Ancient China and Early Modern Europe* (Cambridge University Press, 2005).

54. For a more nuanced view of this story see Chen Kaige's film *The Emperor and the Assassin* [*Jing Ke ci Qin Wang*] (1999). But Zhang's *Hero* version is more influential

both with the critics and at the box office; as we saw in the 2008 Olympics ceremonies, it sets the template for China's national aesthetic.

55. See Alexandra Munro, "Cai Guo-Qiang: I Want to Believe," in *Cai Guo-Qiang: I Want To Believe*, edited by Thomas Krens and Alexandra Munro (New York: Guggenheim Museum, 2008). This passage is taken from the exhibition Web site, which contains pictures and video of Cai's art: http://www.guggenheim. org/exhibitions/exhibition_pages/cai.html.

56. Geremie R. Barmé in Munro "Cai Guo-Qiang," 23; Wang Hui, "The Dialectics of Art and the Event," in Krens and Munro, *Cai Guo-Qiang*, 43.

57. Munroe, "Cai Guo-Qiang," 20.

58. Munroe, "Cai Guo-Qiang"; Barmé, *In the Red*, 226–7.

59. Miwon Kwon, "The Art of Expenditure," in Krens and Munroe, *Cai Guo-Qiang*, 70.

60. Kwon, "The Art of Expenditure," 70. See Qiao Liang and Wang Xianghui, *Chaoxianzhan: quanqiuhua shidai zhanzheng yu zhanfa* [Unrestricted Warfare: War and Strategy in the Globalization Era] (Beijing: Social Sciences Press, 2005 [1999]); for the FBIS translation of the 1999 edition see http://www.terrorism. com/documents/TRC-Analysis/unrestricted.pdf.

61. Kwon, "The Art of Expenditure," 65.

62. Wang, "The Dialectics of Art and the Event," 45.

63. John K. Grande, "Shock and Awe: An Interview with Cai Guo-Qiang," *Yishu: Journal of Contemporary Chinese Art* 6:1 (2007): 39–44.

64. Wang, "The Dialectics of Art and the Event," 47.

65. Philip Tinari in Munro, "Cai Guo-Qiang," 23.

66. Fei Dawei in Arthur Lubow, "The Pyrotechnic Imagination," *New York Times*, February 17, 2008.

67. Wang, "The Dialectics of Art and the Event," 47.

68. Cai in Lubow "The Pyrotechnic Imagination."

69. Wu Hung, *Transcience: Chinese Experimental Art at the End of the Twentieth Century* (Chicago, IL: University of Chicago Press, 2005), 25, 179.

70. Munro, "Cai Guo-Qiang," 31; Barmé, *In the Red*, 228.

71. "Interview with Zhang Jigang, Deputy Director of the Beijing Olympics Opening Ceremony," *Liberation Daily*, August 1, 2008, translated for *China Digitial Times*, August 6, 2008.

Character List

bainian guochi	百年国耻
da yitong	大一统
duoyuan ti	多元体
fenge	分割
fenqing	愤青
guochi	国耻
haiwai huaren	海外华人
han	汉
hanjian	汉奸
hua	华
huaqiao	华侨
huaxia	华夏
huayi	华裔
huayi zhi bian	华夷之辨
jiangyu	疆域
jiuguo	救国
kangRi zhanzheng	抗日战争
kangzhan	抗战
Liji	礼记
mieguo	灭国
minzu shibie	民族识别
shaoshu minzu	少数民族
taoguang yanghui	韬光养晦
tianxia	天下
tianxia wei gong	天下为公
woxin changdan	卧薪尝胆
wujiu guochi jinianri	五九国耻纪念日
xixue guochi	洗雪国耻
xuechi	雪耻
Yuanming yuan	圆明园
zhengyou	诤友
zhenjing	震惊

zhenshi de Zhongguo	真实的中国
Zhonghua minzu	中华民族
zhongyuan	中原
zhuquan lingtu	主权领土
zunwang rangyi	尊王攘夷

Index

act of resistance 73
All-under-Heaven *see* Tianxia
Almanac (1912) 99, 100
Ang Lee 207, 210–12, 217
  Crouching Tiger, Hidden Dragon
    210–12
angry youth *see* indignant youth
Anti-Secession Law 12
Assimilation policy 135, 136
The Atlas 116, 118

backward/modern distinction 45
Bainian guochi see Century of National
    Humiliation
Barabantseva, Elena 140, 150, 152
Barmé, Geremie R. 167
Book of Rites 16, 132
Border diplomacy 111–16
bounded sovereign territory 94, 95
Boxer Uprising 23, 36, 39, 53,
    72, 78

Cai Guoqiang 191, 207, 212–16
Cao Zengmei, 135, 244
Center for Citizen Media 122
Center for the Study of Borderland
    History and Geography 114
Central Propaganda Department 16,
    25, 31, 32, 34, 35, 52, 55, 56, 105,
    107, 111, 195
Chang, Iris 164, 181, 185, 188
Chiang Kai-shek 19, 25, 35, 135, 136,
    168, 198, 199

China:
  China Central Television 20, 127
  China threat 33
  Chinese diaspora 129
  Chinese foreign policy 15, 28, 192–3,
    218
  Chinese historiography 168
  Chinese identity 19
  Chinese irredentism 111
  Chinese nationalism 13, 25, 28, 63, 69
  Classical Chinese texts 23
  Imperial frontier policy 133
  "the real China" 29, 32, 34, 53, 55,
    57, 121, 129, 155, 167, 192, 197
China Construction Materials 80
China-Japan Joint History Research
    Committee 188
China Youth Daily 52, 72, 165
Chinese Academy of Social
    Sciences 114, 208
Civilization:
  civilization/barbarian distinction 19,
    21, 22–7, 42, 50, 96, 130, 131,
    134, 136, 140, 142, 155, 157, 158,
    189, 195, 209, 211
  civilization and barbarians in imperial
    China 132–3
  civilization discourse 21–2
  material civilization 32
  spiritual civilization 32, 140
Colbert, Stephen 28
Confucianism 157
  Confucian Institutes 4, 12, 150, 152

Confucianism (*cont.*)
  Confucian quotes 2, 3
  Confucian values 3
Contemporary Auditing 79
Cultural Revolution 52

da yitong see Great Unity
Dai Yi 46
the Dalai Lama 24, 122, 127, 141, 156, 194
Daode Jing 209
Deng Xiaoping 9, 24, 29, 32, 36, 51, 55, 61, 151, 191, 195, 203
Diplomacy:
  friendship diplomacy 20
  triangular diplomacy 189
duoyuan ti 136

East Asia Summit 4, 12
Ethnic minorities 127, 128, 133
expansionist policies 20

Fei Xiaotong 136–7, 138, 139, 140, 142
fenqing see indignant youth and angry youth
Film Censorship Committee 165
foreigners, Chinese view of 41, 43, 53, 56
Freezing Point 183
Fu Ying 196

Gandhi 26
Garden of Perfect Brilliance imperial palace 16, 38, 41, 53, 63, 86–9
geobody 93–4, 95, 98, 99, 101, 105, 107, 109, 111, 122
  Alternative geobodies 116–21
Global Daily 81
Great Unity 22, 98, 109, 111, 132, 136, 157
Greater China 143, 147
guochi see national humiliation

Haiwai huaren 144
Han Chinese 127, 128, 131, 135, 141, 154, 157, 159
Hanjian see race traitor
hard power 3, 6, 13, 20, 94, 125
harmonious society 9, 20, 24, 56, 140
harmonious world 37, 121, 191, 208, 216
hero 42–4, 53
heping jueqi see peaceful rising
history issue 162, 166, 187, 195
  history question 165
  history war 162
Honor and shame dynamic 81
Hu Jintao 24, 33, 56, 140, 195
Hua 20
huaqiao 144, 145, 149
Huayi zhi bian see civilization/barbarian distinction
humiliation 16, 23

identity 13, 14, 16, 23, 28, 45
  ethnic identity 127
  national identity 12, 35, 59, 74, 82, 88, 93, 114, 127, 129, 150, 154, 165, 169, 171, 188, 194
  identity dilemma 13, 192, 193, 205
  identity distinctions 194
  identity politics 88, 94, 95, 96, 121, 125
  political identity 128
  popular identity 162
imperial domain 94, 95–8, 99, 100, 107, 109, 110, 111, 120, 121
indignant youth 10, 32, 56, 57, 156, 193, 207, 217
insecurity 13
international society 112, 158, 191
international system 12, 13, 45, 46, 52, 96, 97, 109, 192, 209
Internet bulletin boards 74
Internet opinion 6

Jiang Rong 130, 155–8, 171
Jiang Wen 165
Jiang Zemin 24, 30, 32, 34, 39, 48, 50, 51, 140, 198, 202
Jiangsu Statistics 80
jiangyu see unbounded domain
Jin Xide 53–5, 59, 201
Journey of Harmony 9, 12, 128
June 4th massacre 36, 56, 191
Junichiro Koizumi 161
Just War 81

Kang Youwei 134, 162
King Goujian 203
Koguryo controversy 113–15

Lang tuteng see Wolf Totem
Laozi 209
Leonis, Ted 185, 189
Li Hongzhang 43, 53
Liang Qichao 128, 134
Liaowang see Outlook
Lin Zexu 42, 43, 49, 51, 59
Lin Zexu (film) 48, 50
Long March, 137
lost territories 100, 101, 104, 109, 110, 112, 115, 120, 204
Lu Jiamin 156 *see* Jiang Rong
Lü Simian 34

Ma Rong 131, 132, 137–8, 142, 143
Manchurian Incident 78
Maps:
  cartographic aggression 111
  convention of imperial Chinese maps 96
  Change the Perspective to View Taiwan map 118
  Maps of China's National Humiliation 94
  Maps of Chinese National Humiliation between 1912–1937 99–105
  Maps of Chinese National Humiliation after 1989 105–9
  Map of Civilization and Barbarism 96, 97
  national maps 110, 111, 125
  normative maps 95, 96
  Tibetan protest map 122
May 4th Movement 34
Mao Zedong 16, 31, 44, 55, 62, 128, 137, 198
Mencius 133
Mukden Incident 71

Nanjing Massacre 39, 40, 71, 78, 164–7, 172–8, 183, 187, 189 *see also* Rape of Nanjing
Nanjing massacre in the century of national humiliation 169–70
Nanjing massacre in the war of resistance 170–2
Nanjing massacre memorial 175–8
Nanjing 1937: A Love Story 185–7, 190, 205
Nanjing Safety Zone 174, 189
Nanking (film) 185, 189
nation-building 65
national aesthetic 1, 4, 6, 9, 11, 16, 19, 29, 48, 51, 63, 80, 92, 93, 98, 111, 120, 121, 129, 136, 155, 178, 187, 193
national character 52, 56, 157
National Defense Education Day 63, 66, 70, 72, 74, 83, 84, 88
National Defense Education Law 15, 63, 71, 80, 201
National Day 67, 68, 75, 193
  National Day celebration 61–3
national humiliation:
  Century of National Humiliation viii; 8, 12, 14, 15, 19, 20, 27, 28, 31, 32, 40, 42, 43, 45, 59, 68, 82, 84, 105, 120, 128, 149, 162, 163, 169, 183, 194, 198, 205

national humiliation: (*cont.*)
  cleanse national humiliation 11, 44,
    199, 202
  Deflating national humiliation
    205–7
  history of national humiliation 34,
    35, 55, 147
  National Humiliation Day 15, 16,
    26, 30, 31, 59, 63, 65, 66, 193,
    201
    Proclaiming National Humiliation
      Day 67–75
    Ritual performances on National
      Humiliation Day 75–82
    national humiliation activities 85
  national humiliation discourse 15,
    16, 19, 25, 26, 29, 30, 57, 67,
    74, 84, 105, 162, 193, 194, 201,
    205
  national humiliation education 12,
    14, 35, 37, 47, 56, 69, 75, 81, 105
  National Humiliation Fund 83
  national humiliation history
    textbooks 38–44, 135
  new national humiliations 32
  political economy of national
    humiliation 44–6
  resisting national humiliation
    education 52–5
  Rhetoric of national humiliation
    39–40
national minorities 129, 130, 133
  distinguishing nationalities
    project 138–9
  national minorities' policy 131, 136,
    137–9
National People's Congress 71, 72, 74
national territory 135
national time 65, 66, 70, 73
nationalism:
  Chinese nationalism 134
  Consuming nationalism 82–9, 125
  emotional nationalism 195

ethnic nationalism 127
forging nationalism in Republic
  China 134–6
militant masculine nationalism 166
nationalist resistance 167–9, 170,
  173, 180, 181, 186, 190
patriarchal nationalism 178–9, 180,
  181, 182, 186, 189, 204
pessoptimist nationalism 196
rational nationalism 55
resistance to nationalism 167, 173,
  190
Resisting nationalism 183–7
xenophobic nationalism 55
nationalist historiography 168, 183
nationalist insecurities 192
nationalities work 132, 136–43, 155
Navigation Day 20
1989 mass movement in Tiananmen
  Square *see also* Tiananmen
  movement 32
nonofficial intellectuals 208, 212,
  217
Northeast Asia Project 114–15

Olympics
  a central goal of Beijing's foreign
    policy 3, 8
  opening ceremony 2– 6, 19, 21
  iconic new buildings 191
  success 196
One World, One Dream 208, 209, 210,
  217
open door policy 145, 151
Opium War 36, 38, 40, 44, 51, 53, 57,
  63, 78, 80, 88, 94, 111, 145, 172
The Opium War (film) 48–52, 80, 107,
  189
overseas Chinese 128, 129, 143, 163
  identity 145–50
  Oversea Chinese Affairs Offices
    (OCAO) 150, 152
  overseas Chinese work 150–5

patriotic cosmopolitanism 208, 216
patriotic education 12, 14, 16, 19, 26,
        43, 44, 48, 57, 59, 67, 79, 98, 105,
        116, 141, 162, 166, 194, 195, 205
    patriotic education policy 32–8, 57,
        167, 188, 193
    patriotic education textbooks 41, 45
    popularization of 46–52
People's Daily 122, 202, 203
pessoptimism 24, 25, 26, 54, 56
    pessoptimist discourse 195
    pessoptimist nation 9, 11–14
    pessoptimist nationalist
        narratives 168
    pessoptimist nationalism 25, 27,
        196, 198, 199, 204
    pessoptimist patriotism 80
    pessoptimist performance 88
    producing and consuming
        pessoptimism 14– 19
    rise of pessoptimism 24
Please Don't Call Me Human 205–7
pluralist-unitary structure 136, 142
policy toward frontier ethnic
        groups 130
political performances 66, 67
political theatre of resistance 70
political unity-cultural pluralism
        framework 142
popular performances 67, 79
propaganda campaigns 65, 67
    resistance 65–6
propaganda system 33

Qi Kang 175, 177
Qi Shan 49, 50

race traitor 10, 44, 56, 128
Rape of Nanjing 39, 78, 154 *see also*
        Nanjing Massacre
The Rape of Nanjing 164, 167
Red Guards 53
Ren Guixiang 148, 245

Rent Collection Courtyard 216
Republic of Five Races 131, 134
right and wrong 81–2
rise of China 13
    peaceful rise 1, 3, 8, 12, 20, 21, 191,
        192
    peaceful rising 33, 37
    threat 8

Sarkozy, Nicolas 122
security 14, 16, 23, 31
    cultural security 1, 35, 63
    ideological security 63
    military security 63
    national insecurity 65
    national security 1, 13, 35, 45, 65,
        112, 125
    regime security 1, 35, 63, 112
    security dilemma 13, 192, 205
    state security 162
self-criticism 26, 27, 45
self-determination 137, 142
separatist movements 112
Shanghai Cooperation Organization 4,
        11, 211
shared memory 188, 189
shaoshu minzu see national minorities
Shenbao 85
Shinzo Abe 161
Sick Man of East Asia 6–8, 15, 40, 94,
        157
Sino-Indian War 111
Sino-Japanese War 38, 39, 40, 78, 134,
        162, 194
Sino-Russian border 113
soft power 2, 3– 4, 6, 13, 20, 21, 28, 94,
        125, 193, 197
Sons of the Yellow Emperor 147, 148,
        170–1
sovereign territory 94, 95–8, 99, 100,
        107, 110, 111, 120, 121
sovereignty performances 66, 83,
        116

Spring and Autumn Annals 23
strategic partnership 12
structure of feeling 9, 10–11, 12, 14, 19,
    21, 23, 28, 32, 40, 48, 51, 55, 56,
    65, 93, 96, 111, 129, 155, 162,
    193, 195, 205
  pessoptimistic structure of feeling 82,
    194
Sun Yatsen 23, 128, 129, 134, 135, 149
symbolic politics 96, 116, 125, 163

Taiping Rebellion 39
Taiwan 11, 12, 32, 33, 43, 91, 92, 116,
    192, 194, 204
  Taiwanese discourse 19
taoguang yanghui 203
Three People's Principles 134
Tiananmen movement 35, 37, 78, 98,
    156, 167 *see also* May 4th
    Movement
Tianxia 20, 132, 134, 142, 209, 213
The Tianxia System 208–9, 210, 211
Tibet controversy 57
Tibetan unrest 9, 24
Tibetan uprising 122, 127, 128, 131
traitor 42–4, 53
Tributary 20
Twenty-one Demands 65, 68, 69, 73, 83

unbounded imperial domain 95
United Nations Education, Scientific,
    and Cultural Organization
    (UNESCO) 113–14

Wang, Grace 128, 152
Wang Shuo 205
War of Resistance 170–1, 172, 183, 187,
    189

War of Resistance Museum 170, 172
War pornography 178–82
Wolf Totem 155–9, 171
woxin changdan 203

Xiao Hong 186, 187
Xiao Jun 186
Xie Jin 48
Xinjiang 116, 120, 209
xixue guochi 202 *see also* cleanse
    national humiliation
  xuechi 74, 199, 202, 203, 204

Yasukuni Shrine 161
Ye Zhaoyan 185, 186–7, 205
Yellow Horde 113
YouTube 56, 57, 122
Yuan Shikai 68
Yuan Weishi 52–4, 55, 59, 156, 183
Yuan Xiaoming 81–2
Yuanming yuan see Garden of Perfect
    Brilliance imperial palace

Zeng Guofan 43
Zoellick, Robert 13
Zhang Jigang 8
Zhang Yimou 207, 210
  Curse of the Golden Flower 6
  Hero 6, 210, 211
  Olympics opening ceremony 1–6
Zhao Tingyang 207, 208, 210
Zheng Bijian 20
Zheng He 3, 20, 91, 92
zhenshi de Zhongguo see "the real China"
Zhonghua minzu 128, 132, 134
zhongyuan 133
Zhou Shan 147, 246
zhuquan lingtu 94